AF660266

Political Elite among Scheduled Castes

Political Elite among Scheduled Castes

Aluri Sundar Kumar Das
IPS (Retd.)

RAWAT PUBLICATIONS
Jaipur • New Delhi • Bangalore • Guwahati • Kolkata

ISBN 978-81-316-0947-7

© Author, 2018

No part of this book may be reproduced or transmitted in any form or by any means, electronic or mechanical, including photocopying, recording or by any information storage and retrieval system, without permission in writing from the publishers.

Published by
Prem Rawat for **Rawat Publications**
Satyam Apts, Sector 3, Jawahar Nagar, Jaipur 302 004 (India)
Phone: 0141 265 1748 / 7006 Fax: 0141 265 1748
E-mail: info@rawatbooks.com
Website: www.rawatbooks.com

New Delhi Office
4858/24, Ansari Road, Daryaganj, New Delhi 110 002
Phone: 011 2326 3290

Also at *Bangalore, Guwahati* and *Kolkata*

Typeset by Rawat Computers, Jaipur
Printed at Chaman Enterprises, New Delhi

To

Those hapless known and unknown victims of
Kanchikacherla, Padirikuppam, Neerukonda, Karamchedu,
Chunduru, Laxmipeta and other places of
erstwhile Andhra Pradesh

Contents

Foreword

Dr Aluri Sundar Kumar Das's *Political Elite among Scheduled Castes* not only deals with the brief political history of the erstwhile State of Andhra Pradesh (now divided into two) but also emphasizes the role of the members of the Scheduled Castes. It outlines the political events of the erstwhile State of Andhra Pradesh in the twentieth century.

The various political events discussed by Dr Das reflect his own perception of the events and the motives of the dramatis personae of the events. There could be other perceptions too.

The point is that the problems which the members of the Scheduled Castes faced in the past and some of which they still continue to face at present, may be different but real. Essentially, at the core is the problem of poverty which leads to all kinds of unwarranted other problems. If the Telugu society, for that matter even the Indian society, is to live in harmony and secure progress it must necessarily attend to the problem.

Attendance to the problem is possible only when the society understands the problem and its causes. The understanding of the causes necessarily depends upon the examination of the various possible perceptions of the cause.

The work of Dr Das certainly would be a valuable input for such an examination.

I congratulate Dr Aluri Sundar Kumar Das and I wish him all the best.

4 March 2017

Justice J. Chelameswar
Judge, Supreme Court of India,
New Delhi

Preface

Social science teaching and research were initiated in our university system only after the Western concept of university ushered in the 19th century. Political science as a subdiscipline of social science discourse and the study of Kautilya along with other texts started in the formal education system only after 1858. The syllabus, the text books and references for the study of these social science issues including political science were almost the same as they were in London University in the beginning. Even after a few generations of scholars trained here and produced treatises, the influence of the West in our academic life continued. The 1950s saw a plethora of studies either sponsored or collaborated with American and other universities saw the emergence of Political Sociology, as a subdiscipline to enrich our knowledge of the political process, elections, political behaviour, party politics, etc. Along with the proliferation of the studies, concepts like Clientalism, Competition, and the huge data compilation of election studies by Centre for the Study of Developing Societies (CSDS) and other institutes have inspired scholars to take up studies on different social groups that included Scheduled Castes and Other Backward Classes (OBCs). The present study by Dr Aluri Sundar Kumar Das, an IPS officer of the rank of IG who had a stint in JNU for M.Phil. is an important addition to the limited literature on the subject to advance our understanding on the political transition in Andhra Pradesh.

The study on *Political Elite among Scheduled Castes* is a critical study on the behavioural pattern of the so-called Dalit leaders in the combined state of Andhra Pradesh. The scholar has adopted Western and popular concepts in political science such as Clientalism, and Elite to capture the nuances of political sociology of Andhra Pradesh. But, there seems to be some limitations in the use of these concepts since Scheduled Castes were considered as untouchables till 1950 and thereafter in a subtle manner in our public life. Clientalism as part of feudal construct of an equivalent of Jajmani-Kamin under the Jajmani system which kept the caste system alive in India. Several western scholars used the terms that emanate from Sanskrit literature without much scrutiny of these concepts in their application to those who remained outside the system, the untouchables. The traditional Vettichakiri-begar system appears to be more relevant to the conditions of the Dalits today, whether they are in public service or in political platforms. The author, however, tries to bring out the relevance of Jajmani system flourishing among Dalits who are becoming clients of the upper caste patrons in the party that gives them the ticket. In fact, Kanshiram coined a term *'chamchagiri'* to describe the character and process of political assimilation of Dalit leaders. As Dr Sundar Kumar Das has an academic background and was trained in JNU in the discipline of political science, he has used the standard concepts to describe and analyse the political transition of Scheduled Caste leaders in Andhra Pradesh. It seems the term, Elite is not an appropriate term as far as Scheduled Castes and their socio-economic status is concerned. At one time it was used as derogatory by the upper caste elite academics and intellectuals to characterize the emergence of first generation educated few among the Dalits and separate them both from the Dalits and from others by calling them as Dalit elite. But, the character, the status and dignity of the so-called elite has not undergone any change even if they gain access to modern life through some constitutional provisions. We can find some of the shades in the present study.

The author has divided the study into 6 chapters with excellent data on SC legislators, bibliography and references. The study has contributed a unique chapter on Dalit Movements in Colonial Andhra and Telangana, describing the indigenous nature of the movements through cultural and literary upsurge before Babasaheb Ambedkar entered Andhra Pradesh. The prominent leaders like Bhagya Reddy Varma, Kusuma Dharmanna, Jashua, Dalit

Left and others who have reacted to the inhuman and exploitative conditions under which the Dalits of Telugu speaking areas were subjected to. The author has brought in relevant excerpts of Babasaheb writings and speeches at the Round Table Conference, Poona Agreement, Constituent Assembly debates to substantiate his argument that how Jothi Rao Phuley and Ambedkar were responsible for the educational advancement of the Dalits bereft of the British policy and the missionary charity. He has narrated the political awakening among the Dalits in Nizam and Andhra regions through the Scheduled Caste Federation, Independent Labour Party before independence and RPI and Bahujan Samaj Party later. It is proved that the SCF and RPI are found to be more spirited in Telangana and less vibrant in Andhra regions by giving the names of important personalities and the seats won by Dalits on their own. His training in JNU and the competent academic guidance are reflected in some of his elucidations.

The author needs to be congratulated for bringing out a detailed account of the political career of forgotten leader of Dalits, Dr Damodaram Sanjivayya. It is strange to notice the psyche of the Dalits who simply ignore their leaders and are very critical of their own men who stood for them and do not apply the same parameters in critiquing the 'other caste' leaders under whom they serve. This is true in the case of Dr Jogendranath Mandal, the ignored Dalit leader of Bengal who became the Chairman of the Pakistan Constituent Assembly and Constitution-making. In Chapter 4 on Dalit participation in electoral politics, Dr Das has given the emergence of Sanjivayya as a tall leader not only in Andhra politics but also at the national level at a young age. He was perhaps the only Dalit leader in the country who had become a minister at the age of 31, under the C. Rajagoplachary Ministry in Madras Presidency. He got elected again in the mid-term elections to Andhra Assembly in 1955 and played a crucial role in the formation of the state. He was a prominent lawyer practising in Madras was brought in to politics by K.B. Narasappa and K.V. Vema Reddy. He was made Chief Minister of AP when Sanjiva Reddy became President of AICC and the tussle between two upper castes enabled him to occupy the seat at a young age. He was instrumental in providing reservations to Backward Classes in AP and led the Congress Party to thumping victory in 1962 elections. However, being a Dalit, he was marginalised by the Reddy and upper caste leaders and was ultimately accommodated as a Cabinet Minister in Nehru's Cabinet at the age of 43. The Reddys of Rayalaseema got him defeated when he joined Mrs Gandhi and later died at an early age of 51. This is a case study of how Dalits would never be allowed to occupy the positions of power where they can take independent decisions. Then, how is it possible for them to join the Elite Club?

The core part of the study is analysed in two chapters where necessary data, information and analytics are used to show the transition of Dalit politicians from members of SCF to being representatives of Congress and TDP and the fiasco created with BSP under 'Dalit Disease'. Dalit disease is a phenomenon where the Dalits can sincerely work under the leadership of anyone other than Dalits, but within themselves there will be splits and infighting leading to surrender to the adversary. This character seems to have dented the formation of a sustainable Dalit political class of its own to carry the label Dalit Elite. Though the author has not explained it in so many words, it is evident from the analysis that the parties have given seats to Dalits only in reserved seats making the pre-Poona Pact era 'separate electorate' as a fact of political process in independent India. The author has narrated how reform movements in India and the role of enlightened rulers like Baroda Maharaja to sponsor Babasaheb Ambedkar for higher studies to emerge as leader of the Dalits in India. He has explained how the movement for subcategorization started by the enlightened Christian converts like Elia, alias Krishna Madiga and others with the astute support of upper caste elite who got threatened with the emergence of Bahujan ideology in the South. He has also narrated the gruesome incidents where Dalits were butchered in Karamchedu, Chundur, Laksmipet and other incidents and the dismal outcome of the legal battles where the culprits were by and large acquitted. It is interesting to note that the author has given some instances where he was an observer as a police officer to give credence to the argument that nothing happens as long as Dalit leaders work under the beck and call of upper caste political formations, be it Congress, TDP or something else. However, the transition from clientalism to competition of Dalit politicians has been moderately established within the parameters of mainstream political theory. It is definitely an excellent study to corroborate the hypothesis that Dalit politicians are emerging as agents of upper castes in the established parties to a large extent, under the rubric of dominant caste patrons. Dalit politicians have neither an agenda nor a programme of action for the emancipation of the poor and exploited Dalits.

The dissertation on the Dalit political elite of Andhra Pradesh from the pre-independence days to the present has brought out clearly that Dalits were more organized and focussed with independent agenda when they were under SCF, as the electorate were exclusive of Dalits. It has also noted that not a single economic issue was projected by the Dalit representatives either in the form of leading a movement or raising issues in the legislature as long as they were under the tutelage of an upper caste political party. Political elite is a group of politicians who are to be distinguished from others with their economic and social status. But, except Venkata Swamy's family and Geetha Reddy in the combined state of Andhra Pradesh, there is not a single sustainable political group within each subcaste to threaten the hegemony of upper castes in any party. Most of the elected representatives behave as if they are paid servants, if not slaves of the upper caste party leadership. It is expected that the advanced districts of Coastal Andhra where majority of the gruesome incidents against Dalits took place due to land related issues, would create a leadership to carry on the message of Babasaheb Ambedkar and Kanshiram to the logical end. Sadly, it is in these districts the subcaste movement for categorization of Dalits took place belying the emergence of political elite and it may be in the negative sense that competition among the Dalits led to the present impasse. The study has definitely opened several issues for a dispassionate academic debate by scholars and others. I congratulate Dr Sundar Kumar Das for bringing out a study that might prompt more of such studies in future to broaden our understanding about the political process in an upper caste dominated polity today.

Professor K.S. Chalam

Chairman, Institute for Economic and Social Justice

Former Member, Union Public Service Commission

Vice-Chancellor, Dravidian University

Special Rapporteur, NHRC South II

Acknowledgements

First and foremost, I express my deep gratitude to Justice Jasti Chalameswar, Judge, Supreme Court of India for sparing his valuable time to go through my work to write the foreword. I am profoundly thankful to Dr Yarlagadda Lakshmi Prasad, former Member of Parliament who treated me as his younger brother since my student days and encouraged me to take up this work. I profusely thank Professor K.S. Chalam, former Vice-Chancellor, Dravidian University, Kuppam, Andhra Pradesh, and former Member, Union Public Service Commission (UPSC) for writing a highly insightful and erudite preface. I am grateful to my research supervisor and a distinguished academician of international repute - Professor K. Srinivasulu, for suggesting a topic with immense research potential as also for his valuable inputs at several stages of this work.

I am grateful to Ch. Madhusudana Rao, IRSE, Executive Director, Research Designs and Standards Organisation (RDSO), Ministry of Railways, Government of India, Lucknow for arranging the accommodation and transport during my fieldwork in and around Lucknow in the year 2009. I am indebted to Chandra Bhan Prasad, freelance journalist and my fellow alumnus of Jawaharlal Nehru University (JNU), New Delhi for introducing me to several key functionaries of the Bahujan Samaj Party (BSP) including R.K. Chaudhary, one of the founders of BSP. I am thankful to Dr V. Sreemannarayana Murthy, Assistant Professor, Centre for SAARC

Studies, Andhra University for going through the manuscript before the work assumed its final shape. I express my sincere thanks to my fellow alumnus of JNU and eminent journalist Ashok Tankasala for offering his critical comments and for proofreading. I am highly thankful to Sri P. Ratnam, Additional Registrar (Admin.) (Retd.), Co-operative Department, Government of Andhra Pradesh for inspiring me to carry out my academic endeavours. I express my sincere thanks to Sri Pranit Rawat of Rawat Publications for accepting my work for publication.

Being a police officer on security duty on several occasions, I had the ringside view of some of the incidents described in this work. In the saga of my career, I did witness prejudicial treatment against Dalit officers. Yet some Dalit politicians helped me in my career. Late Sri Neethipudi Ganapathi Rao, the then MLA of Nagaram constituency in East Godavari district got me posted as DSP Vijayawada East. Similarly, Late Sri B. Sanjeev Rao, the then MLA, Gajwel and Dr G. Vijaya Rama Rao, Member of Parliament of Siddipet were instrumental in my retention as DSP in Medak District against the transfer orders. Also I express my gratitude to Sri K. Madhav Rao, IAS (Retd.), former Chief Secretary, Government of Andhra Pradesh, Sri S.V. Prasad IAS (Retd.) former Chief Secretary, Government of Andhra Pradesh, Dr P.K. Mohanty, IAS (Retd.), former Chief Secretary, Government of Andhra Pradesh, and Sri Roddam Prabhakara Rao, IPS (Retd.) former Director General of Police, Government of Andhra Pradesh for helping me to overcome challenges in my career at various stages.

Aluri Sundar Kumar Das

CHAPTER 1

Introduction

The Scheduled Castes, also referred to as Dalits are the ex-untouchables* of the Indian society and are not a part of four-fold Varna system, which is a pan-Indian phenomenon. The word 'Dalit' in Sanskrit means 'broken' or 'downtrodden'. It was drawn into Marathi from Sanskrit. Dr Ambedkar described the 'untouchables' as broken people. The word 'Dalit' was used as early as 1931 in journalistic writings. Eleanor Zelliot observes that 'Dalit implies those people who have been broken, ground down by those above them in a deliberate and active way.[1] They have been an excluded group from the mainstream society though the policy of protective discrimination reserved some space for them in education, employment and political power structure. Before the implementation of affirmative action in independent India, several social movements were launched seeking their liberation from the socio-religious sanctions. Social reformers like Jyothiba Phule, Narayana Guru, Periyar Ramasami, Sahu Maharaj, B.R. Ambedkar and others worked for the emancipation of these outcastes. The Christian missionaries reached out to the masses in course of propagating their religion and found potential adherents in them as they remained excluded from the Hindu social structure and thus were easily attracted to the liberal Western religion. They opened schools for them and exposed them to Western education and

---

* The ex-untouchables in India in this thesis are interchangeably referred to as Scheduled Castes, Dalits, and Depressed Classes.

ideals, which ultimately ignited them to action to demand their just rights. Reformist organizations like Brahmo Samaj also supported their education by condemning the discriminatory treatment meted out to them by the rest of the society adhering to the Institutes of Law which enjoyed the blanket support of the Hindu religion.

The reform movements and peasant struggles formed two different strands of movements during the British rule. The reform movements had the support of the progressive thinkers of the ruling establishment and derived support of the regime. The nationalist movement, however, did not seriously touch upon the issues of the oppressed masses.

Though the political elite of today are far alienated from the people, their predecessors, namely the leadership of the reformist social movement appears far better by any standard of the measure considering their proximity to the people. The reformist social movement of the Scheduled Castes gradually acquired political dimensions and joined the political stream of the day. Thus, the reformist social movement faded away. Nevertheless, Andhra Pradesh continues to be a State with politically conscious masses and economically oppressed people, often challenging the dominant castes.

Andhra Pradesh in this study refers to the erstwhile composite state of Andhra Pradesh, which comprised the regions of Coastal Andhra, Telangana and Rayalaseema. The study encompasses the period from the formation of Andhra Pradesh in 1956 till its bifurcation in 2014 into two successor states of Andhra Pradesh (comprising Coastal Andhra and Rayalaseema), and Telangana. The study has taken 2009 General Elections as a conclusive benchmark. Hence, the mention of Andhra Pradesh, hereinafter, refers to the composite state of Andhra Pradesh in this thesis.

An attempt is made in the following pages to describe the historical conditions, in the framework of which alone can we understand the present setting. A general description of the historical background in the sense of the origin and growth of an oppressive ideology running through ages is followed by an attempt at understanding the Adi-Andhra movement.

Owing to India's exposure to the West, consequent to the advent of British rule, the process of modernization was set in motion. It marked many a departure in the cultural and social structure of the traditional Indian society. As such the British rule, within the broad framework of imperialism, contributed to modernization as was evident in the largely successful attempts to establish new social institutions, which were essentially modern and pan-Indian in nature.

As a corollary of the Indian contact with the liberal concepts of the West, there emerged certain sections evolving a distinct culture or subculture marked by their tendency to be gradually socialized along the Western lines. This was the case especially in the 17th century Bengal, Madras and Bombay where certain sections like interpreters, trader-cum-middlemen emerged, seeking to modify or replace the existing social structures along the Western lines. It also led to the birth of certain social movements like the Brahmo Samaj, Prarthana Samaj etc. wedded to the task of eliminating the obscurantist traditions of Hindu religion. With this initial impact of Western values on the Indian society and also the subsequent consolidation of British hegemony towards the middle of the 19th century, a tradition of modern norms gripped the Indian society. It found expression in the demands for a universalistic legal system, expansion of Western form of education, urbanization and industrialization, development of modern communication and transport network and social reforms per se. Along with such new social norms, there had been structural changes in the Indian society along modern lines. Some, altogether new social structures were created and some older institutions were sought to be replaced or conditioned to the new social situation.

The administration was revamped along rational lines with concrete bureaucratization in the administrative and judicial realms. New classes of business elite and entrepreneurs emerged, accompanied by the emergence of a political elite and a nationalist leadership by the middle of the 19th century. It is against this background that the rise of working class, because of the emergence of industrial entrepreneurship, and the subsequent formation of trade unions on corporate lines as in the West should be viewed. Thus, the modernization process and the subsequent development of its structures, which pervaded the entire Indian society, saw the articulation of nationalist aspirations, which by itself was a major contribution to the growth of modernization in India.

However, the process of modernization in India was confined largely to certain segments of the Indian social life under the British rule. There were many substructures of the Indian society, which were conspicuously unaffected as was reflected in the continuance of caste system, joint family systems, village community etc. It is not difficult for us to understand the reasons as to why the traditional caste system and such other ethnic factors were not sought to be replaced by Western concepts.

The 1857 'mutiny' and the nationalist movement later during the twentieth century laid severe constraints on the British. They found in the existing social stratification an easy ploy to play one section against the other. In fact, we find the British seeking to divide the Indian society into watertight compartments along the lines of caste, religion and such other ties. Thus, given the imperialist designs of British to perpetuate its hegemony in India, it is not strange that caste and other ethnic factors were given importance in matters of employment etc. The same is the reason for the creation of communal electorates and the consequent communal tensions. These historical factors have had massive influence on the affairs of modernization. The post-colonial India as is evident by the social categories such as caste etc. has taken deep roots in the contemporary Indian society as well.

However, with the advent of independence the attempts at modernization have undergone a basic change from the colonial pattern. As a part of the general developmental strategy, the efforts of modernization are now sought to percolate to all aspects of Indian social life. The introduction of adult franchise, the federal set-up, popular administration at the grassroot level because of elections to the village Panchayats, Community Developmental projects etc. clubbed with the introduction of land reforms, politicized the countryside in all aspects of social life. The villagers are gradually sucked into a bureaucratic form of participation in local level management and administration of justice. As such, caste has found a different role in the new socio-economic and political situation. It now functions as an important structural network in the process of socialization in general, and modernization in particular.

In the traditional Indian society caste commanded a functional value. The Jajmani system portrays functional interdependence fostered by caste. While it contributed to social order and social stability, it conferred differential privileges on various groups. Though the system supported the conventional economic processes, the evolution of modern economy and the inevitable adoption of modernization owing to the British rule, along with the emergence of new institutions and the value system surrounding them, necessitated social change. Social reforms led to demands for political reforms.

The political reforms undertaken by the British rulers from time to time recognized the need for separate electorate for the depressed classes after Ambedkar convinced the imperial government of the necessity. The outcome of the second Round Table Conference was the declaration of separate electorate in favour of depressed classes. Gandhi's strong opposition to the Award, his subsequent fasting to recall the Award leading to the Poona Pact[2] in the year 1932 provided for joint electorate in select constituencies. This formula found place in the Constitution of independent India. Though political reservations were meant only for ten years, they have been extended thereafter. Despite space in legislative bodies, the status of the excluded groups has been that of clients in Indian politics. The political parties cautiously picked up weak and docile candidates who would toe the party line and not take radical steps to improve the lot of their backward brethren.

Clientelism

The present study deals with evolution of the Scheduled Caste political elite in Andhra Pradesh from clientelism to competition. It is pertinent in this context to throw some light on the concept of Clientelism. It is a relationship in which an individual of higher socio-economic status as patron uses his influence and resources to provide protection or benefits or both, for a person of lower status, his client who on his part reciprocates by offering generous support and assistance including personal service to the patron.[3] Viewed in political context, it is a tool for building a loyal network of supporters. It involves creating socio-economic dependence on the regime and consequently political subservience on the part of the targeted group.

Jean Louis Briquet[4] describes Clintelism as relationship between individuals or parties of unequal social and economic status, which involves reciprocal exchange of material and services because of personal relationship and moral obligation. This phenomenon occurred at various stages of history whether it was between patricians and their henchmen during ancient Roman age or between lords and serfs in feudal era, or between landowners and peasants in various rural communities. Clientelistic relations continued even in modern states even after their democratization towards the later part of the nineteenth century. In the process of transition, these relationships transformed into two ways. On the one hand, they acquired political dimension i.e. their insertion into the political institutions. On the other hand, they are criticized as obstacles to the efficiency of democratic institutions and to the respect of democratic values.

To further dwell on the history of clientelism, the introduction of elections strengthened the power of notables. In the French Third Republic or the French government from 1870 to 1940, the bourgeoisie, landowners, aristocrats and industrialists won political office through wealth and social advantages, which enhanced their electoral chances. Until the mid-twentieth century, the same phenomenon was in vogue among the peasant communities of Southern Europe and agrarian elites in numerous developing countries. Voting patterns strengthened social hierarchies. Votes were exchanged for goods or services like employment, land, charitable donations, etc. which could be given to loyalists. Democratization thus resulted in formation of clientelistic networks, which became first political parties for the notables. When mass parties were founded, these notables had to compete with new political entrepreneurs from the middle classes and the trade unions. These professional politicians had no endowment that could be converted into clientelistic resources. Instead, they sought vote due to sharing of convictions, ideology and defence of collective interests.[5]

The fact that democratically elected governments act in the interests of the poor is attributed to clientelism. Clientelism requires buying votes to secure power. It is undertaken by a cadre of political elite called patrons. Having received direct benefits the clients support the patrons. Thus, in a quid pro quo arrangement the patrons control the government while promoting the benefits of government.[6]

Richard Graham[7], the historian, characterized clientelism 'as action-set built upon the principle of 'take there, give here', enabling clients and patrons to benefit from mutual support as they play parallel to each other at different levels of social, political and administrative articulation. In the political domain clinetelism involves electoral support extended in exchange for employment and other resources. It is an effective strategy for electoral victories and for building political support base. It also involves select release of public funds to the supporters, or appointing political nominees into the government structure. Thus, it is a means of political mobilization.

According to Jonathan Hopkin, political clientelism constitutes direct exchange between citizens and those who hold the political authority.[8] Thus, the SC elite entered into clientelistic relationship with patrons running major political parties. They obliged them by offering various positions in the power structure. This drives home the point that the patrons are not only trying to woo the SC electorate with a temptation that there lies ahead an opulent life if they supported them but the SCs themselves feel that clientelism offers them quick benefits or access to potential resources which otherwise are not accessible to them.

The excluded groups in India are vulnerable to clientelistic politics due to the difficulties in accessing the resources and services of the State, given the social stigma attached to their status. Within the framework of joint electorate model of political reservations, the Scheduled Caste elites' approach has been clientelistic towards the Indian National Congress (INC).

Commenting on the Poona Pact, Ambedkar observed:

> The second misdeed of the Congress was to subject the Untouchable Congressmen to the rigours of party discipline. They were completely under the control of the Congress Party Executive. They could not ask a question which it did not like. They could not move a resolution, which it did not permit. They vote as they wished and could not speak what they felt. They were there as *dumb driven cattle*. One of the objects of obtaining representation in the Legislature for the Untouchables is to enable them to ventilate their grievances and to obtain redress for their wrongs. The Congress successfully and effectively prevented this from happening.[9]

The inroads of Republican Party of India (RPI) founded by the followers of B.R. Ambedkar in the initial years post- independence and the Bahujan Samaj Party (BSP) founded by Kanshi Ram in the later years showed signs of movement from clientelism to competition. With the emergence of the Telugu Desam Party (TDP) on the political landscape of Andhra Pradesh in 1983, the Dalits oscillated between the Congress and the TDP to raise their clientelistic stakes. The Mahajana Socialist Party[10] founded by Manda Krishna Madiga, a Dalit leader who spearheaded a movement demanding apportioning of Scheduled Castes reservation in accordance with the population of various Scheduled Castes and their subgroups, is a glaring sign of Dalit assertiveness and entry into electoral politics looking for political alliances in the era of coalition politics where a few seats can catapult a political party to positions of power. The rise of BSP in Uttar Pradesh has encouraged the Dalits to develop a competitive spirit in electoral politics rather than settling for concessions of clientelism.

This work is divided into six chapters. While the first chapter introduces the theme of the work along with presentation of methodology and review of literature, the second chapter titled 'Caste in Indian Society' discusses the origin and evolution of caste and the genesis of untouchability to focus on the origin and evolution of Dalit castes in the country as a backdrop to the emergence of Scheduled Caste political elite.

The third chapter on 'Dalit Movements in Colonial Andhra and Telangana' exposits on the social conditions and challenges which spurred the Dalits to launch campaigns demanding the State to initiate measures for their welfare. It throws light on the different social milieu prevailing in the two regions of Andhra and Telangana which determined the distinct trajectories of the social movements.

The fourth chapter on 'Evaluation of Dalit Participation in Electoral Politics' examines the trajectory of Scheduled Caste political elite from clientelism to competition in the State's electoral politics. It focuses on the changing political and socio-economic factors, which led to their transition to competition.

The fifth chapter on 'Dalit Elite Response to Atrocities against Dalits' narrates the significant atrocities on Dalits so far, and the response of the Dalit political elite in the present framework of political reservations where the concept of joint electorate made the Dalit politicians dependent on the votes and patronage of the upper castes.

The final chapter concludes the thesis by drawing upon the analysis from the preceding chapters.

Methodology

The methodology adopted in the present study is to partly make use of secondary sources of knowledge pertaining to caste, caste movements and politics of Andhra Pradesh, along with field studies wherein the researcher interacted with politicians of all the three regions given his professional advantage to access the political representatives of all hues. The researcher has analysed the knowledge so gathered using 'content analysis' technique within the framework of the theme. It is, however, admitted that the interpreter's unconscious bias may creep into the analysis of the subject. The researcher is nevertheless cautious about these methodological delicacies and has taken necessary care to maintain objectivity and value-neutrality.

The author's observation of some specific incidents and developments from close quarters is reflected in this work. He personally interacted with many Dalit leaders and activists as a research student while pursuing his higher education, and also in the course of executing his official work on numerous occasions. Thus, he could gather first hand information from the subjects in this research work. He was privy to many closed-door political developments as he was posted to oversee security arrangements to top brass politicians. Through the methodological tools of observation and participant observation though by virtue of professional obligation, the author gathered authentic information useful for this study.

Review of Literature

A review of literature on Scheduled Caste political elite in the State of Andhra Pradesh shows that this work is first of its kind. However, some studies which are proximate to the present themes are given below.

Sachchidananda's[11] study of elite covers status, mobility, network and the role of Scheduled Caste elites etc. in the social transformation of their own community. His study covers three categories of elite viz. legislators, civil servants and social workers. The following are his findings:

(1) Among the elite, the economic status of legislators and some categories of civil servants is higher than that of others.
(2) A large number of elite suffers from inferiority complex.
(3) The political elite are conscious of the value of their vote.
(4) The elite has been most active in propagation of education through which social change of the betterment of Scheduled Castes is possible.
(5) Majority of the Scheduled Caste elite in the state of Bihar were found to have taken less interest in solving the problems of their kith and kin.
(6) Some who have improved their social status have forgotten their ties with their past.

Abbasayulu's[12] study of elite covered three categories of elite viz. (i) Political elite consisting of MLAs, MLCs and ministers in Andhra Pradesh; (ii) Administrative elite – IAS officers, Doctors and Engineers; and (iii) Intellectual elite – university teachers and lawyers.

His findings are:

(1) Occupational mobility is initiated by the individual and later spreads to family lineage and then to the group. There is not only intra-generational but also inter-generational occupational mobility among the Scheduled Castes elite in Andhra Pradesh.
(2) The fruits of reservations are being enjoyed by the second generation.
(3) Majority of the high positions in the State are occupied by Malas, though Madigas are numerically preponderant when compared to the Malas.
(4) Contrary to the popular belief, the Scheduled Castes political elite of Andhra Pradesh are educated.
(5) The number of Scheduled Castes woman in elite positions is very low.
(6) The majority of Scheduled Castes elite falls in the category of middle income group, while a few of them belong to the higher income group.

Thus Sachchidanada's study is confined to the Scheduled Castes elite who have come up the social ladder by making use of the economic as well as political reservations. He did not touch upon the level of political consciousness elaborately since his main focus of the study was on economic status of the elites.

The study fails to address as to why there has not been a marked change in the socio-economic status the Scheduled Castes despite the space earmarked for them in the form of reservations in education, employment and political power structure.

Abbasayulu categorized Scheduled Caste elite into three types, viz. political, administrative and intellectual elite. His main focus was on the economic status and their occupational mobility. The political aspect seems to have been almost totally ignored. Besides, his study is limited in its scope as it touched upon only the IAS cadre of the state. The same is true with his study on the intellectual elite. His omission of MPs as well as the representatives of local bodies from the scope of the study is arbitrary. All these serious lapses together make the study look non-serious.

Thus, an account on the above studies shows that the political aspect is either totally ignored or did not find its due share as a factor of social change. Therefore arises the need to highlight the political aspect in all its ramifications.

Doneti Sivaji[13] in his study of Adi-Andhra reform movement in colonial Andhra covers the commercialization of agriculture and its impact on Dalits, their religion; reform movements changing the interpretation of certain religious concepts to rope in the excluded groups; the impact of missionary activities which stood as a challenge to the native religion by seeking to educate the Dalit masses; the autochthonous Adi-Andhra Movement and the status of Dalits as a result of these attributes. This study does not specifically deal with the measures adopted by the British government in breaking the barriers of caste-Hindu orthodoxy to rope in the Dalits into the mainstream society.

Kumara Swamy Nagam's[14] study on Dalits' struggle in Andhra Pradesh deals with colonial rule and Dalit movement in Coastal Andhra; Nizam's state and Dalit interventions; various modes of Dalit articulation wherein the Dalit issue of injustice have been espoused by Dalit organizations like Andhra Pradesh Dalit

Mahasabha led by Katti Padma Rao. The issue of one caste among Scheduled Castes cornering a major portion of reservations disproportionate to its population has been a subject of discussion for a long time. But such policy imbalances have been highlighted not by the Scheduled Caste political elite, but a Dalit organization 'Madiga Reservation Porata Samthi' (MRPS) led by Manda Krishna Madiga. Similarly, Nagam observes that the legal inconsistencies in the process of classification of Scheduled Castes reservations in Andhra Pradesh have been highlighted by another Dalit organization – Mala Mahandu led by P.V. Rao. All along, it was for the Dalit organizations to take up the issues and not their political elite.

K.Y. Ratnam's[15] 'Dalit Movement and Democratization of Andhra Pradesh' deals with Dalit movements in Andhra and Telangana regions in the pre-independence era. It traces the concessions accorded by government and the reprisals on the part of dominant castes which could not accept the attempts of upward social mobility by the Dalits. This development is akin to cultural gap where changes in material culture do not reflect in non-material culture thereby leading to cultural gap. In this context if the Dalits attempt to change their social status by accessing the institutional channels, the dominant castes unable to bear the mobility of Dalits resist the change, often violently. This work highlights the efforts of the Dalit organizations in taking up the Dalit issues within an ideological framework. It does not specifically deal with the limitations of Scheduled Caste political elite in dealing with the Dalit issues, which could be resolved with their serious and active interventions.

The works covered do not comprehensively deal with the present study. They touch upon certain areas of the present study. Most of the information apart from the secondary sources is gathered by the author's personal observations.

Area of Study

The erstwhile composite state of Andhra Pradesh is taken as the area of study. In order to assess the transition of Scheduled Caste political elite from clientelism to competition, the election results from the first general elections in Andhra Pradesh for Parliament and State Legislative Assembly up to the 2009 elections have been studied.

The researcher in the course of discharging his duty as a police officer met and interacted with the Legislators and Parliamentarians who constitute the political elite of Scheduled Castes of the state.

Objectives of the Study

Sixty-two years elapsed since the first elections were held under the system of joint electorate. Article 334 of the Constitution originally extended reservation of seats in Lok Sabha and State Legislative Assemblies up to 1960 i.e. for a period of ten years. But this was extended up to 1970 by Constitution's Eighth Amendment. Subsequently, the Constitution's 23rd, 45th, 62nd, 79th and 95th Amendments extended reservations up to 1980, 1990, 2000, 2010 and 2020 respectively. An attempt is made in this study to investigate the following aspects:

1. The emergence of Scheduled Castes political elite.
2. Whether the Dalit movements in the regions of Andhra and Telangana inspired the Scheduled Castes political leaders to carry forward the ideology in the post-independence era.
3. Whether the Scheduled Caste political elite who were subject of dominant caste clientelism have transitioned to compete with the other castes.
4. Whether there has been a conspicuous movement from clientelism to competition with every succeeding general election. Whether there is resistance by Scheduled Castes elite to the dominant caste politics.
5. Is the rise of Scheduled Castes leaders attributed to clientelism or their competence?
6. Why the Uttar Pradesh's formula of Scheduled Castes victory in elections could not be replicated in Andhra Pradesh?
7. What is the response of Scheduled Castes political elite to the atrocities committed against their brethren.
8. Why political reservations and the rise of Dalit leaders to prominent positions in the politics of the State and Centre did not act as deterrence on the atrocities against Dalits.

Notes

1. S.M. Michael, 'Dalit Vision of a Just Society in India' in S.M. Michael (ed) *Dalits in Modern India: Vision and Values,* Sage Publications, New Delhi, 2007, pp. 108–131 and Eleanor Zelliot, *From Untouchable to Dalit,* Manohar Publishers, New Delhi, 2001, p. 267.
2. S.N. Sen, *History of Modern India,* New Age International Publishers, New Delhi, 2006, pp. 195–196.
3. Allen Hicken, 'Clientelism' *The Annual Review of Political Science* accessed on 05.07.2013 www.polisci.annualreviews.org
4. http://www.britannica.com/EBchecked/topic/1916881/clientelism accessed on December 23, 2014
5. Ibid.
6. Siwan Anderson et al 'Clientelism in Indian Villages' Vancouver School of Economics, accessed on 5 January 2014 http://faculty.chicagobooth.edu/workshops/AppliedEcon/pdf/Francoisclientilism.pdf
7. Luis Roniger, 'Political Clientelism, Democracy and Market Economy' in *Comparative Politics,* Vol. 36, No. 3 April-2004, Published by New York University Press, pp. 353–375 www.Jstor.org/stable/4150135 accessed on 14 March 2015.
8. Jonathan Hopkin, 'Conceptualizing Political Clientelism: Political Exchange and Democratic Theory', Paper prepared at London School of Economics, London, 2006, p. 4, http://www.academia.edu/2588134/Conceptualizing_Political_Clientelism_Political_Exchange_and_Democratic_Theory accessed on 14 February 2015.
9. Kanshi Ram, *The Chamcha Age: An Era of Stooges,* published by Kanshiram, New Delhi, 1982, pp. 98–99.
10. *The Hindu*, 5 January 2014.
11. Sachchidananda, *Harijan Elite,* Thomson Press (India), Faridabad, 1977.
12. Y.B. Abbasayalu, *Scheduled Caste Elite: A Study of Scheduled Caste Elite in Andhra Pradesh,* Osmania University, Hyderabad, 1978.
13. Doneti Sivaji, 'A Study of Adi-Andhra Reform Movement in Colonial Andhra: A Historical Perspective' in *Journal of International Academic Research for Multidisciplinary Studies,* Vol. 1, Issue 5, June 2013, www.jiarm.com/Jun/paper3782.pdfý accessed on 14.11.2013.
14. Kumara Swamy Nagam, 'Dalits' Autonomous Struggle for the Annihilation of Caste: An Appraisal of Experiments in Andhra Pradesh, *The International Journal of Social Science Research,* April, 2013: Vol. 1, No. 4, pp. 35–55, www.ijssr.org/Aprilissue.html accessed on 23.11.2013.
15. K.Y. Ratnam, *The Dalit Movement and Democratization of Andhra Pradesh,* East-West Centre, Washington, 2008.

Chapter 2

Caste in Indian Society

The Hindu society, hereinafter referred to as Indian society, stands stratified-based on caste. Though the number of castes runs into few thousands, there is a pattern underlying the hierarchical gradation of these castes. The pattern is the pan-Indian four-fold Varna system. Caste as a basis of Hindu social organization has tremendously influenced the pattern of living of other religious communities in India. It was, therefore, rightly commented that caste system continued to be the 'steel frame of Hinduism'[1] and the 'sheet-anchor of popular Hinduism'.[2]

Before we define the term 'caste', we should be clear about the distinction that exists between the terms 'varna' and 'jati' which conceptually differ from each other though they are often used interchangeably.[3] The 'varna' literally means 'colour'. But in the context of Hindu social organization it was designed as a functional category. According to Vedic theory, the Hindu society was then organized into four broad functional categories according to the attributes of individuals. Thus, Brahmins were entrusted with the work of conducting religious and priestly functions; the Kshatriyas had to perform occupation of defending the territory; the Vaishyas were to engage in agriculture, trade and commerce, and Shudras had to serve all the above three varnas.

Thus, there was broad categorization of people into four definite and distinct varnas and this has sanction of Vedic religion on the basis of functions entailed. Undoubtedly, there was some mobility in the varna system in the beginning, but this was a very temporary phenomenon. As the first three groups by creating certain laws and practices became more and more socially exclusive groups, forces generating social mobility eventually disappeared.

'Jati' is different from 'varna' in that a certain degree of purity is maintained here in terms of heredity, endogamy and birth, while the 'varna' theory divides society into four hard and fast categories with Brahmins and Shudras occupying the top and bottom layers of the social hierarchy.

Definition of Caste

The term caste originated from the Portuguese word 'casta' signifying breed, race or kind (caste derived from the Latin word 'castus' meaning pure).

According to Ambedkar:

> Caste is a self-enclosed social unit which limits social intercourse including messing etc., to members within it. Consequently this absence of messing with outsiders is not due to positive prohibitions, but it is a natural result of caste i.e. exclusiveness. No doubt this absence of messing originally due to exclusiveness, acquired the prohibitory character of a religious injunction but it may be regarded as a later growth.[4]

> Caste in India means an artificial chopping off of the population into fixed definite units, each one prevented from fusing into another through custom of endogamy.[5]

M.N. Srinivas defines 'jati' as follows:

> ... a hereditary, endogamous, usually localised group having a traditional association with an occupation and a peculiar position in the local hierarchy of castes. Relations between castes are governed, among other things by the concept of pollution and purity and generally maximum commensality occurs within the caste.[6]

Some Indologists find it worthwhile and realistic to explain the meaning of the caste in terms of its characteristics rather than give it a specific definition. For instance, P.V. Kane, chooses this course of analysis. He identifies the following features: (i) hereditary, i.e. in theory a man is assigned to a particular caste by birth in that caste; (ii) endogamy; (iii) restrictions as to food; (iv) occupation;

(v) graduation of castes; (vii) the caste council with powers to regulate the conduct or the fines or excommunication for lapses.[7]

Another theory of caste[8] propounds that caste came into being because of a long practice of colour bar. It is held that thousands of years ago, India was inhabited by small dark skinned people. Then she was invaded by waves of a tall fair-skinned race from the north who either came and enslaved the earlier inhabitants or pushed them southwards or into the hills and jungles. Those dark skinned people who were conquered and subjugated were despised by their conquerors and were forced to do menial tasks. Further, they were kept outside the social system of the conquerors forbidding every conceivable mix such as intermarriage. This kind of social arrangement based on the distinction between the fair-skinned and the dark-skinned people clearly gives us an idea that varna then meant a category of people having same colour.

Controversy about the Varna System and Origin of Shudras

There is a controversy not only about the origin of Varna system but also about the origin of Shudras. According to Purushasukta of the Rig Veda, Shudras existed as fourth Varna right from the beginning of Chaturvarna system that originated during the Vedic period. Ambedkar however does not accept this view. He argued that the Vedic Aryan society recognized only three varnas, viz. Brahmins, Kshatriyas and Vaisyas. The Shudras were not then a separate Varna but a part of Kshastriya Varna.

According to him, there was a continuous struggle between the Shudra kings and Brahmins, in which the latter were subjected to many tyrannies and indignities. As a result of the hatred towards the Shudras the Brahmins refused to invest the Shudras with the sacred thread. Due to the loss of the sacred thread the Shudras became socially degraded, fell below the rank of Vaisyas and came to form the fourth Varna. In support of his contention Ambedkar advances two arguments: (i) he states that the Rig Veda excluding the 'Purusha sukta' mentions Brahmins, Kshatriyas and Vaisyas but does not mention Shudra as a separate Varna. Hence, there were only three 'Varnas'; (ii) his second argument is that the 'Satpatha' and 'Taitreya Brahamana' speak of the creation of three Varnas and not of the fourth 'Varna' as separate.

On the basis of these two arguments, Ambedkar holds that originally there were only three 'Varnas' and that the Shudras were part of the second, i.e. Kshatriya Varna. Ambedkar further explains that those Kshatriyas who became degraded and constituted a fourth 'Varna' belonged to the Solar Line. They were higher than the Kshatriyas of Lunar Line in material spirit, learning and pride. It was these Kshatriyas of the Solar Line who often conflicted with the Brahmins and challenged the Brahmins. On the other hand, the Lunar Line Kshatriyas compromised with the Brahmins and thus gave up themselves to the superior force of the Brahmins. Though the Institutes of Law like *Manu Smriti* regard Shudras as the fourth Varna on the lines of Purusha Sukta, a critical analysis on the evidence adduced by Ambedkar necessitates a deeper investigation of the Hindu sacred texts and the Institutes of Law.

Genesis of Untouchability

Another important aspect of the Indian caste system is the prevalence of the institution of untouchability. There is plenty of literature now being presented by the Indian as well as foreign scholars about this subject. Different approaches are adopted and different views are expressed about the emergence of untouchability. The study of the untouchability has become still more an intricate issue. In this part of the analysis an attempt will be made to disentangle coils of intricacies surrounding the origin of untouchability, by throwing light on a few select theories of untouchability as the constraints of time, space and scope of the current theme of study do not allow us to go into all theories,

It is generally seen that this practice of untouchability is peculiar to Hindu society. Because of the existence of untouchability, Ambedkar commented that 'the Hindu civilisation could hardly be called civilisation. It is a diabolical contrivance to suppress and enslave humanity'.[9]

Untouchability means pollution by the touch of certain persons by reason of their birth in a particular caste or family. The untouchables were known by different names in different parts of the country. They were called as outcastes, *Atishudras, Avarnas, Antyajas, untouchables, paraiahs, panchamas,* and *namasudras.* Their social disabilities were specific, severe and numerous. Their touch or any kind of contact, shadow, voice and even sight were deemed by the caste Hindus to be polluting. Furthermore, they had to clear the way at the approach of a caste Hindu.

The untouchables were forbidden to keep certain domestic animals and to use certain metals for ornaments, were obliged not to wear footwear, and were forced to occupy the dirty and unhygienic outskirts of villages and towns for habitation where they lived in dark, unsanitary and miserable smoky shanties or cottages. The dress of the male consisted of a turban, a staff in the hand, a rough blanket on the shoulder and a piece of loin cloth. The women wore bodices and rough sarees barely reaching the knees. These people are considered so inferior and excluded from the ordinary life of the society. And they are part of that caste system, unique to India, which fixed a man's social and economic status by the group into which he is born.[10]

As pointed out earlier, the origin of untouchability appears to be enigma to historians, anthropologists and sociologists. However, it is generally believed that it is a perverted outcome of the caste system.[11]

It will be seen that the origin of untouchability dates back more than two thousand years. Untouchability is first mentioned in a later vedic text and by the time of Manu.[12] Manusmriti speaks of chandalas and antyajas at various places. According to Manu, the most extreme of these extra-varnaic marriages produced the chandalas. The chandalas is the result of a hypogamous marriage of the most unequal type, between a Shudra male and a Brahmin female and he is described as the lowest of man.

There is a racial theory of Stanley Ross[13] which explains the phenomenon of untouchability in terms of an interplay of racial factors. According to him, the untouchables were non-Aryans, non-Dravidian aboriginals and that they were conquered and subjugated by the Dravidians. The outcastes were not the races conquered by Aryans. The untouchability was thus explained to have been rooted in the ideas of race and occupation.

Ambedkar who championed the cause of the untouchables and spearheaded the militant movement for the eradication of untouchability put forward his theory of 'Broken men' becoming untouchables. He points out that the untouchables were initially the 'Broken men' who were subsequently treated as untouchables.[14] There are settled communities based on territorial affiliation, as the earliest form of wealth is cattle, the primitive society had been nomadic with the pressure of dangerous difficulties, and advancement in man's thinking to resolve them a new stage arrived in the life of the roaming tribals. These new stages indicate progress of agriculture leading to settled life of some tribes. Thus, there emerged a new situation of settled tribes and roaming tribes.[15] There was a continuous warfare between them. Some tribes emerged conquerors while others got defeated. Those defeated in the warfare subsequently split into small groups, thus becoming 'Broken men'. Ambedkar further said that due to the continuous aggression of roaming tribes and settled tribes, the problem of security and protection of wealth arose. At the same time the 'Broken men' also were facing the problems of protection and shelter. The 'Broken men' depended for this on the settled tribes.

According to the agreement, the 'Broken men' had to do the work of watch and ward for the 'settled communities' and the 'settled communities' agreed to give them food and shelter and the 'Broken men' began to live outside the village.[16] In course of time they were regulated: unpleasant duties were imposed upon them and in the end they were condemned as 'untouchables'.[17] He further said that untouchables were outside the 'varna system'. They were 'avarnas'.[18] He holds that these untouchables originally were 'Broken men' and like the settled tribes they also ate beef. No doubt, every settled village had 'Broken men' living at the outskirt of the village and there was a distinction between the settled tribes and the 'Broken men' in the pattern of religious and social living. But there did not exist an abominable distinction of sort of untouchability then. However, later with the rise of Buddhism, the 'Broken men' became Buddhists. Buddhism had influenced the way of life of the settled tribes considerably. In order to defeat the Buddhism, Brahminism dominated settled tribes gave up beef eating. They further hated the 'Broken men' for having become Buddhists and also for having continued the practice of beef eating. That is to say, in their fallen days they did not assimilate themselves into the Vedic Hindus, or give up beef eating and so they were segregated as 'untouchables'.[19]

Whatever may be the views of the thinkers about the origin of the untouchables, it is indubitable that the untouchables are the most degraded and enslaved class of Hindu society. Moreover, graded inequality gave ascribed advantage to one group against the other. While Shudras are considered to be the least stratum in the society, they have below them the untouchables whose least position gave them (Shudras) the psychic advantage.

Social Position of Untouchables

The untouchables do not have the same social position in relation to other groups everywhere in the country. Their position varies from one group to another. However, they are underprivileged, poor, illiterate and subjected to many oppressions and indignities. At the root of all their subjection is the idea of untouchability. The untouchables live segregated from the caste people in a separate part of the village.

In South India, they actually live in a separate village half-a-mile or a mile away from the main village. They are not allowed to enter caste Hindu houses, except for the necessary purpose of scavenging, and in many villages, they are not allowed to enter the high caste dwelling places. The untouchables are not allowed to draw water from tanks and wells of caste Hindus. Even for shopping, they have to stand in a separate place, until the caste Hindus finish their shopping. They are not allowed to enter into hotels. Separate glasses, cups and plates are kept for them. They have to take it outside the hotel. Education is denied to them. And they are not entitled to sit along with the caste Hindu students. There is a discrimination of caste Hindu teachers towards the depressed class students. They are not allowed to enter the barber saloons at village level. The untouchables have their own barbers from their own community.

In the villages, the caste Hindus have contributed both in words and practice to the inferiority of the untouchables. This has been affected in many ways. Even if the untouchables improve their standards of living, they are not allowed to do so. The Hindus insisted that untouchables should not dress well, men should not wear shoes or women, gold jewellery. They should not possess the brass vessels which are the pride of every Indian housewife, but must cook and fetch water in cheap earthen pots. Atrocities by caste Hindus on them were increasing every year. The untouchable women are sexually exploited. The caste Hindus do not tolerate even little amount of resistance from the untouchables. Once they start organizing themselves for their rights they are being brutally suppressed and are often killed en masse.

Economic Position of Untouchables

So far, we have seen the social position of untouchables in relation to other castes of the Hindu society. Another dimension of untouchability is its pernicious influence on the economic life of the untouchables. The Hindu Smritis fixed the way of life of untouchables. They have to do all the work of the community. The untouchables are the scavengers, removers of dead animals and are involved in leather based jobs. Their earnings are very low. In the villages they are often paid in kind, and during the harvest time, they received a certain portion of grain which is too inadequate for their subsistence. In many parts of the country they are forced to do much unpaid work. Only after the advent of the British rule that Western laws came to be applied to all the people of the land. Social reform movements and the lower caste movements infused consciousness about the rights of the untouchables.

Benevolent reformers of the upper castes also were instrumental in awakening the depressed classes. Western education and the policy of protective discrimination resulted in the emergence of a class of government employees and political elite. As such, the depressed classes lack capital to invest in business. Of late the government has been focusing on Scheduled Castes sub-plan to assist them financially. But the state governments are arbitrarily diverting the grants earmarked for the welfare of the SCs. There are a handful of Scheduled Caste entrepreneurs across the country. Moreover, given the ages of discrimination against them, they have not developed the acumen for business.

Religious Position

Though the untouchables are treated as Hindus, they are not allowed to worship the Hindu gods in temples. In this context it is pertinent to note that freedom fighters like M.K. Gandhi averred that untouchables are part and parcel of the Hindu society and they were Children of God (Harijans) and hence not entitled to separate electorate.

The doctrine of 'karma', transmigration of souls and its dogmas are the main guiding principles of the Hindus. The Hindus believe in the 'theory' of transmigration of souls with the terminating point being the union with the 'Ultimate Reality' and that its actions in one incarnation will affect its 'karma' in the next. Good actions will result in a good incarnation leading to a man's birth in a high caste or a wealthy or a happy family. Evil actions on the other hand will result in a bad incarnation and would make a man an 'outcaste' or place him in miserable circumstances. The miserable position of untouchables is regarded by many Hindus as the outcome of evil action or their bad 'karma' in previous lives. It is regarded as the working out of the justice of the infinity and all the untouchables can do is, by accepting his lot humbly and doing his lowly duties well, to shake off the burden of past misdeeds and earn for themselves a better birth in future.

However, the concept of untouchability kept them away from mainstream of the society and especially from temples. Though by virtue of constitutional safeguards and rights they are able to secure government jobs and political positions, the discrimination continues in one form or the other. The atrocities against them to check their assertiveness are discussed in the succeeding chapters. In rural areas the discrimination continues though not as virulently as it used to be. In urban areas, it must be noted that they are not given houses on rent by caste Hindus so liberally. Dalits often conceal their caste status to obtain a house on rent in urban areas, if it is far away from their native village where they are familiar. As a police official the author interacted with many Dalits during his service at various places in AP. He found that certain Dalits were not forthcoming when enquired about their social status. They told him that anonymity enables them to take up private jobs where they lie to the owner or the supervisor about their caste.

The Movements towards Equality

In order to know the position of untouchables in the caste Hindu society, it is important to find out as to whether the conditions of the untouchables remained static over the time or whether there was any change in their conditions. If the answer is in the affirmative in the sense that change is taking place, it becomes pertinent to know its nature and extent.

With the advent of British, Indian society witnessed some new changes. The British government upheld the principle of equality for all and equality before law. In 1831 the courts refused to recognize the validity of slave status and in 1860 it was finally made illegal to possess slaves.[20] The British government opened schools for all castes irrespective of caste, creed and colour. It also reserved the right to withdraw grants from private schools refusing education to depressed class pupils. The British government opened the doors of public service to the untouchables. They were recruited in army in different provinces. The recruited untouchables were Mahars, Mangs and Mazhabi Sikhs.[21] There was a separate Mahar regiment in the British Army. The Mahar Regiment fought heroically during the World War II. For the first time the Mazahabi Sikhs were recruited in the British Army after the Sepoy Mutiny, whereas the Mahars were recruited in the army from mid-17th century.[22] Thus, the British elevated the socio-economic status of the untouchables.

The Missionaries and Untouchables

One of the biggest influences in altering the position and outlook of the untouchables is the work of Christian missionaries in India. The Christian missionaries attracted the untouchables towards their religion by way of preaching ideals of equality of all men before God, and challenged the whole Hindu conception of human inequality under the system of caste.[23] The result was two-fold; they brought about many conversions. And they catalysed a change in the Hindu thinking. Conversions over a period of time, it was thought, would drastically reduce the strength of Hinduism and would strengthen the foreign religions.

The effect on the untouchables was direct, for they started looking inwards. The Christian community in India had been drawn largely from converts of untouchables. Christianity altered the outlook of the untouchables. The untouchable acquired a sense of human dignity and a sense of realization of his own existence as a man. At the same time, the Christian missionaries worked out a practical programme of uplift of the untouchables.

They started schools for their children. The untouchables were the most poverty-stricken strata of the Hindu society as they were without means of their subsistence. The missionaries realized this plight of the untouchables and provided them new means of earning their livelihood such as lands for cultivation, starting of schools, colleges, enterprises etc. they also worked for bettering their health conditions. Thus, new cultural and social atmosphere generated by Christian Missionaries enabled the untouchables not only to elevate them to a better position but also contributed to the growth of new leadership within own community. Ranga Rao[24] who studied Dalit Christians in erstwhile Andhra Pradesh observed that conversion helped the Dalits in escaping from pejorative names of their castes as Mala or Madiga. Any Christian when enquired about caste answered that he or she is a Christian instead of naming the caste. Given the predominant number of Dalits among Christians, 'Christians' became synonymous with 'Dalits'. Further Rao observed that Christians of Reddy caste when enquired about their social status answered that they were Reddys. Some of the Kamma Christians in order to make their caste identity conspicuous, suffix the appellation 'Chaudhary' to their names. In Andhra Pradesh, Kammas use the appellation 'Chaudhary' by considering themselves as analogous to Jats of Northern India. Thus, it is inferred that Christianity was used as a shield against untouchability by the Dalits.

Reform Movement

Various social reform movements were started during mid-19th century to eradicate the then existing evils in the Hindu society and thereby uplift the untouchables. Earlier, 500 years before the birth of Jesus Christ, Buddha challenged the social order prescribed by 'Purusha Suktha'.[25] In the succeeding centuries, saints like Chakradhar, Ramananda, Nandanar, Ravidas and Chokamela succeeded to a great extent in propagating equality through the Bhakti movement. The later saints were from the untouchable community.[26]

Basava who was a minister of a Kannada king during 12th century, tried in his own way to dismantle this system.[27] Brahma Naidu, a powerful Prime Minister of Malideva Raju of Palanadu in Andhra in the 14th century was a great social reformer among the higher and lower castes. He had adopted Kannama Dasu, Mala (untouchable) caste as his beloved son. Perhaps Barahma Naidu might be the first caste Hindu in the history of India who had adopted an untouchable as his son. Later, he appointed Kannama as the chief of his army. Further, Brahma Naidu had brought up eight boys of different castes along with his son in his own house to encourage others to have human outlook and equality towards the oppressed people in the society. In the name of universal brotherhood, irrespective of caste and religion, he enacted laws for the entry of untouchables into the temples. In fact, Barahma Naidu belongs to 'Padmanayaka Velama'.

Then, this was followed by other religious reform movements started by men like Raja Ram Mohan Roy, Dayananda Saraswati, Ramakrishna Paramahamsa and Vivekananda. They fought against the evils that existed in Hinduism, particularly against untouchability in their own ways.

However, considering the radical ideology, revolutionary steps of reform and their tremendous impact on the lower strata of the Hindu society, the movements started by Jyotiba Phule, Narayana Guru and Dr B.R. Ambedkar for eradication of caste and untouchability are significant and notable among all other movements.

Chandra Bhan Prasad, a Dalit intellectual called upon the Dalits to celebrate 25 October as English Day to mark the birthday of Lord Macaulay whom he calls Father of Indian modernity. When discussions were in progress in the English East India Company's administration on whether to adopt English or vernaculars as medium of instruction from the mid-19th century in the institutions of higher learning funded by the Company, in 1835, Lord Macaulay the member of the Supreme Council of the Company favoured English with his Minute on Indian Education. Macaulay's minute broke the dominance of Sanskrit, Persian and Arabic – a privilege reserved for the elite castes. English, according to Macaulay would promote European type of modern education with focus on modern sciences. It would also promote liberal political and economic ideas and a representative government. Macaulay hoped that through English education, Indians in future would demand European institutions. English could usher in an era of cultural rejuvenation for Dalits. A temple dedicated to 'English – the Dalit Goddess' was built in Bankagaon village near Lakhimpur Kheri in Uttar Pradesh in 2010 with the inspiration of Chandra Bhan Prasad.[28]

Dr B.R. Ambedkar (1891–1956) and Emancipation of Untouchables

Ambedkar was born in Mahar caste, an untouchable community in Maharashtra. He emerged as the champion of downtrodden. He dedicated his life for the cause of his community which had been subjected to all kinds of suppression and exploitation for centuries together. He took many steps to reform the way of life of his people. He urged them to give up beef-eating and menial services like dragging of the dead cattle out of the village. He appealed to his people to become literate and send their children to schools. He started a paper called *Mook Nayak* in 1920 which means the leader of the voiceless.

Ambedkar led the temple entry movement. The most important part of this movement was Kalaram Temple Satyagraha in Nasik in 1930. It was the most important large scale satyagraha led by him. His movement for temple entry was more of social than religious nature. Ambedkar took this temple entry programme in order to establish the rights of the untouchables. Following 1930, Ambedkar concentrated on the improvement of the educational standards of his community and establishment of their political rights.

By 1930, Ambedkar came to be regarded as the only powerful leader of the untouchables of the whole country. He played an historical role in the Round Table Conference (RTC) with regard to the achievement of rights of the untouchables without opposing struggle for national freedom. In the RTC, he emphasized that the untouchables constitute a distinct social group and could not be considered as an integral part of the Hindu community. So, on the basis of this argument he wanted separate electorate for untouchables.

However, this move by Dr Ambedkar was opposed by Gandhi. He rejected separate electorate for untouchables on the plea that the untouchables were Hindus and separate electorate would create a schism in the Hindu society. When separate electorate was obtained by Ambedkar, Gandhi protested against it by starting 'Fast unto death' in 1932 in Yerwada Jail at Poona (now Pune). The aim of the fast was to force Ambedkar to give up a plan of 'separate electorate' for the untouchables. This created tension in the whole country. To resolve this deadlock and to save Gandhi's life, Madan Mohan Malaviya and other Hindu leaders decided to hold a conference in Bombay (now Mumbai) on 19 September 1932 and invited Ambedkar to participate in the Conference.

On the eve of the conference, Ambedkar issued a statement asserting:

> There have been many Mahatmas in India whose sole object was to remove untouchability and to elevate and absorb the depressed classes but every one of them failed to solve the problems of untouchables. Mahatmas have come and Mahatmas have gone but the untouchables remain untouchables for ever.[29]

Later an agreement was reached between Ambedkar and Gandhi. Ambedkar gave up the demand for separate electorates which he won in the RTC and accepted the 'Joint electorates' in which the caste Hindus constituted majority. This agreement is known as the famous 'Poona Pact'.

Christophe Jaffrelot observes that in conversation with Sardar Patel on the second day of his fast against the Communal Award, Gandhi said '*the untouchables do not realize that a separate electorate will create division among Hindus so much that it will lead to bloodshed. "Untouchable" hooligans will make common cause with Muslim hooligans and kill caste Hindus. Has the British Government no idea of all this? I do not think so*'[30] (emphasis added).

John C.B. Webster observes that Gandhi was wedded to the communal view of caste. He not only opposed the Communal Award for the Depressed Classes but also instructed that the Harijan Sevak Sangh activities be confined only to Hindu Harijans.[31]

The Motilal Nehru Committee established by Congress in reaction to the appointment of the Simon Commission, consulted Muslim, Sikh, Christian, Parsi, Anglo-Indian and non-Brahmin organizations, but it completely ignored the Dalit movements. It included no provisions for the protection of 'untouchables'.[32]

Ambedkar himself observed that the Poona Pact was accepted because of the coercive fast of Gandhi and because of the assurance given at the time that the Hindus will not interfere in the election of the Scheduled Castes.[33]

Another important step taken by Ambedkar to improve the lot of the untouchables was the establishment of 'Independent Labour Party' in 1937 on the model of Labour Party in Britain. In 1942,

Ambedkar was appointed as a member in Viceroy's Executive Council, which is the supreme body to decide all the administrative matters in India. Ambedkar was invited to take up Labour portfolio. Before assuming office Ambedkar attended the All India Depressed Classes Conference in Nagpur in July 1942. In this conference, Ambedkar appealed to his people thus – 'Educate, Agitate and Organize, have faith in yourself. It is a battle cry'.[34] This conference also announced the formation of 'Scheduled Caste Federation' which was officially established in 1946.

Ambedkar was elected to the Constituent Assembly and later was elected Chairman of the Drafting Committee of the Indian Constitution. He submitted the draft Constitution to the Constituent Assembly for its approval which officially came into force on 26 January, 1950. In fact, Ambedkar did not find a place among the 296 members initially sent to the Constituent Assembly. It was left to Jogendra Nath Mandal, a noted Dalit leader from East Bengal, to take up the challenge. He was nominated to the Constituent Assembly from East Bengal. To enable a genius like Ambedkar to enter the Constituent Assembly, Mandal withdrew his candidature to the Assembly. During the six months between 9th December 1946 and 3rd June 1947, the Assembly was immensely dependent on the excellent and dedicated work of Ambedkar. But Ambedkar lost his seat after East Bengal became a part of Pakistan. Without his presence Vallabhbhai Patel and the President of the Assembly Rajendra Prasad felt that the work of the Assembly would be crippled. Hence, there was a great urgency on their part to get back the services of Ambedkar for the Assembly. Rajendra Prasad wrote a letter on 30th June, 1947 to B.G. Kher, the Premier of Bombay Presidency[35]:

> ... Apart from any other consideration, we have found Dr Ambedkar's work both in the Constituent Assembly and the various Committees to which he was appointed to be of such an order as to require that we should not be deprived of his services. As you know, he was elected from Bengal, and after division of the province he has ceased to be a member of the Constituent Assembly. I am anxious that he should attend the next session of the Constituent Assembly commencing from 14th July and it is therefore necessary that he should be elected immediately ...[36]

On 1 July 1947, Vallabhbhai Patel too wrote a letter to B.G. Kher:

> ... Confirming my conversation with you last night, you have to make arrangement for Dr Ambedkar's election, if possible before, the 14th. If the date of nomination is 4th, then the only way to finish the work before the 14th is to persuade other candidates to withdraw. Anyway, you do your best ... .[37]

The above two letters written to B.G. Kher by Rajendra Prasad and Vallabhbhai Patel prove that the stalwarts of Congress also recognized the indispensability of Ambedkar's services in drafting the Constitution. Few weeks before the dawn of independence, Jawaharlal Nehru accompanied by Sarojini Naidu met Gandhi who enquired the progress of the Constitution making. Nehru replied that he was not satisfied with the progress and hence sought Gandhi's permission to seek the services of Sir Ivor Jennings, an international authority on constitutional law who helped many countries in drafting their Constitutions. By then Gandhi learnt from Rajendra Prasad, Rajagopalachari, Vallabhbhai Patel and even Jagjivan Ram of the erudite contributions of Ambedkar as member of various committees. Hence, he instantly suggested the name of Ambedkar and also recommended his inclusion in the Union Cabinet. Though Nehru expressed his displeasure over the recommendation by alleging that Ambedkar was a blockade to the freedom struggle, Gandhi's word prevailed as he emphasized that Ambedkar's 'talent and capacity' should be utilized for building modern India. Thus, Ambedkar became Law Minister in Nehru's Cabinet and also the Chairman of the Drafting Committee.[38] Ambedkar observed:

> I came into the Constituent Assembly with no greater aspiration than to safeguard the interests of Scheduled Castes. I had not the remotest idea I would be called upon to undertake the most responsible function. I was, therefore, surprised when the Assembly elected me to the Drafting Committee. I was more than surprised when the Drafting Committee elected me to be its Chairman.[39]

Before his death, on 6 December 1956, Ambedkar and his followers embraced Buddhism. During this ceremony, it was decided to establish a political party. After his death, his followers established a political party i.e. Republican Party of India (RPI).

Ambedkar was the most outstanding and tireless fighter on behalf of the untouchables and he exposed the caste Hindus' hypocrisies and reactionary policies of the Congress. He initially demanded separate settlements for the untouchables. Later, he advocated the nationalization of land as a socialistic programme – a programme of equitable distribution which was expected to dismantle the iniquitous social structure.

Still in India, the untouchables continue to face social and economic disabilities. Though the Constitution abolished the practice of untouchability and a separate Act called the 'Untouchability Offence Act of 1955' was introduced, the practice of untouchability still exists in the villages and some urban places. The Scheduled Castes and Scheduled Tribes (prevention of atrocities) Act 1989 has not been able to act as a total deterrent against the atrocities against the vulnerable sections of the society. Often the upper castes use this Act in the name of a Dalit against their rivals to settle their personal scores.

However, the phenomenon of atrocities on the Scheduled Castes after independence appears to be distinct from that witnessed in the past. There has been a great change among the Scheduled Castes people due to the spread of education and they became conscious of their rights guaranteed by the Constitution. This led to tensions between Scheduled Castes and caste Hindus. The caste Hindus are disquieted over the rights guaranteed to the Dalits by the Constitution. Atrocities against Dalits, be it the Khairlanji killings in Maharashtra or the Laxmipet killings in Andhra Pradesh only reflect the intolerance of caste Hindus against the assertiveness of Dalits. In both the incidents cited the killers belonged to Other Backward Castes (OBCs). It is significant to note that while the OBCs demand benefits on par with Scheduled Castes, in the village context in particular, they undermine the Dalits. Accommodation of the interests of the Dalits is an ordeal to the backward Castes.

Reservations and Distributive Justice

Though Ambedkar advocated for annihilation of caste, the concept of reservations stands twined with politics. Caste has pivotal importance in the politics of India. It became a symbol of identity and hence it gathered major stakes in politics.

Reservations guaranteed to the SCs by the Constitution are being cornered by those who have an advantageous start in their life. The urbanites and the succeeding generations of those who already availed themselves of the reservations, continue to preemptively grab the reservations before their economically backward caste brethren could reach for them. These consequences have rendered the reservation policy lopsided.

Owing to lack of a thorough review of the reservation policy, certain erroneous features which outlived their utility continue to be a part of the law. The political parties or the ruling class are not inclined to correct the imbalances, for it amounts to antagonizing the vote banks. On the other hand, the poor among the Dalits are not educated enough or strong enough to espouse their own cause. Any such movement even if initiated would not sustain for long. It needs the support of the enlightened groups, who must plan to sustain the movement and to lead it to its logical end.

Though democracy is a better form of governance compared with dictatorship, the former is fraught with its own demerits – the concept of majoritarianism being a major threat. Since 'majority' is a decisive factor in the formation of the government, the political parties take extreme care lest they incur the wrath of their vote banks. Every opportunity is explored to create assured vote banks. Among backward castes in Andhra Pradesh there are certain castes which are fairly advanced but were included in the list of backward castes and the political parties also could not oppose their inclusion. Any objection on the part of a political party would result in a backlash and the parties fear loss of patronage by the caste in question. Political parties in their desperate bid to acquire political power, devise often irrational or one-sided policies which defy reason. The decision of the INC government in Maharashtra to promulgate an ordinance granting 16 per cent reservation to Marathas and five per cent reservations to Muslims on 9 July 2014[40] is a case in point. This was stayed by the High Court on 14 November 2014 on the ground that the reasons cited in support of the condition are not convincing. In fact, the Government of Maharashtra led by the INC and the Nationalist Congress Party knew fully well that there is a Supreme Court stricture limiting the total percentage of reservation to 50. The Ordinance increased the percentage of reservation to 73 in violation of the Supreme Court verdict. In course of legal whetting, the violation might have been reported. Yet the government in its anxiety to construct a vote bank on the eve of elections went ahead with the ordinance despite knowing that such a step would not stand judicial scrutiny. As anticipated the Bombay High Court stayed the 16 per cent quota to Marathas and partially stayed five per cent reservation to Muslims in its order issued on 14 November 2014.[41] The INC's intention was to retain political power by resorting to an offer of sops to a caste group. Political parties in a bid to outmanoeuvre each other, design such policies which are not usually in keeping with the spirit of the Constitution although they justify the letter of it.

In 1983 elections to the AP State Legislative Assembly, N.T. Rama Rao swept the polls in coastal Andhra but could not perform equally well in the Telangana region. Hence, he devised a strategy to expand his support base in Telangana. He aimed to create a vote bank of Backward Castes (BCs) in Telangana. He always claimed to have worked for the welfare of BCs. He preferred them at his party's organizational level, and also while fielding candidates at various levels of election.

In 1986, Rama Rao as Chief Minister announced the increase in the quota of BC reservation from 25 per cent to 44 per cent in government jobs and educational institutions. He learnt through intelligence sources that the Congress Party under the leadership of the then External Affairs Minister P. Shiv Shanakar was planning to call for a mammoth gathering of BC leaders. This convention was expected to swing the BCs behind Congress. As the BCs constituted 52 per cent of the State's population, Rama Rao was alarmed. On 4 July 1986 he ordered that the N.K. Muralidhara Rao Commission report on reservations submitted in 1982 be examined immediately. The same day he declared that the recommendation of the Commission to increase the percentage of reservation from 25 to 44 as accepted by the government in a precipitously convened cabinet meeting. However, he added a rider that only those below an annual income of ₹ 12,000 were eligible for reservation.[42]

Though Rama Rao's decision managed to take the wind out of the sails of convention presided by Shiv Shankar, the latter described it as a political stunt and cautioned that the increase in reservations to BCs is a ploy to provoke the upper castes to challenge the government's decision in the court of law, whereupon it would be struck down by the court. The convention ended up in the formation of Andhra Pradesh Backward Classes Sangham with the Congress MP, T. Bala Goud as its President.[43] In fact the Sangham was critical of Rama Rao for stipulating an income limit to avail reservations. It demanded the deletion of income limit to enjoy reservations.

The Muralidhar Rao Commission was constituted in February 1982. The Commission submitted its report in September 1982. It recommended 44 per cent reservation of government jobs and seats in educational institutions for the 52 per cent of BC population. The Commission also included ten more castes or subcastes in the list of BCs and the total rose to 102 castes. This recommendation was not implemented by the Congress government. It was believed that due to non-implementation of this policy that the Congress government was defeated at the hustings in 1983 paving the way for the TDP to come to power.[44]

The Commission recommended the increase of quota in respect of Backward Castes from 25 to 44 per cent. While accepting the Commission's recommendations, Rama Rao also increased the Scheduled Castes quota from 14 to 15 per cent and the Scheduled Tribes from five to six per cent. As the increase of BC quota was challenged in AP High Court, a three Judge full bench of the Court on 5 September 1986 struck down the increase as unconstitutional.[45] Despite filmic charisma, Rama Rao had to resort to political manoeuvres to sustain people's support, for the politicians bartered attractive concessions for people's patronage.

Of late a demand for inclusion of Kapu caste in the BC list has gained ground after being dormant for about a decade. In 1953, the Union Government appointed the Kakasaheb Kalelkar Commission to identify Socially and Educationally Backward Castes to consider them for SEBC reservations as a policy of protective discrimination. As the Government was not convinced with the vague criteria prescribed by the Commission, it asked the state governments to evolve their criteria to identify the Backward Castes. Subsequently the state of AP in 1963 issued a Government Order (GO) specifying a list of Backward Castes and granting them 25 per cent reservations. This was challenged in the AP High Court and the Court struck down the GO as unconstitutional and directed the Government to provide financial assistance to such backward caste people whose annual income is below ₹ 1500.[46]

The AP Government issued another GO by identifying 112 Backward Castes in 1966 and it was also struck down by the AP High Court on the grounds that no proper investigation was carried out in determining the list of BCs, and the Director, Social Welfare and the Law Secretary who prepared the list were no experts in carrying out such an exercise. The AP Government then challenged it in Supreme Court which upheld the High Court's verdict. In 1968, the AP Government appointed the Anantha Raman Commission to prepare a list of BCs. The Commission prepared a list of 93 castes and accordingly the government issued a GO in 1970 reserving 25 per cent of jobs in government recruitment and equal percentage of seats in educational institutions. The challenged GO was struck down by the AP High Court but it was later on upheld by the Supreme Court. The State government again appointed the Muralidhar Rao Commission in 1982 to review the list of BCs. The Commission was to determine the nature of social and educational backwardness of different sections of citizens. The Commission in its report did not recommend the inclusion of Kapus, Ontaris, Balijas and Telagas in the list of BCs.[47]

In 1994, Mudragada Padmanabham, a Kapu leader of the East Godavari District, undertook hunger strike demanding the inclusion of Kapus (Kapus, Ontaris, Balijas and Telagas are collectively referred to as Kapus in this thesis). By then the Backward Classes Commission headed by Justice K.B. Puttuswamy was already studying the demand of 53 castes demanding inclusion into BCs list. Padmanabham, apart from the concessions accruing to the BCs, demanded state owned Finance Corporation to fund the Kapu entrepreneurs.[48]

The agitation in the districts where Kapus were predominant had intensified. In order to placate the agitating Kapus, the then Chief Minister Kotla Vijaya Bhaskara Reddy heading the Congress government, issued a GO providing certain non-statutory educational benefits and economic schemes to poor people. Another GO was issued providing non-statutory educational and economic support schemes to poor among Kapus whose annual income is below ₹ 12,000 But this step of state government did not appease the Kapus. The agitation continued with added vigour. Then the State Government issued GO Ms No. 30 dated 25.08.1994 declaring 14 communities as Backward Classes which included various groups of Kapus. As this GO was challenged in the High Court of Andhra Pradesh, the Court quashed it in a majority judgment. This was not challenged by the Government in the Supreme Court.[49]

Thus, populist schemes and policies aimed at creating vote banks to perpetuate political power endanger the stability of the society. But in democracy, pleasing the electorate is one of the ways of securing their mandate. Often the politicians do not hesitate to fracture the unity of the people by patronizing some and being non-committal on others.

While presenting the Constitution to the Constituent Assembly Ambedkar observed:

> On the 26th of January 1950, we are going to enter into a life of contradictions. In politics we will have equality and in social and economic life we will have inequality. In politics we will be recognizing the principle of one man one vote and one vote one value. In our social and economic life, we shall, by reason of our social and economic structure, continue to deny the principle of one man one value. How long shall we continue to live this life of contradictions? How long shall we continue to deny equality in our social and economic life? If we continue to deny it for long, we will do so only by putting our political democracy in peril. We must remove this contradiction at the earliest possible moment or else those who suffer from inequality will blow up the structure of political democracy which this Assembly has so laboriously built up.[50]

Thus, unless efforts in that direction are made to remove the contradictions, social and political stability in the country cannot be achieved and democracy would be rendered unsalutary.

Notes

1. B.R. Ambedkar, *Annihilation of Caste,* Bheem Patrika Publications, Jalandhar, 1975, p. 34.

2. Jagjivan Ram, *Caste Challenge in India,* Vision Books Pvt. Ltd., New Delhi, 1980, p. 33.
3. M.N. Srinivas, *Caste in Modern India and Other Essays,* Asia Publishing House, Bombay, 1977, pp. 7–8.
4. B.R. Ambedkar, *Castes in India, their Mechanism, Genesis and Development,* Bheem Patrika Publications, Jalandhar, 1973, p. 10.
5. Ibid., p. 11.
6. M.N. Srinivas, No. 3, p. 3.
7. Kane's definition of Caste, cited in an Article: 'Dialectics of Caste and Class Politics' by Sharad Patil, *Economic and Political Weekly,* Vol. 7 and 8, Annual Number, 1979.
8. B.R. Ambedkar, Ibid., No. 1, p. 49.
9. Ibid., p. 57.
10. S.K.S. Natham, 'The Star among the Revolutionaries' in *Thoughts on Dr Ambedkar,* Hotlal Nim (ed), Siddhartha Educational and Cultural Society, Agra, 1969, p. 2.
11. B.R. Ambedkar, *The Untouchables,* Bheem Patrika Publications, Jalandhar, 1948, Preface.
12. Michal Moffatt, *An Untouchable Community in South India,* Princeton University Press, New Jersey, 1979, p. 33.
13. Stanley Ross, 'Hindu Customs and their Origins', cited in Kuber's *Ambedkar: A Critique*, PPH, New Delhi, 1977, p. 41.
14. B.R. Ambedkar, No. 11, pp. 41–50.
15. Ibid., p. 34–39.
16. Ibid.
17. Ibid.
18. Ibid., p. 42.
19. Ibid., pp. 109–160.
20. Lousie Ouwerkerk, *The Untouchable of India,* Oxford University Press, London, 1945, p. 17.
21. Ardythe Basham, *The Untouchable Soldiers,* Balaji Traders, Bangalore, 1980, p. 13.
22. Ibid., p. 18.
23. Lousie Ouwerkerk, No. 20.
24. Author's interview with Professor K. Ranga Rao, Department of Sociology, Andhra University, 14 August 1993.
25. B.R. Ambedkar, *Buddha and the Future of His Religion,* Bheem Patrika Publications, Jalandhar, 1973, p. 4.
26. Ibid., No. 11.
27. B. Kuppuswamy, *Social Change in India,* Vikas Publishing House, Ghaziabad, 1972, p. 176.

28. *The Times of India*, 9 May 2010.
29. Dhananjay Keer, *Life and Mission of Dr Ambedkar*, Popular Prakashan, Bombay, 1962, p. 163.
30. Christophe Jaffrelot, *Dr Ambedkar and Untouchability: Analysing and Fighting Caste*, Permanent Black, Delhi, 2005, pp. 64–65.
31. John C.B. Webster, 'Who is a Dalit?' in S.M. Michael (ed), *Dalits in Modern India: Vision and Values*, Sage Publications, New Delhi, 2007, pp. 76–88.
32. Christophe Jaffrelot, No. 29, p. 56.
33. B.R. Ambedkar, *States and Minorities: What are Their Rights and How to Secure Them in the Constitution of Free India*, Dr Ambedkar Memorial Society, Hyderabad, 1970, p. 64.
34. Dhananjay Keer, No. 28, p. 173.
35. H.V. Hande, *Ambedkar and the Making of the Indian Constitution: A Tribute to Babasaheb Dr B.R. Ambedkar*, Macmillan Publishers India Ltd., New Delhi, 2009, pp. 8–23.
36. Ibid.
37. Ibid.
38. Ibid.
39. Ibid., pp. 22–23.
40. *The Hindu*, 10 July 2014.
41. *The Hindu*, 15 November 2014.
42. *India Today*, 15 August 1986.
43. Ibid.
44. B.L. Mathur, *Encyclopedia of Backward Castes: Commissions*, Vol. 2, Kalpaz Publications, Delhi, 2004, pp. 31–32
45. *India Today*, 30 September 1986.
46. http://indiankanoon.org/doc/1869869/?type=print accessed on 23.03.2014
47. Ibid.
48. *India Today*, 31 July 1994.
49. http://indiankanoon.org/doc/1869869/?type=print accessed on 23.03.2014
50. http://www.outlookindia.com/article/The-Grammar-Of-Anarchy/289235 accessed on 23.03.2014.

CHAPTER 3

Dalit Movements in Colonial Andhra and Telangana

The Dalit movements in colonial Andhra and Telangana form a prelude to the evolution of political elite among the Dalits. Thus, it is to be examined as to how, from the state of oppression by virtue of occupying the lowest rung of social ladder, these sections developed political consciousness and began to participate in electoral politics. The trajectory of the Dalits' progress from the rigidities of a closed society to democratically governed system needs to be studied. While the Andhra region before India's independence was within the Madras Presidency under the British rule, the Telangana region was part of the Princely State of Hyderabad under the rule of Nizams.

The state under study was ruled by Satavahanas during whose reign the four-fold caste system became very rigid as they were champions of Hinduism, though their queens followed Buddhism. Though foreign invaders like the Sakas and Yavanas settled in India and got absorbed into the Hindu fold, the attempts of Gautamiputra Satakarni (78–102 AD), the Satavahana ruler to resist the absorption of foreign tribes into the Hinduism further rigidified the caste system. The Ikshavakus, the successors of Satavahanas, the Brihat Palayanas, Anandas, Salankayanas, Kalingas, Pitrubhaktas, Marathas, Vashisthas, Vishnkundins, Chalukyas, Kakatiyas, Reddis, Vijayanagara kings ruled over various parts of Andhra Pradesh at different times in the history of the state.[1] During this period most of the rulers proved to be the champions of Hinduism. They respected the institutes of Law or the Smrithis, which were attributed religious sanctity.

Though Buddhism was patronized by some of the rulers, in course of time it was absorbed into Hinduism with Buddha being declared as one of the ten incarnations of Lord Vishnu, the Hindu god. It is thus understood that the avenues for mobility for the untouchables were not yet open as Hinduism continued to remain rigid. Later the Qutubshahis of Golconda followed by the Nizams of Hyderabad and the British ruled over various territories of the present state.

Brahmins enjoyed the patronage during this period given their knowledge of revenue collection and administration. A sect called *Golconda vyaparulu* emerged among the Brahmins of the state with the patronage enjoyed by 'Akkanna and Madanna', the two Brahmins who occupied prominent positions in administration during the Qutubshahi rule. It is with the advent of British rule that the western values of liberty, equality and fraternity gradually entered the Indian educational system. For the ground level administration, the British East India Company needed ministerial staff. Hence, they encouraged English as a medium of education as the language would act as a lingua franca of the British governed territories. They also introduced the civil and penal code or their concept of jurisprudence, which marked the end of indigenous institutes of Law, which contained discriminatory provisions. The social disabilities in the Indian culture, which were inconsistent with western values, were sought to be dispelled. Thus, began the socio-religious reform movements.

Prior to the reform movements, which took place during the British rule, there were instances of Hindu saints attempting to fight for the rights of Dalits. Dnyaneshwar, one of the greatest reformer saints of Maharashtra, who was excommunicated from Brahminism, opened the gates of Vedic spiritualism to the Hindu masses including the Dalits. Another excommunicated Brahmin saint, Eknath also fought for the liberation of the untouchables. The fourteenth century saint poet, Chokhamela was initiated into devotional poetry by another saint Namdev.[2] The Bhakti movement thus tried to interpret the religious scriptures liberally and broadly by dispensing with obscurantism. Drawing spirit from the Bhakti movement and the charitable approach of Christian missionaries towards the Dalits, rulers like Gaekwad of Baroda and Sahu Maharaj encouraged education among Dalits.[3] B.R. Ambedkar, who relentlessly championed for the rights of the Dalits was financially supported by them in pursuit of his higher studies.

Many non-Dalits generously contributed to the welfare of Dalits. Their munificence gave the Dalits access to knowledge and education, which were hitherto denied to them. In Andhra, Kandukuri Veeresalingam (1848-1919) started a school for Dalit children with the financial support of the Maharaja of Pithapuram. He established Prarthana Samaj in 1878 at Rajahmundry. Another branch of the Samaj was started at Kakinada in 1888. The same was changed into Brahmo Samaj in 1910. The Maharaja of Pithapuram Sri Venkata Mahipate Surya Bahadur (1885–1965) established two hostels for boys and girls at Pithapuram. The other social reformers like Chilakamarthy Lakshmi Narasimham (1867–1945), Raghupati Venkataratnam Naidu (1862–1939), Sri Nallapati Hanumanth Rao, Sri Vellanki Krishna Murthi and many others devotedly contributed to the uplift of the depressed classes.[4]

The Dalits also built schools and hostels to educate their children. The Burma factor helped them in the process. Vundru Tatayya (1850–1930) was one of the Burma returned Dalit reformer who owned about 150 acres of land in Ponnamanda village in Razole Taluk of East Godavari district. In 1920s, he built a school at Ponnamanda and also funded establishment of some other schools for Dalits. He extended financial assistance to schools established at Annavaram, Allavarm and Mogalikuduru villages of East Godavari District. In 1928, Jala Rangaswamy established two separate hostels for Dalit boys and girls at Rajahmundry. In 1930s, Eeli Vadapalli (1911–1972) established a school and a hostel for Dalit students at Mandapeta. He also established Lakshmi Industrial Training School at Ramachandrapuram. In 1936, Golla Chandraiah (1918–72) established a hostel at Razole for Dalit students. Pandu Lakshmana Swamy (1892–1960) and Moka Meerayya also established hostels for Dalit students.[5]

Vemuri Ramjee Rao (1891–1963)[6] established a school for the children of depressed classes at Bandar now known as Machilipatnam in Krishna District, as early as in 1907, much before

Gandhi gave a call to undertake Harijan welfare activities. His idea was to draw all the otherwise socially distanced children to the school and initiate them into education. By 1914, it transformed into a primary school. Ramjee Rao was a bachelor who dedicated his life to impart education to the deprived children.

He offered education to children of all castes in this school. The remarkable feature of the school was that children of upper castes were to share the same bench with the depressed class children. Apart from spending his own money on the school, he mobilized funds from various quarters including the Andhra Dalit migrants in Burma. Having toiled to run the school till 1927, he handed it over to the Labour Department of the Madras government.

In 1923, he established a hostel for the children of depressed classes. This was to create an ideal atmosphere, which would otherwise not be available in their villages. He set up a library in the hostel and also engaged teachers to tutor the students during study hours. The students were provided good quality food. This hostel was known as Depressed Classes Hostel. He encouraged students to play sports and games. He arranged training for the students in vocations like tailoring, welding, etc. as alternative sources of livelihood should they not secure a job in government service. Owing to his dedication to the service of the children of depressed classes, his fellow Brahmins nursed resentment against him and imposed a social boycott on him. They stopped entertaining him, and refused to offer him even a glass of water.

In 1929-30 when Gandhi was on a tour to Andhra visited Bandar and having learnt about the charitable activities of Ramjee Rao paid a visit to his hostel, extolled his services and fondly called him 'Deenabandhu'. The school started by him in 1907 and handed over to the Madras government in 1914 was later upgraded into High School by 1947. Velmula Kurmaiah who was a Minister in the Madras government was a product of Ramjee's charity. He used his good offices to develop the school further. Other prominent individuals who were products of Ramjee's charity were Koneru Ranga Rao who rose to the rank of Deputy Chief Minister, Neethipudi Ganapathi Rao who became MLA in 1978 and 1989, K. Madhava Rao who became Chief Secretary of Government of Andhra Pradesh and a host of civil servants and government functionaries including M. Dharmaiah, IAS, B. Sundara Rao another noted beneficiary became Chief Security Officer, New York, USA. Though Ramjee funded both school as well as hostel, which came to be known as Seva Sadan, they were gradually taken over by the government. Ramjee suffered a brief illness and breathed his last on 13 June 1963.

In Telangana, Arya Samaj played a serious role in preventing the Hindu Dalits from converting to Christianity and Islam. The Brahmo Samaj also played an active role in Hyderabad. The prominent social reformers of the region were Rai Balmukund, Baji Krishna Rao, Justice Keshav Rao and Vaman Rao Naik.[7]

Dalit Movements in Colonial Andhra

The colonial Andhra of pre-independence era was within the jurisdiction of Madras Presidency. It comprised twelve Telugu speaking districts of Ganjam, Vizagapatnam, East Godavari, West Godavari, Krishna, Guntur, Nellore, Chittoor, Cuddapah, Kurnool, Anantapur and Bellary.

The colonial education system, as such, could not meet the aspirations of the lower castes for socio-economic advancement. In the initial years of their rule, the British desisted thrusting on the system, concessions to the lower castes for, such precipitant steps could challenge the existing social system and may further antagonize the dominant castes. Hence, they were cautious in implementing such unprecedented measures, as commercial benefits were paramount for them. Nevertheless, the role of Christian missionaries in Andhra signalled a new epoch in the emancipation of Dalits from caste oppression.

Christian missionaries were the pioneers of western education in Andhra in the early decades of nineteenth century. Many missionaries worked in the midst of untouchables and carried out their proselytizing activities. Spread of education became a sine qua non for conversion to Christianity. Thus, the Dalits began to acquire the benefits of education. They obtained noticeable gains in education and employment. Missionary elementary schools provided access to education. This contributed to new awakening among the underprivileged. Education induced them to gradually contest for equality and social respect. Though there were provisions under the Woods Despatch 1854, for the education of the Depressed Classes, there was resistance from the upper castes. Hence, the colonial government yielded to the pressure of upper caste prejudices on the pretext that 'no principle however sound could be forced upon an unwilling society in defiance of social and religious sentiments'.[8]

The Hunter Commission in 1882 recommended the establishment of separate schools for the children of Depressed Classes. Thus, Labour Department of the Madras Presidency opened separate schools for the untouchables. This proposal encountered certain challenges like the shortage of teachers, as the upper caste teachers were unwilling to work in such schools. Such a precipitant step by the government was not acceptable to the upper and intermediary castes. Though the government had the will to promote the education of the Depressed Classes, resistance by the upper castes was manifest in the refusal of the upper caste teachers to work in the government run schools meant for the Dalits. Thus, the government decided to revert to the concept of common schools. It was decided to relocate the schools in areas which were distant to all the communities. Earlier, schools with Government aid were located in *Agraharams,* temples and in the other upper caste localities.[9]

Adi Andhra Mahasabha and the Struggle for Dalit Emancipation and Self-respect

A total number of sixty castes are recognized as Scheduled Castes (SCs) in Andhra Pradesh. They account for 15 per cent of total population of the state. Malas and Madigas are numerically significant SCs together accounting for a major percentage of the total SC population.

The Malas and Madigas are scattered all over the state. The Malas (also called Dher, Antyaja or Panchama) are considered as a subcaste of menials and servants. In the villages, they work as private servants, labourers, messengers, grooms and watchmen and live on the outskirts. Actually, the term Malas means hill men, probably because in the hill tracts of Telangana, by the pressure of later immigrants of higher castes, the indigenous sons of soil were driven to the hills for shelter. Their proportion in the population is considerable in the four delta districts (East Godavari, West Godavari, Krishna and Guntur), Chittor and Nellore. In Telangana, they are less in numbers than the Madigas. The Malas occupy the lowest and the most degraded position in the Indian society. Their touch is regarded as unclean by the higher castes. The village barbers do not shave their heads nor will the village washermen wash their clothes. The wells of the higher castes cannot be used by them. They eat the leftovers of all castes.

The Madigas in terms of caste hierarchy are the lowest in relation to Malas. They are sometimes referred to as Ettiwandlu, true to their occupation. Ettiwandlu are those who do the 'vetti' or 'begari' (forced labour). Chambar or Chamar (adoption of the Sanskrit Charmakar – leather worker), Kamati (menial worker), Gosangi (cow killer). To indicate their low births, members of other castes refer to them by approbations like *chandal, dher, and antyaja.* The latter two terms are also applied to Malas. In a bid for acquiring social respectability, the Madigas, on the other hand call themselves as *Panchamollu* (members of the fifth caste), *Peddinti Wandlu* (dwellers of big house) or *Matangi Makkalu* (children of mythical Goddess Matangi). Those who join the Army, refer to themselves as *Bandars.* They live like Malas on the outskirts of the villages and suffer all the indignities as do Malas. The extent of the rigours surrounding uncleanness can be measured by the fact that if a Brahman is touched by Madiga, he is required by the tradition to regain purification by bathing, washing clothes and changing the sacred thread. While the original occupation of the Madigas was skinning of dead animals and doing leather work, generally they also work as scavengers, village watchmen and village musicians. They have a larger population in Rayalaseema and Telangana. In smaller numbers they are found in all the districts of the State.

Apart from Malas and Madigas, there are 58 castes constituting a meagre proportion of about 8.5 per cent. Within the Malas and Madigas, there are so many subcastes. Among the most important Mala subcastes are Reddi-Bhoomi, Pakanati, Mala Masteen (protection force of Malas), Mala Dasu (also called as Sri Vaishnavaite, who perform the rituals of Malas), Sarrajulu (by profession they are weavers), Mala Devara (by profession they beg by displaying the images of God), Mala Jangam (by profession they beg and also perform religious rituals of Malas).

Among the important Madiga subcastes are: Madiga Bhogama (devadasis of Madigas), Madiga Dasulu (who perform the religious rituals of Madigas), Madiga Masteen (who constitute the protection force of Madigas).

Access to education either through the aid of Christian missionaries or by the steps taken by the British government aroused the Dalits to think about their deprivation and take an initiative to fight for their legitimate rights. The British rule provided an ambience of neutrality for the Dalits to ponder over their ascribed low social status and explore solutions to reform the oppressive and discriminatory system. Moreover, they were under the administration of rulers who were not supportive of the existing social system.

The educated Dalits dedicated themselves to work for the welfare of the excluded communities. The emergence of organic intellectuals among Dalits enabled them to organize themselves to launch a mass movement to articulate their grievances. Thus came into existence, the Adi-Andhra Mahasabha which held its first conference at Bezawada during 4 to 6 November 1917 under the presidentship of Bhagya Reddy Varma who already emerged as a crusader for the Dalit rights in the Nizam ruled Princely State of Hyderabad.

A series of conferences was held between 1917 to 1938 to discuss the strategies to improve the lot of the excluded groups. Prominent Dalit leaders who participated in the movement were Bhagya Reddy Varma, Sunduru Venkaiah, Kusuma Dharmanna, Vemula Kurmaiah, etc. These first generation Dalit intellectuals were products of Western education through Brahmo Samaj and Christian missionaries.[10] The main objectives of the movement were: abolition of untouchability, caste oppression and discrimination; negation of Brahmanical Hinduism, to counter the socio-cultural hegemony of the upper castes, and to organize the Dalit masses for achieving socio-economic and political equality.[11]

The periodic reforms in British administration, and the Western institutions of governance gave freedom to launch movements within a certain permissible framework e.g. the Indian National Congress motivated the Dalits to follow the methods adopted by some existing organizations in the freedom struggle. The self-respect and anti-caste movement of Periyar Ramasamy Naicker (1879–1973) also inspired the young Dalits into action.

With the freedom struggle in progress across the country, the Dalits organized their movements to highlight their grievances.

Adi Andhras

The Dalits claimed that they are Adi Andhras or the 'sons of soil' which means they are the original inhabitants of the land. Based on the demand of the Adi Andhra Mahasabha, the Dalits were designated by the then Government as Adi Andhras.[12] In fact, the terms Mala and Madiga, used to address the Dalits, carried a pejorative purport and hence a dignified and honourable term to strengthen the claims of the Dalits as the original inhabitants of the land was preferred. Jala Ranga Swamy observed that the *Panchamas* or the Dalits are *Anaryas* and were subjugated and enslaved by the Aryans. Hence, the Dalits as per their postulation, constitute the original inhabitants of India and are free from the concept of caste while the very concept of 'caste' is an Aryan import.

The Dalit intellectuals articulated their ideology and advocated their goals through writings. The liberal means of propagating the thought to inculcate reformative ideology was adopted by the Dalit intellectuals from the British and the Indian National Congress.

Kusuma Dharmanna wrote *Makoddu ee Nalladoratanamu* or 'We Do Not Want the Rule of Black Landlords'. Boyi Bheemanna's *Paleru* (annual servant) and *Coolie Raju* (the labour king) portrayed the miseries of Dalits and inspired them to overcome the challenges thrown up by the tradition guided society. 'Paleru' play was staged in Godavari, Krishna and Guntur districts. It is the story of a son of 'annual servant' evincing interest in education. Resisting a reprimanding father he leaves home, studies and becomes Deputy Collector and marries a girl of upper caste.[13] This play focused on the facilities available for education and how a determined low caste boy could attain a high position by defying the existing oppressive social system. It was staged in several villages especially in East and West Godavari districts. The author's father Aluri Narasimha Rao, son of Aluri Bheemiah, who hailed from Neerullipalem village in the erstwhile Narasapuram taluk and in the present Achanta mandal was an acclaimed Dalit harmonist and was deepiy associated with the background music of the play. He migrated to Rangoon (Burma) at a young age and was educated there. In course of his education, he had an opportunity to learn music. It is learnt through his personal experiences that Dalits who were normatively excluded from education and fine arts like music in India could acquire education and have access to music in Rangoon.

Nakka China Venkaiah wrote *Antu Dosham* or the sin of untouchability and *Harijana Keertanalu* or Harijana psalms. Jala Rangaswamy wrote *Antaranivarevvaru* or 'Who are the untouchables?' and *Malasuddi* or purification of the polluted. Some of the demands of the Adi-Andhra Mahasabha regarding education, employment and political representation were responded to favourably by the Justice Party in the Madras Presidency. A new department called Labour Department was created and apart from opening separate schools for Dalits, it also enabled assigning of government wastelands and *lankas* to Dalit rural poor peasants and labourers.[14]

Reaching out to the oppressed through writings, developed in them consciousness about their deprivation and infused in them the spirit to collectively fight for their rights. This was another effective tool of mobilization used by the Dalit intellectuals to enkindle revolutionary spirit in the Dalits. On the other hand, it conveyed to the government and also to the caste Hindus that the Dalits are no more the old tolerant lot and in the changing social and political milieu, they have developed awareness about their legitimate rights.

Journals like Kusuma Dharmanna's *Jayabheri*[15] and B.S. Murthy's *Navajeevana*[16] brought to light the atrocities committed against Dalits across the Telugu speaking districts and successfully moulded Dalit consciousness and articulation. The activists also rejected the term *Harijan* as patronizing. They were not looking for concessions from the caste Hindus. They firmly believed that they deserved a legitimate space in all spheres of life and having developed awareness, they would fight for it.

The Dalit movements aspired for secularization, humanization and liberalization of civil society on the lines of elite nationalists.[17] Aspiring to convert to Christianity was to delegitimize the traditional notions of status and rank. Though the earliest Protestant Christian Missionary activities among the Telugu speaking people in Madras Presidency took place in the second decade of the 18th century, the mass conversion of the lower castes in the rural and urban areas of colonial Andhra took place principally during the second half of the 19th century and first quarter of the 20th century. Apart from Roman Catholics Missions, the Church Mission Society, American Baptists, Lutherans and Anglicans played a catalytic role in socio-cultural transformation of Dalits.[18] They had the spirit and rigour to reach out to the excluded groups whose shadow was considered pollution by the caste Hindus. The Dalits on their part saw a hope for their welfare. Thus, Christianity became a potent channel to work for delegitimizing the ascriptive social order.

Kandukuri Veeresalingam's Brahmo Samaj facilitated Dalit sponsorship of education. Guduru Ramachandra Rao started a Sevashram at Gudivada and called upon the activists to work in all Telugu speaking districts. Those who were active during 1920s were Sunduru Venkaiah, Kusuma Venkatramaiah and Kusuma Dharmanna. In fact, in 1917 it was Guduru Ramachandra Rao who took the initiative to convene the Bezawada conference which was considered as the First Provincial Panchama Mahasabha with his protégé Sunduru Venkaiah acting as Chairman of the Reception Committee. As already stated Bhagya Reddy Varma, the Dalit leader from Hyderabad, presided over the conference. The delegates reconstituted themselves as First Adi-Andhra Mahajana Sabha. The Kanaka Durga temple which is now open for members of all the social strata was then closed for three days fearing forced entry by the delegates.[19]

After 1930, the Adi Andhra activities slackened for about five years and the Gandhian scheme of Harijan emancipation acquired prominence taking advantage of the lull in the Dalit movement. The Andhra branch of Harijan Seva Sangh was formed at Vijayawada in November 1932. The President was K. Nageswara Rao of Krishna district – a caste Hindu. M. Bapineedu was the General Secretary. The Joint Secretaries were Vemula Kurmayya of Krishna district and Naralasetty Devendrudu of West Godavari district. The Dalit leaders have been co-opted by the Congress to showcase their efforts towards Dalit emancipation. Earlier Devendrudu was nominated to the Madras Legislative Council.[20] The Congress swung into action to prove their concern for the problems of the

Dalits and in turn to prove to the British government that they represent all sections of the Indian society.

During 1934–35, N.G. Ranga, a leader belonging to Kamma caste, in order to move close to the Congress took up some Dalit emancipatory work which was a part of Gandhian scheme in the Congress. He formed 'Harijan Sevadal' by actively involving his wife, and both of them toured the Guntur and Krishna districts after launching a temple entry campaign at Govada village. Associated with them in this work were social reformers like Unnava Lakshminarayana the author of *Malapalle,* an acclaimed novel, and Guduru Ramachandra Rao M. Bapineedu was picked up from West Godavari district to be the General Secretary of Andhra branch of the Harijan Sevak Sangh.[21]

Unnava Lakshminaryana's *Malapalle*[22] or the 'Hamlet of the Untouchables' written in the year 1922, portrays the nexus between capitalists (including landed aristocrats) and bureaucrats who systematically crushed the rights of the Dalit masses. Various wings of the government – police, magisterial and judicial worked in league with each other to suppress the Dalits. The affected people become conscious of their exploitation work for their own emancipation along with peasants. The novel concludes with India achieving independence and Lakshminarayana conceives of a government structured to meet the demands of peasants and labour class, where all lead happy and stable lives. The novel stresses the need for cooperation between peasants and agricultural labourers. To buttress his proposition he shows a Kamma landlord's son helping a Dalit agricultural labourer in his endeavour to secure minimum wages for his brethren. This book was banned by the Government for its criticism of government departments.

In 1933 N.G. Ranga wrote a novel *Harijana Nayakudu*[23] or 'the Harijana Leader', which calls for cooperation between peasants and labourers. The story is about a harijan agricultural labourer's efforts to reform his community. He succeeds in his endeavour with the help of his Kamma landlord's son. Though Ranga narrates some instances which depict the cruelty and greediness of peasants, he ultimately concludes that the agricultural labourers could lead a harmonious life, if they coordinate their efforts with the peasants.

Irrespective of the advice to coordinate their efforts towards emancipation with the peasants, the writings did play an important role in awakening the Dalits. Upper caste writers themselves exposing the exploitation of Dalits by the government and upper caste administrative functionaries, have further alerted, encouraged and awakened the Dalits.

Gudipati Venkatachalam wrote *Malapilla,* a social drama, which portrays a love story between a Brahmin girl and an untouchable boy. Later a film was produced based on this story in 1938. It was directed by Gudavalli Ramabrahmam. The story is based on discrimination against Dalits of the village. Some try to work against the discrimination. They are opposed by Sundararama Sastri, a priest. His son Nagaraju, a photographer, falls in love with Shamapalatha a dalit girl. They both elope to Calcutta and the boy teaches the girl to read and write. The strained relations in the village between people of the two castes continue. As Sastri's wife is saved by dalits in a fire accident, his views begin to change. In the end both Nagaraju and Shamapalatha are married.

Eali Vadapalli (1911–71) and Geddada Brahmaiah (1912–50) organized a number of district conferences between 1938-40 and edited the Adi-Andhra Patrika to sensitize the Dalit masses and prepare them for a movement against upper caste hegemony and injustice meted out to them by the upper caste functionaries in the government.[24]

The state level Adi-Andhra Mahasabha resumed in 1935 (10th sabha) at Rajahmundry. It was inaugurated by Diwan Bahadur M.C. Rajah and presided over by Kusuma Venkataramaiah. The Eleventh Conference was held in 1936 and the Twelfth and final conference was held at Tallarevu in East Godavari district in 1938. In this conference, there was confrontation between the young radicals and the old organizers. The latter sought a resolution on temple entry but the former led by Pamu Rama Murthy of East Godavari district opposed it as a mere concession to Hinduism and hence did not serve a progressive purpose.[25] The youth envisioned beyond Hinduism for their emancipation as they believed that clash with orthodoxy only sapped their energies.

The final resolution included demands for reserved seats from Panchayat to Legislative Councils; sanctions against those opposing the education of untouchable children in schools; job reservations; formation of labour co-operatives and credit banks; to give forest and waste land to dalits. It must be noted that after the last conference, a large section of Dalit leadership was getting absorbed into the Congress with its Harijan terminology and its reiteration of Hindu identity. Under the influence of clientelistic politics, the Scheduled Caste elite who were in the forefront of the Dalit movement saw an opportunity to enter the power structure.

The joint electorate system of reservation emanating from the Poona Pact conveys that the SCs cannot win the elections from the reserved seats without the assent of the non-Dalits of the constituency. With regard to inclination towards Hinduism, there were some factors which played a catalytic role in the process. Boyi Bheemanna's writings gave fillip to the Hinduization of Dalit movement. In *Raaga Vasishtam* (1940) one of his published writings, he describes the marriage of Vasistha and Arundhati by emphasizing strong casteless Hindu nation and arguing that Harijans are Aryans.[26] By 1940s, the Adi Andhra movement in the coastal districts had disappeared. The elite were attracted to the power structure. The concessions they had been aiming for had been to a certain extent achieved by champions of the Dalit cause at national level like B.R. Ambedkar. As political space and opportunities in education and employment were created for Dalits, it was time for them to vie with each other to occupy various positions of power. Thus, the leading activists of the Dalit movement were either absorbed into Congress or the Communist parties.

Later, many young Dalits joined the Communist agricultural labour movements from 1940s including Guntur Bapanayya, Prasad Rao, M. Sriramulu – all of Krishna district; K. Rangarao, R.A. Kolayya, Kandikatla Nagabhushnam, Kaneti Mohan Rao, and Neethipudi Ganapathi Rao of East Godavari district. Guntur Bapanaiah became General Secretary of the Agricultural Labour Union and K. Suryaprakash its President from 1941–43. Suryaprakash Rao left the organization after the S.C. Federation was dubbed by them as a communal organization while Muslim League a political organization.[27]

Other prominent leaders who worked for the uplift of Dalits were Gurram Jashua (Guntur), Gottipati Brahmayya (Mausulipatam), B.S. Murthy, B.V. Ramanayya (East Godavari); Sardar Nagappa (Kurnool), Konada Suryaprakash Rao, Ravuri Ekambaram (Vijayawada), V.C. Keshav Rao (Krishna), Nandanar

Harishchandra (West Godavari); Mangalagiri Nanadas (Nellore) and many others.[28]

Ambedkar's impact was limited during this period because he was preoccupied with Maharashtra and Delhi. However, the concessions he won for the Dalits at national level did make an impact on the movement. The independent Dalit movement of Coastal Andhra faded away after the late 1940s. The space provided by various political organizations to Dalits impelled them to join such organizations. The formula of joint electorate, however, arrested their freedom to air their views freely for their success in electoral politics depended on the mercy of the dominant castes. Despite the influence of clientelism on the SC elite towards the leading political parties, most of the first generation Dalit leaders who did not yield to the overtures of the political parties, especially the Congress, stood their ideological ground. But it was not sustainable for long under the joint electorate system of reservations as was noticed from the results of second and third Assembly and Lok Sabha elections. Though the leaders belonging to the era of Dalit movements won the elections on the ticket of Communists or other non-Congress parties in the first General Elections, a shift towards the Congress due mainly to clientelistic politics was evident from the second and third General Elections as will be discussed in the fourth chapter.

Dalit Movements in Telangana

The Dalits in the state of Hyderabad were in a feudal structure. Their choice either in industry or agriculture was limited. The Nizam suppressed any kind of a political movement though it did not directly target his administration. The devadasi system involving Mala/Madiga girls called *bsavis or matangis* prevailed in the state where the said *basavis or matangis* established liaison with affluent or noble Muslims of Hyderabad. In 1910, Dalits launched a movement amidst differences over Muslims physically exploiting Dalit girls. This movement was led by Bhagya Reddy Varma and Arigay Rama Swamy. Varma's original name was Madari Bhagayya. He changed his name after joining the Brahmo Samaj. This is a reflection of the process of Sanskritization where the low castes emulated the culture and lifestyles of upper castes or frequently the twice-born castes to gain legitimacy to their acculturation in the Hindu social structure. The Dalit organizations stressed internal social reform. Propagation to give up alcohol and meat-eating at social functions and abolition of devadasi system are cases in point. These Dalit groups even set up alternative courts to settle disputes within the castes outside the state courts.[29]

Radicalization of Dalits began with the appellation 'Adi'. The Adi-Hindu conferences were organized between 1912 and 1924. Arigay Ramaswamy who formed a social reform group in Secunderabad was active in the depressed classes movement in that area. The idea that Dalits are the original inhabitants of the country was developed in the Madras presidency. This was manifest in the three main 'Adi' names. Adi-Dravida or original Dravidians/Tamils, Adi-Andhras or the original people of the Telugu speaking country; and Adi-Karnatakas for the Dalits of Karnataka region. In Secunderabad it was coined as Adi-Hindu. In 1922, Arigay Ramaswamy started the 'Adi-Hindu Jatiyonnati Sabha with Konday Venkataswamy as President, and J. Papaiah and Arigay Ramaswamy as Secretaries. The association in 1927 was renamed as Adi-Hindu Mahasabha. Venkataswamy became a staunch lieutenant of Ramaswamy and eventually the General Secretary of the association. B.S. Venkata Rao, Madari Govindaraju, C.S. Ethirajan, P.R. Venkataswamy and others joined as members. About that time, Bhagya Reddy Varma transformed his Manya Sangam into Adi-Hindu Social Service League. This became the main organization for the agitating Dalits against the oppressive system. The Adi-Hindus claimed to be the descendents of the original inhabitants of the country before the advent of Aryans, and held the view that 'caste' is completely an Aryan concept.[30]

More radical and anti-Hindu approach began to evolve by 1930s. The demand to reform caste cultures began to make way for assertion of rights by the Dalits, having understood the exploitative mechanisms adopted by the dominant castes. They aimed to move beyond Hinduism in course of their struggle for emancipation. The British hegemony in the neighbouring provinces had weakened the Hindu Institutes of Law and the scope to fight for liberty appeared to be encouraging. There was free interaction between the leaders of coastal Andhra and Telangana in course of Dalit movements. It was Bhagyareddy Varma who presided over the first meeting of the Dalits at Bezwada.

Meanwhile, Venkataswamy who was profoundly impressed by the groundswell of support to the Ambedkarite conferences parted ways with Arigay Ramaswamy and in association with a businessman, B.S. Venkat Rao who had been supportive of Adi-Hindu Mahasabha for some years, formed the Youth League of Ambedkarites. This organization was recruiting educated Dalit youth to spread the awareness on the exploitation of Dalits by the caste Hindus. This movement focused more on religious issues rather than political issues. Venkatswamy's obsession with anti-Hindu stand annoyed the other members as it did not look beyond Hindu religion. After two years of crusade against Hinduism, an organization with a different orientation was needed to meet the emerging challenges mostly political in nature. Hence, the Youth League was transformed into the Hyderabad State Depressed Classes Association (HSDCA). The limitation with the new organization was that its activities were mostly confined to the urban areas without expansion of its base to the rural areas.

Venkataswamy strained his relations with the President of HSDCA, Venkat Rao and was finally expelled from the association. A good number of followers of Venkatswamy left the association with him and joined Arigay Ramaswamy's old organization and renamed it as Hyderabad State Adi-Hindu Mahasabha (HSAM). J.H. Subbaiah was named as President and Venkatswamy, the General Secretary. This new organization was in conflict with Adi-Hindu Social Service League founded by the prominent Dalit leader Bhagya Reddy Varma. But after the death of Varma the organizations worked in league with each other.[31]

Madigas who became conscious about their numerical preponderance over the Malas after the 1941 census, began to contest the dominance of Malas in the organizational structure of all the existing associations.[32] Though Malas and Madigas are considered as polluting castes in the Hindu religious perspective at macro level, at micro level there is hierarchy of castes among the Scheduled Castes. Though the goal of all the Dalit castes is the same, often there has been rivalry between Malas and Madigas in terms of leadership and the quantum of institutional concessions utilized by each caste. Such rivalry has been traditional.

Venkataswamy who met B.R. Ambedkar at the All-India Depressed Classes Conference at Nagpur in July 1942 as a representative of HSAHM decided to rename their organization as Hyderabad State Scheduled Castes (Adi-Hindu) Federation – a variant of the All-India Scheduled Castes Federation which was envisaged by Ambedkar to bring all the depressed classes organizations under a common umbrella. Personal differences between Venkataswamy and Subbaiah had dissipated the vigour of their organization.[33]

Rama Swamy opposed Ambedkar's call for conversion into Buddhism in 1935 and joined the nationalist Andhra Mahasabha, staying with right-wing Gandhian Congressmen. Following the Congress path, he later joined the All-India Depressed Classes League founded by Jagjivan Ram. This League was also referred to as Harijan League. Though some village schools were founded to facilitate the education of Dalits, the vigour of the movement was confined to urban Hyderabad. The Dalit politics of Hyderabad was marked by competitive struggle, especially between Rama Swamy and Varma. Similar struggles took place between B.S. Venkatrao and Rama Swamy and later between Venkatrao and Subbaiah. These leaders failed to organize any mass movement. The Dalit leaders in later years were to be divided between Hindu Congress and the Nizam.[34] Ravi Narayana Reddy headed the Hyderabad branch of the Harijan Sevak Sangh.[35]

In Hyderabad, B.S. Venkatrao (1890–1953), originally Bathula Ashaiah, dominated the scene for two decades. He was known as Hyderaba Ambedkar. He sacrificed all that he earned from various jobs in Engineering and public works department and died a pauper. J. Subbaiah was Ambedkar's man in Hyderabad. He later headed the Scheduled Castes Federation. In 1938 Venkatrao took the initiative of forming Hyderabad State Depressed Classes Association (DCA). This was politically oriented to Nizam regime and in 1939 demanded a separate electorate within Hyderabad state. In 1940 there was a split in DCA with Subbaiah opposing the Venkatrao line of propagating Islam. The Youth group joined Arigay Ramaswamy in reviving the Hyderabad State Adi Hindu Mahasabha. In 1942, the Adi Hindu Mahasabha voted the change of name to S.C. Federation with Subbaiah as President and Venkata Swamy as General Secretary. The DCA and SCF contested for hegemony in the Dalit community of Hyderabad state and on behalf of SCF Sukum Achalu in Nalgonda and Butti Rajaram in Karimnagar tried to build the organization at rural level. Achalu was denied SCF ticket in 1952 General Elections and hence he contested on People's Democratic Front and won the election.[36]

Bhagya Reddy Varma

Bhagya Reddy Varma's services to the Dalit movement in Hyderabad need a special mention. Varma made an outstanding contribution to the Dalit movements in Telangana and Andhra regions. As already mentioned, Madari Bagayya renamed himself as Bhagya Reddy Varma. Later in 1913, the Arya Samaj honoured him with the title Varma. He was the forerunner of Ambedkar in fighting for the emancipation of Dalits in Hyderabad princely state as well as in Andhra region. It is noteworthy that he influenced Dalit movements in coastal Andhra region as well. He did not receive any formal education but could read and write Telugu. Though employed in a private service, he took to the welfare of the Dalits of the region, moved by their plight.

In 1906, he founded the Jagan Mitramandali to enlighten the illiterate masses through *Harikathas* and *Bhajans*. He encouraged the Mala Dasus and Mala Jangalu to perform *Harikatha,* a form of storytelling on mythological themes accompanied by musical instruments. It must be noted that this had been the privilege of the upper castes and more particularly the 'twice born castes'. Since Dalits were denied entry to watch such programmes, Varma wanted to create such facility for the masses through Dalit performers. In 1912, he founded Manyam Sangam which after a decade was renamed as Adi-Hindu Social Service League. The League's objectives were to eradicate the evil habits that, had crept into the Dalit society such as drinking liquor, sacrificing animals, dedicating girls to the temples and performing child marriages. He organized a band of volunteers called Swastikdal to achieve these objectives. He also founded Adi-Hindu Murali Nirvan Mandali to eradicate prostitution.[37]

The Adi-Hindu Social Service League started around 40 primary schools in Hyderabad for the untouchable children. He also constructed a hostel for the students by collecting funds from philanthropists. However, due to want of funds, the administration of these schools was handed over to the Government. As a pioneer of Adi-Hindu movement in Andhra, he was invited to preside over the Andhra-Panchama conference at Vijayawada. In his presidential address, Varma observed that the depressed classes were the original inhabitants of India and hence, must be addressed as Adi-Hindu and not Panchama. Consequently, the conference adopted the name Adi-Andhra Mahajana Sabha. Later, he was invited to preside over the Adi-Andhra conferences held at Masulipatnam in 1919, Eluru in 1925, Anantapur in 1925 and Nagpur in 1933. He also participated in Adi-Hindu conferences held at Allahabad and Lucknow.

In order to resolve the caste differences among the depressed classes, he started Adi-Hindu Sammelana in 1919. In 1925, he organized handicrafts art exhibition to showcase the skills of various Dalit groups. He established a printing press in 1930 and started a Telugu weekly *Adi-Hindu.* He appealed to the Nizam to officially address the untouchables as Adi-Hindus. Nizam responded positively and in the 1931 census, they were designated as Adi-Hindus. On 18 February 1939 Varma passed away at the age of 51.[38]

Other prominent Dalit leaders who worked for the emancipation of their brethren were M.L. Adaiah, K.R. Veeraswamy, Rajamani Devi (Secunderabad), Easwari Malliah (Golkonda), Puli Ramaswamy, Bollepalli Premdas, B. Shyamsunder, Suthrapu Babaiah, Mudigonda Laxmaiah, Rao Saheb B.S. Venkat Rao (Hyderabad), Butti Rajaram (Karimnagar), K. Antaiah (Medak), Sukum Achalu, Edla Gopaiah (Nalgonda), Ambadas (Medak) and many others. Venkat Rao became a minister in Nizam's government after India gained independence. He obtained a substantial amount of one crore rupees from the government for the welfare of the depressed classes.[39]

Despite internal differences, the Dalit movements in Telangana region took up one activity or the other to sustain the movement. Especially, the contributions of Bhagya Reddy Varma are significant. He not only led the Dalit movements in Telangana, he guided the movements also in Coastal Andhra region. The Dalit movements in Telangana generated awareness in their subaltern brethren. The frontline leaders could not continue with their ideology for long after independence. They were sucked into major political parties. Leaders like Arigay Ramaswamy, Butti Raja Ram and others had to move towards clientelistic politics as ideological stand without sufficient finances rendered them helpless in the joint system of electorate in the Scheduled Caste-reserved constituencies.

Notes

1. P.R. Rao, *History and Culture of Andhra Pradesh From the Earliest Times to 1991,* Sterling Publishers Pvt. Ltd., New Delhi, 1994, pp. 17–18.
2. H.C. Sadangi, *Emancipation of Dalits and Freedom Struggle,* Delhi, Isha Books, 2008, pp. 41–72.
3. Mahesh Ambedkar, *The Architect of Modern India: Dr B.R. Ambedkar,* Diamond Pocket Books Pvt. Ltd., New Delhi, 2005, p. 57.
4. R.K. Kshirasagar, *Dalit Movement in India and its Leaders, 1857–1956,* M.D. Publications, New Delhi, 1994, pp. 381–382.
5. L.V. Reddy, *Education for Dalits,* Discovery Publishing House, New Delhi, 2004, p.22.
6. Souvenir published by Sri Vemuri Ramjee Rao Trust, Machilipatnam, 2000.
7. R.K. Kshirasagar, No. 4, p. 382.
8. A. Satyanarayana, *Dalits and Upper Castes: Essays in Social History,* Kanishka Publishers, New Delhi, 2005, p. 62.
9. Ibid.
10. Ibid., p. 85.
11. A. Satyanarayana, 'Dalit Protest Literature in Telugu: A Historical Perspective' in *Economic and Political Weekly,* Vol. XXX, No. 3, 21 January 1995, Sameeksha Trust, Mumbai, pp. 171–175.
12. A. Satyanarayana, No. 8, p. 86.
13. Ibid., p. 92–93.
14. Ibid., p. 102.
15. Thummapudi Bharati, *A History of Telugu Dalit Literature,* Kalpaz Publications, Delhi, 2008, p. 62.
16. Sanjay Paswan and Pramansi Jaideva (eds), *Encyclopedia of Dalits in India: Struggle for Self Liberation*, Vol. 2, Kalpaz Publications, Delhi, 2004, p. 122.
17. A. Satyanarayana, No. 8, p. 125.
18. Chandra Mallapalli, *Christians and Public Life in Colonial South India: 1863–937: Contending with Marginality,* Routledge Curzon, London, 2004, p. 8.
19. Gail Omvedt, *Dalits and the Democratic Revolution*, Sage, New Delhi, 1994, pp. 115–117.

20. Ibid., pp. 288–89.
21. Y. Ashok Kumar, *Struggle for Economic Freedom and Social Justice of Scheduled Caste in South India,* Kalpaz Publications, New Delhi, 2005, p. 254.
22. Sisir Kumar Das, *History of Indian Literature 1911–1956: Struggle for Freedom, Triumph and Tragedy,* Sahitya Akademi, New Delhi, 1995, pp. 310-312.
23. N.G. Ranga, *Harijana Nayakudu,* Guntur Kisan Publications, Guntur, 1987 (Reprint).
24. Gail Omvedt, No. 19, p. 289.
25. Ibid.
26. Ibid., p. 290.
27. Ibid.
28. R.K. Kshirasagar, No. 4, p. 383 and learnt through author's filed studies.
29. Gail Omvedt, No. 19, pp. 120–121.
30. Ibid., p. 122.
31. Simon Charsley, 'Evaluating Dalit Leadership: P. Venkatswamy and the Hyderabad Example, in *Economic and Political Weekly*, Vol. 37, No. 52, Sameeksha Trust, Mumbai, pp. 5237–43.
32. Ibid.
33. Ibid.
34. Gail Omvedt, No. 19, pp. 124–125.
35. Ibid., p. 293.
36. Ibid., pp. 295–297.
37. R.K. Kshirasagar, No. 4, pp. 179–181.
38. Ibid., p. 383.
39. Ibid., p. 334.

CHAPTER 4

Evaluation of Dalit Participation in Electoral Politics

With the Indian Constitution providing for joint electorate system of reservations in the Lok Sabha and provincial legislatures for the Scheduled Castes as per articles 330 and 332, the Dalit representation in the law making bodies became inevitable. The Indian National Congress which led India to independence, tried to rope in the depressed classes into the freedom movement to make it representative of all groups, and to wean them away from social reform movements which were meant to liberate them from the rigidities of tradition. Gandhi called for the emancipation of the depressed classes by encouraging temple entry and taking up their cause. He gave them the significant name 'Harijans' or the Children of God. Thus, Harijan upliftment prominently became a part of Congress agenda in the freedom movement. The anti-untouchability campaign was manifested in the 1937 Congress ministries. Several Dalit leaders were appointed ministers and Parliamentary secretaries.[1] There were Scheduled Caste cabinet ministers in Assam, Bihar and Madras (now Tamil Nadu). In Bihar, Jagjivan Ram became Parliamentary Secretary.[2] Measures for removal of caste disabilities were adopted in many states. Special grants were provided for the education of Dalits.[3] With Dalit upliftment being a part of the Congress agenda coupled with the policy of political reservations, it gave way to clientelistic politics between the Congress and the

Scheduled Castes. The efforts of the Dalit leaders to float political parties did not yield encouraging results. The system of joint electorate placed the Dalits at the mercy of the dominant castes. Hence, clientelism became the order of the day for them.

The Independent Labour Party floated by B.R. Ambedkar contested the 1937 elections and won 11 out of the 13 reserved seats and 3 out of the four general seats it contested to the Central Legislative Assembly from Bombay (now Mumbai).[4] In July 1942, the Independent Labour Party was replaced by the Scheduled Castes Federation. In the 1946 elections, the Scheduled Castes Federation fared very badly driving home the message that joint electorate system of reservations is not oriented towards the welfare of scheduled castes. It only subjects them to the mercy of the dominant castes. Ambedkar's idea of a new political party called The Republican Party of India (RPI) became crystallized in 1956, few months before his death but was formally launched in1957. Without a unifying force, the RPI could not progress as a monolithic organization and was splintered into groups. Nevertheless, some Dalit leaders profoundly subscribing to the ideology of Ambedkar filed their nominations for Legislative Assembly and Lok Sabha elections from reserved constituencies of East Godavari district, representing the RPI. Though such moves strived to keep the spirit of Ambedkarism alive, they did not yield electoral benefits for the Dalits in the state on the lines envisioned by Ambedkar.

Dalit Electoral Politics

Since the first elections to the Lok Sabha and the State Legislative Assembly, the AP politics was dominated by the Indian National Congress (INC). Only Communists were the major challenging force though instances of their victory in elections were limited. Till the emergence of Telugu Desam Party in 1982 and its formation of government in 1983, there was no party in Andhra Pradesh (AP) which could match the influence of the INC which was viewed by the electorate as a party which brought freedom to India. Freedom fighters like Jawaharlal Nehru, Sardar Patel, etc. who earned the laurels of the people for their role in India's liberation, were leading the INC in independent India. Hence, they did not require a major electoral plank as they were credited with winning freedom for India. The development model of Congress included programmes for the welfare of the Dalits and weaker sections of the society. Hence, Dalits in particular were an assured vote bank of INC. The Dalit parties like the All India Scheduled Castes Federation (SCF) and the Republican Party of India (RPI) did enter the electoral politics of the AP. But their influence was limited to a few seats. Nevertheless, it is significant to note that the SCF and RPI scored some victories in SC reserved constituencies, which marks the inclination of the electorate towards ideology. An examination of the results of General Elections would be more informative to support the analysis.

Lok Sabha Elections 1951

In the 1951 Lok Sabha elections, the Dalit leaders entered active politics. In the composite state of Madras, Andhra region had a share of 24 Lok Sabha seats in which four were double-seat constituencies represented by General and Scheduled Castes candidates. B.S. Murthy, a Dalit activist won from the Eluru constituency on Kisan Mazdoor Praja Party (KMPP) ticket. Kaneti Mohana Rao another influential Dalit leader won from Rajahmundry double member constituency on CPI ticket. Rama Danayya who contested on Scheduled Caste Federation (SCF) ticket stood third securing 12.72 per cent of votes as against 16.41 per cent secured by the winner. In the Ongole double member constituency, Mangalagiri Nanadas, a Dalit activist, won as an independent. From Chittoor double member constituency the Scheduled Castes seat was won by M.V. Gangadhara Siva on Congress ticket. Here Rajah Mohan Vitthal contested on SCF ticket and secured 5.12 per cent votes. Ealy Vadapalli, a prominent Dalit leader who not only participated in Dalit movements but was noted for charity towards Dalits, contested from Kakinada constituency and stood in fifth place by securing only 5.01 per cent of the valid votes.

Multiple factors determined the outcome of the electoral result at this point of time in Indian democracy. Though the Congress was riding on the claim of Indian freedom, it could not sweep all the SC constituencies. In the double member constituencies reserved for SCs, each voter had two votes and he or she could cast only one vote to a single candidate. The Congress could win only one out of the four seats reserved for SCs. It is interesting to note that from Ongole constituency, it was not the Congress candidate who was elected but it was an independent candidate – Nanadas who was a Dalit activist chosen by the electorate. During the tour of Ambedkar to Andhra in 1944, Nanadas had an opportunity to interact with him at Nellore. In course of the interaction Ambedkar learnt that Nanadas passed his Intermediate and could not pursue further studies for want of resources. Ambedkar supported his higher education and thus he pursued his studies at Siddartha College, Bombay between 1946 and 1949. The college was established by the People's Educational Society founded by Ambedkar. On completion of his studies, he met Ambedkar to thank him for his support. In his discussion with Ambedkar, he opined that it would be advantageous for Dalits to forge alliance with others caste groups or like-minded political organizations to broaden the support base and ensure victory. But when Ambedkar posed a volley of questions Nanadas trembled and returned without giving any reply. But Nanadas who contested the Lok Sabha polls in 1951, won from Ongole constituency with the support of Communists while Ambedkar was defeated from Bombay North Central constituency by his Private secretary Narayan Sadoba Kajrolkar.[5] The INC which utilized the services of Ambedkar for drafting the Indian Constitution ensured his defeat by co-opting his Private Secretary Kajrolkar who was motivated to part ways with his master in a clientelistic bargain. However, after Ambedkar was elected to the Rajya Sabha from the Bombay state, Nanadas met him in the Parliament and persuaded him to consider the inclusion of other like-minded caste groups or political parties to expand the support base. Ambedkar concurred with the view of Nanadas. His own assessment of the political journey since the floating of Independent Labour Party propelled him to cogitate in the direction of floating Republican Party of India. He was in touch with Socialist, Ram Manohar Lohia. Both of them exchanged letters. But before the concept of political party could materialize with their combined effort, Ambedkar passed away in December 1956.[6]

Similarly, Kaneti Mohan Rao was elected from Rajahmundry as the electorate reposed faith in his leadership. B.S. Murthy was preferred from Eluru constituency by virtue of his activism. This result indicates that it is not the political party which mattered for the electorate in the double member reserved constituencies but it was the competence of the candidate which indeed mattered.

The erstwhile state of Hyderabad had 21 Lok Sabha constituencies including few constituencies of the present States of Maharashtra and Karnataka. There were three double member constituencies reserved for SCs. P. Ramaswamy of the Indian National Congress (INC) was returned uncontested from the Mahabubnagar constituency. M.R. Krishna won from the Karimnagar constituency on SCF ticket. Sunkum Atchalu won from Nalgonda constituency on PDF ticket. The SCF also fielded a candidate from Nalgonda. It is significant to note that the SCF candidate won from Karimnagar constituency. Dalits collectively chose SCF candidate, for the ideology and manifesto of the party were meant emphatically for their benefit. Similarly, Sunkum Atchalu won, though on PDF ticket based on his face value as a Dalit leader espousing the cause of Dalits. Mahabubnagar constituency is an exception where no one challenged P. Ramaswamy, a prominent Dalit leader, though he contested on Congress ticket. This result illustrates that the Congress could not sweep the constituencies as a whole and the Dailts maintained their individuality as leaders.

The Dalit movements in Coastal Andhra and Telangana seriously aimed for the welfare of the Dalits. The leaders who entered politics as a part of the movement contested either as independents or on the tickets of non-Congress parties. Moreover, Ambedkar was critical of the Congress's disposition towards Dalit welfare. But the clientelistic politics adopted by the Congress shifted the disposition of Dalits in favour of that party. Nevertheless, the Dalit parties like the Republican Party and the BSP at a later stage attempted a shift from clientelism to competition.

Lok Sabha Elections 1957

The 1957 Lok Sabha elections were held in the newborn state of Andhra Pradesh. Out of a total of 35 constituencies, six were double member constituencies where one of the seats in each such constituency was reserved for the Scheduled Castes. As a boost to clientelistic politics, the Indian National Congress won all the six seats reserved for SCs. B.S. Murthy who won on KMPP ticket, from Eluru, this time won from Kakinada constituency on INC ticket. The SCF fielded Ealy Vadapalli, a powerful Dalit leader known for his charitable contributions for the welfare of Dalit students. But there was a division in the Dalit votes with prominent Dalit leader

Neethipudi Ganapathi Rao with Communist leanings contesting as independent, thereby making a dent into the voting share of SCF.

The SCF did not field candidates for the other SC reserved seats. M.V. Gangadhara Siva of the INC was returned uncontested from Chittoor constituency. B. Anjanappa of the INC won from the Nellore constituency while P. Ramaswamy of the INC won from the Mahabubnagar constituency. M.R. Krishna who earlier won on SCF ticket from Karimnagar constituency this time was drawn into the Congress in a clientelistic bargain. He won on INC ticket from the same constituency. D. Rajiah won from the Nalgonda constituency on INC ticket. Though SCF contested in seven states/Union Territories and won six seats, it fielded only one candidate in AP who lost from Kakinada. It should be noted that clientelistic politics picked up momentum in just five years. B.S. Murthy who won on KMPP ticket from Eluru was drawn into Congress within five years. In the next election, Congress offered him ticket. Interestingly M.R. Krishna shifted loyalties to Congress from SCF in just five years. It was easy for Congress to indulge in clientelistic politics, for it was the ruling party with a massive presence across the country with a claim of winning freedom from British rule.

Wooed by clientelistic politics, the Dalits who till then sailed with non-Congress parties by subscribing to their ideology, shifted to the Congress as a matter of expediency and pragmatism. As representatives in the house they could perceive power politics of the ruling dispensation from close quarters and hence easily yielded to the bargain of the ruling party. B.S. Murthy later became central minister and went on winning consecutively for five times from the SC reserved constituencies. He became Deputy Minister in the Cabinet of Jawaharlal Nehru in 1956 and thereafter rose to the position of Minster of state. Till 1975, he held one portfolio or the other in the Union Council of Ministers. In 1975, he became deputy leader of Congress in Lok Sabha and also the Chairman of the Parliamentary Standing Committee on Railways during which period his contribution to his constituency or district in terms of Railways was nil. Thus, it was a temptation for Dalit politicians to rise to positions of power by yielding to clientelistic politics of the ruling party.

Lok Sabha Elections 1962

The number of Lok Sabha seats in AP in the 1962 elections rose to 43 with six SC reserved constituencies. In this election the system of double member constituency[7] was dispensed with and the earmarked seat was exclusively reserved for SCs or STs as per the Two Member Constituencies (Abolition) Act 1961. What prompted the government to consider this Act inter-alia was the contention raised by V.V. Giri over the result of the election to the Parvathipuram constituency. In the 1957 elections to Lok Sabha, Parvathipuram constituency was a double member constituency. The INC and the Socialist Party fielded one candidate each for both the seats. While one seat was General the other seat was reserved for Scheduled Tribes. After the end of counting, based on the votes secured by each candidate, B. Satyanarayana Dora was declared elected to fill the reserved seat, while Dippala Suri Dora was declared elected to fill the general seat. This meant that both the candidates declared elected belonged to Scheduled Tribes in the double seat constituency. V.V. Giri who filed his nomination as for the general seat stood third and he objected to Scheduled Tribes member being declared elected even for the general seat. When the authorities did not take his complaint into cognizance, he moved the Judiciary. The final verdict was delivered by the Supreme Court. In *V.V. Giri vs Dippala Suridora and others*[8] 1959 case Supreme Court in a majority judgment upheld the election of Dippala Suridora for the general seat of Parvathipuram. In view of such objections and controversies arising out of the double seat constituency, the Union Government dispensed with the double seat constituencies and reserved such constituency totally in favour of SCs or STs in tune with the reservation policy.

Out of the six seats, the INC won five and CPI won one. This time in the place of SCF, the Republican Party entered the electoral fray. The winners of INC were B.S. Murthy (Amalapuram), B. Anjanappa (Nellore), C. Dass (Tirupathi), J.B. Mutyala Rao (Mahabubnagar) and M.R. Krishna (Peddapalli). The CPI candidate who won from Miryalaguda constituency was Laxmi Dass. The Republican Party (RPI) contested from three constituencies and lost all. Its candidates were Ganta Arun Kumar from Amalapuram, who secured 10.89 per cent votes; E.V. Chinnaiah who contested from Nellore secured 16.61 per cent votes; Matangi Peddaiah contested from Miryalaguda constituency and secured 8.46 per cent seats. The total percentage of votes secured by the Republic Party was 0.96 per cent. The Dalit leaders' shift towards INC is visible from this election results.

Lok Sabha Elections 1967

In the 1967 Lok Sabha elections the total number of seats in AP was reduced to 41 with six seats reserved for the SCs. This time the shift towards Congress was total. All the six seats were won by the INC candidates. B.S. Murthy continued his winning spree from Amalapuram. Well ensconced in INC, he won every election so far after he was fielded from Kakinada double seat constituency for the reserved seat. B. Anjanappa won from Nellore constituency. C. Dass repeated his success from the Tirupati constituency. Loyalist J.B. Mutyala Rao won from Nagarkurnool constituency after SC reservation was shifted from Mahaboobnagar to Nagarkurnool. The RPI contested from two seats unsuccessfully. It secured a vote share of 15.28 per cent from Amalapuram constituency and stood in fourth position. At Narasapuram in West Godavari district, its candidate secured a vote share of 3.84 per cent and stood in fourth place. In the Nellore constituency, popular Dalit leader E.V. Chinniah contested as independent and secured 28.69 per cent votes. At Nagarkurnool, Y. Danayya who contested as independent stood second by securing 32.42 per cent as against 47.42 per cent secured by the winner J.B. Mutyala Rao of the INC. The percentage of votes secured by E.V. Chinnaiah and Y. Danayya shows that despite the clientelistic politics played by Congress, prominent Dalit leaders and activists continued to challenge the might of Congress and the electorate did not discount them altogether.

Lok Sabha Elections 1971

In the 1971 elections to Lok Sabha, the total number of constituencies stood at 41 and six were reserved for SCs. The INC won three while the Telangana Praja Samithi (TPS) won the same number of seats. The TPS candidates were formerly with the Congress. The TPS later merged with Congress after its leader M. Chenna Reddy gave up the demand of statehood for Telangana region following negotiations with Prime Minister Indira Gandhi.

B.S. Murthy won from Amalapuram constituency. D. Kamakshiah was elected from Nellore constituency. T. Balakrishnaiah was elected from Tirupati. M. Bheeshmadev was elected from Nagarkurnool. G. Venkataswamy was elected from Siddipet. V. Tulasiram was elected from Peddapalli. In these elections the RPI (Khobragade) contested from four constituencies unsuccessfully. B.V. Ramanayya, a prominent Dalit Leader of East Godavari District, contested from Amalapuram constituency and stood third, securing 5.93 per cent of votes. The other RPI(K) candidates contested from general constituencies – Narasapur, Eluru and Hyderabad.

Lok Sabha Elections 1977

In 1977 Lok Sabha elections, the total number of constituencies rose to 42 with six seats reserved for SCs. The INC candidates won from all the six seats. B.V. Ramanayya contested from Amalapurama constituency on the ticket of Bharatiya Lok Dal (BLD) and secured 32.24 per cent of votes as against 64.68 per cent secured by INC candidate Kusuma Krishna Murty, D. Kamakshaiah retained his Nellore seat, T. Balaksishnaiah won from Tirupathi; M. Bheeshmadev retained his Nagarkurnool seat, while G. Venkataswamy won from Siddipet constituency, whereas V. Tulasiram won from Peddapalli constituency. Excepting Kusuma Krishna Murthy from Amalapuram rest others were the new generation leaders who were elected to the Lok Sabha in 1971 elections. Congress' clientelism intensified with the new generation Dalit leaders. Earlier, Dalit leaders who won either as independents or from other party tickets were drawn into Congress. But now it is a fresh bid of clientelism with the new generation leaders who were not exposed to the challenges of Dalit activism and were hence totally dependent on the mercy of the Congress. There has been a pattern in fielding the same candidates in the succeeding general elections by reinforcing clientelism.

The RPI(K) contested from Narasapuram constituency and secured just 3.29 per cent of votes. The hold of INC over the SC elite was total and the Dalit parties hold, at least on Dalit electorate, was minimal as was evident from the percentage of votes secured by its candidate from Narasapuram constituency. Ramanayya shifted to BLD as he could not win on RPI ticket earlier. While he secured only 5.93 per cent of votes on RPI ticket in 1971 elections, on BLD ticket he secured 32.24 per cent.

Lok Sabha Elections 1980

In the 1980 Lok Sabha elections the total number of constituencies remained 42 and six seats were reserved for SCs. Following a split in the INC, the INC faction led by Indira Gandhi won all the six seats. This time the Republican Party had no presence in the elections. Iswari Bai contested from Amalapuram on Janata Party ticket and stood second by securing 31.08 votes. From the Nellore constituency, D. Kamakshaiah sailed with Indira Congress and retained his seat. From Tirupathi there was a new face. As Indira Gandhi was encouraging new entrants mostly owing to lack of trust in the old members, Pasala Penchaliah was fielded by the party. This time, T. Balakrishniah who won the 1977 elections on INC ticket contested on Janata Party ticket. Penchaliah won the seat. On the same lines Mallu Anantah Ramulu was fielded by Indira Congress from Nagarkurnool constituency and Bheeshmadev who won on INC ticket in the 1977 elections from the same constituency contested on Janata Party ticket. Ananta Ramulu emerged victorious from this constituency. K. Rajamallu was fielded from Peddapalli by the Congress(I). V. Tulasiram who won from the same constituency in 1977 contested on Janata Party ticket. But the Congress(I) candidate won. The Congress(I) I fielded Nandi Yellaiah from Siddipet by denying ticket to G. Venkataswamy who won in 1977 on INC ticket. The former won the election.

Being skeptical over the credibility of the candidates who won the 1977 election on INC ticket, Indira Gandhi chose different candidates excepting for Amalapuram and Nellore constituencies for this election. In Tirupathi, Nagarkunool and Peddapalli seats, the INC candidates of 1977 election were found contesting on Janata Party ticket in a clientelistic understanding with the new party that rose to power in 1977.

Lok Sabha Elections 1984

In the 1984 Lok Sabha elections the status of the number of seats remained the same as the previous election. There was a major shift in the electoral politics of AP with the entry of Telugu Desam Party (TDP) founded by N.T. Rama Rao, a famous Telugu film actor. Riding high on the popularity of N.T. Rama Rao, the TDP won from all the six reserved constituencies giving further boost to clientelism. The Republican Party had no presence in AP in these elections.

With the entry of TDP began a new stream of clientelism. The Indira Congress from this election came to be recognized as Indian

National Congress (INC) with the other groups of Congress fading away from the national political landscape. The INC fielded loyalist Kusuma Krishna Murthy from Amalapuram and he lost to the TDP candidate A.J.B. Uma Maheswara Rao. From Nellore, INC fielded a strong candidate O. Venkata Subbaiah against the TDP riding on the filmic glamour of N.T. Rama Rao. But the TDP candidate Puchalapalli Penchaliah emerged victorious. Though the INC reposed faith in Pasala Penchaliah who won the 1980 election from the Tirupathi seat, it was the TDP candidate Chinta Mohan who scored victory. From the Nagarkurnool constituency the INC fielded M. Anantha Ramulu. But V. Thulasiram who earlier represented Peddapalli constituency on INC ticket, this time contested on TDP ticket and won. Though the INC reposed faith in Nandi Yellaiah from Siddipet constituency, the TDP candidate G. Vijaya Rama Rao emerged victorious. From Peddapalli, the INC fielded a new candidate, G. Srihari. But the victor was G. Bhoopathy of the TDP.

Clientelism between the Scheduled Caste political elite received a greater fillip with the entry of the TDP in Andhra Pradesh's electoral politics. The new generation of Dalit elite wielded no political stakes and hence submitted themselves for clentelistic arrangements.

Lok Sabha Elections 1989

In the 1989 Lok Sabha elections, the Bahujan Samaj Party (BSP) entered electoral fray in AP. The BSP contested 245 seats in the country and won three seats - two in Uttar Pradesh and one in Punjab. The BSP in all contested from 20 seats in Andhra Pradesh unsuccessfully by securing a vote share of only 0.48 per cent. The RPI(K) contested from general seat of Tenali and lost. The INC candidates won from all the six reserved constituencies.

This election witnessed shrewd operation of clientelistic politics by the SC candidates. Sensing people's growing disenchantment with the TDP, some of the SC candidates who won on TDP ticket in 1984 elections prepared ground to shift loyalties to Congress. Kusuma Krishna Murthy won from the Amalapuram constituency on INC ticket. From Nellore constituency Puchalapalli Penchaliah who won on TDP ticket in the 1984 elections, this time shifted loyalty to INC and won. Similarly, Chinta Mohan who won the 1984 election from Tirupathi constituency on TDP ticket, this time entered the fray on INC ticket and emerged victorious. The INC candidate Mallu Anantha Ramulu won from Nagarkurnool constituency by defeating V. Tulasiram of the TDP. Nadi Yellaiah the INC candidate won from Siddipet constituency while G. Venkataswamy of the INC won from Peddapalli constituency.

A noteworthy result of these elections is the victory of Salagala Benjamin, a Dalit who contested on INC ticket from Bapatla general constituency and scored a historic victory over the BJP President of the state unit of Andhra Pradesh, M. Venkaiah Naidu. Benjamin's son Salagala Raja Sekhar Babu[9] is an advocate who organized the agitation along with Katti Padmarao against the Karamchedu killing of Dalits by the Kammas. The active involvement of Benjamin and his family in the Dalit movement impressed the Dalit electorate. This constituency is spread over Guntur and Prakasam districts and has a sizeable Dalit population of 24.19 per cent.[10]

Lok Sabha Elections 1991

Ever since launching of TDP, polarization of electorate began in AP. In the 1991 Lok Sabha elections, the total number of general and SC reserved seats remained the same. Out of the six reserved seats, the INC secured five and the TDP one. These elections carried a sympathy wave in favour of INC following the assassination of the party President and former Prime Minister Rajiv Gandhi during electioneering in Tamil Nadu. The BSP contested in 29 seats and lost all, securing a vote share of just 0.38 per cent. The RPI(K) nominally contested from Guntur constituency and lost.

These were mid-term elections necessitated after the dissolution of 10th Lok Sabha by President R. Venkataraman. After the fall of V.P. Singh led coalition government of National Front following the withdrawal of outside support by the BJP over the contentious Rama Janmabhoomi – Babri Masjid issue, there was a split in Janata Dal. A faction led by Chandrasekhar formed a separate party called Samajwadi Janata Party. Chandrasekhar formed a minority government with the outside support of INC. However, the INC withdrew support to the Chandrasekhar government over the allegation that the government ordered surveillance at the residence of Rajiv Gandhi to track his interactions with the visitors. This was the election which saw P.V.

Narasimha Rao the first Telugu to occupy the exalted position of Prime Minister of India.

The TDP fielded G.M.C. Balayogi from Amalapuram against the INC loyalist Kusuma Krishna Murthy. Balayogi won the election. From Nellore there was change of face with reference to the 1989 election. The INC fielded a female candidate, K. Padmasree against the TDP female candidate M. Nagabhushanamma. The INC candidate was victorious. Chinta Mohan was fielded again by the INC from Tirupathi constituency and was elected. From Nagarkurnool constituency, the INC fielded Mallu Ravi, the brother of Mallu Anantha Ramulu, after the latter passed away in 1990. The former emerged victorious. The INC candidates Nandi Yellaiah from Siddipet and G. Venkataswamy from Peddapalli were elected. Salagala Benjamin of the INC who contested against Daggubati Venkateswara Rao, the son-in-law of TDP President Rama Rao, from Bapatla constituency lost to the TDP candidate by a margin of just 1,027 votes. However, in the delimitation of constituencies taken up in 2009, Bapatla has been reserved for the SCs. The delimitation exercise has not been altogether flawless as the ruling class always influenced it to suit their vested interest. As per the Two Member Constituencies (Abolition) Act, 1961,[11] geographically compact areas where the population of SCs or STs, as the case may be, is concentrated shall be identified as reserved constituencies in a system of joint electorate.

Confined to clientelistic politics, the Dalit elite competed to obtain either the ticket of INC or that of the TDP. The presence of RPI was waning, though the BSP was striving to establish a base for itself in Andhra Pradesh by wooing the SC, ST and BC electorate. The Dalit electorate trapped in a limited vision did not look beyond the two major parties in the state. Moreover, there was no charismatic force to sway them towards the Dalit ideology.

Lok Sabha Elections 1996

In 1996 Lok Sabha elections in the six reserved constituencies out of a total of 42, the INC won five and the TDP secured one. The BSP contested two seats and lost. The Republican Party of India (RPI) contested from two seats and RPI(K) contested from one seat. Both the parties forfeited their deposits. The INC did make considerable gains in Andhra Pradesh, for P.V. Narasimha Rao was expecting a good number of MPs from his home state. Though Rao could not form the government for want of majority, the INC fared well in Andhra Pradesh by winning 21 seats out of 42.

A trend of retired bureaucrats or those retiring voluntarily entering politics picked up momentum. These bureaucrats by virtue of their proximity with the ruling party involve themselves deeply in their duties often expanding their domain of operation into the political space. The politicians if convinced of their competence would accommodate them in their party by fielding them as candidates in the elections. K.S.R. Murthy, a retired officer of the Indian Administrative Service, Andhra Pradesh cadre, could secure the ticket from Amalapuram constituency. He was fielded against the sitting MP of the TDP – G.M.C. Balayogi. Though Balayogi had mass contacts across the constituency, his winning prospects were foiled by Palli Babu Mohan who contested on the ticket of NTR-TDP led by Lakshmi Parvathi, the widow of N.T. Rama Rao. Babu Mohan polled about one lakh forty thousand votes thereby making a clear dent into the voting share of Balayogi. Panabaka Lakshmi, wife of Panabaka Krishnaiah a bureaucrat in the South Central Railway, was fielded by INC from Nellore. The TDP in an electoral understanding supported the BJP candidate who lost to the INC. The INC fielded N. Subrahmanyam from Tirupathi as Chinta Mohan its sitting MP was found moving closer to the BSP. The INC candidate won from Tirupathi. Manda Jagannadham of the TDP defeated the INC candidate Mallu Ravi in the Nagarkurnool constituency. The strategy of the TDP President N. Chandrababu Naidu to split the SCs and build a vote bank for his party with the help of Madiga caste paid off. Manda Jagannadham who entered the electoral fray with the blessings of Manda Krishna Madiga who spearheaded the movement seeking classification of SCs into four groups by apportioning the reservations based on their population, won. Madigas are numerically preponderant over Malas, the other major caste among SCs of Andhra Pradesh, in the Nagarkurnool constituency. Ravi being Mala was outsmarted by Jagannadham a Madiga. Nandi Yellaiha fielded by the INC from Siddipet was victorious. So was G. Venkataswamy from Peddapalli. It must be noted that Chandrababu Naidu was the convener of the United Front – a coalition of non-Congress and non-BJP parties, but he never elevated any SC MP of his party to the position of Union Minister.

Lok Sabha Elections 1998

In the 1998 mid-term polls to Lok Sabha, the INC and TDP shared three SC reserved seats. The BSP contested from 15 seats unsuccessfully securing just 0.21 per cent of vote share. This time there was no presence of Republican parties.

G.M.C. Balayogi of the TDP defeated K.S.R. Murthy of INC in the Amalapuram constituency. Panabaka Lakshmi of the INC won from Nellore constituency. She could easily outsmart B. Swarnalata of the CPM. In an electoral understanding, the TDP allotted the Nellore reserved seat to the CPM. Chinta Mohan was fielded by the INC from Tirupathi and he romped home victorious. The INC bagged the Nagarkurnool seat with its candidate Mallu Ravi attaining a marginal lead over TDP's Manda Jagannadham. In the Siddipet constituency, M. Rajaiah of the TDP got the better of Nandi Yellaiah of the INC. With the SC classification issue driving a wedge between Madigas and the Malas and the Madigas constructing an identity for themselves, Manda Krishna Madiga recommended the name of C. Suguna Kumari for the Peddapalli constituency against INC's G. Venkataswamy who belonged to the Mala caste. Suguna Kumari won the polls.

BJP which emerged as the single largest party, gathered the support of other parties in a power sharing deal and thus came into existence the National Democratic Alliance (NDA). For a more comfortable majority in the Lok Sabha, the NDA made overtures to the TDP by promising the post of Speaker of the Lower House. Chandrababu Naidu chose G.M.C. Balayogi for the post and he became the first SC speaker of Lok Sabha in the history of independent India. Such positions which constituted the result of a clientelistic politics attracted more Dalit elite to the major political parties of the state, especially the TDP.

Lok Sabha Elections 1999

In the 1999 mid-term polls to the Lok Sabha, the TDP secured five SC reserved seats while the Tirupathi seat was won by the Bharatiya Janata Party. This time the BSP did not contest the polls. The RPI and RPI(K) contested one seat each and forfeited their deposits.

These polls were necessitated by the fall of NDA government following a defeat at the no-confidence motion moved at the behest of J. Jayalalithaa The President of All India Anna Dravida Munnetra Khazagam (AIADMK). The NDA government fell by just one vote with Giridhar Gomang who was sent as Chief Minister of Orissa (now Odisha) by the Congress Central leadership, and who by then did not resign his Koraput Lok Sabha seat, voting in favour of the no-confidence motion to break the tie in voting.

G.M.C. Balayogi who scaled great heights having been elected to the position of Lok Sabha Speaker was fielded again from Amalpuram constituency by the TDP. The INC fielded Gollapalli Surya Rao a former TDP legislator. Balayogi who was enjoying the exalted position of Speaker was overwhelmingly favoured by the electorate. Jesudasu Seelam, a Dalit, and a retired IAS officer of the Karnataka cadre was fielded by the INC from the Bapatla constituency. However, he was defeated by Daggubati Rama Naidu a film producer, fielded by the TDP. From Nellore, V. Rajeswaramma of the TDP defeated the INC candidate Panabaka Lakshmi. In an electoral tie-up with the TDP the BJP fielded a retired bureaucrat, N. Venkataswamy from Tirupathi. He defeated the INC's Chinta Mohan. In Nagarkurnool constituency, Manda Jagannadham of the TDP defeated INC's Mallu Ravi. M. Rajaiah of the TDP defeated Nandi Yellaiah of the INC from the Siddipet constituency. Suguna Kumari of the TDP who belonged to the Madiga caste once again defeated INC's G. Venkataswamy who was a Mala by caste. G.M.C. Balayogi of the TDP was once again elected as the Speaker of Lok Sabha. In 2002, Balayogi died in a helicopter crash in Andhra Pradesh. His wife Ganti Vijaya Kumari was fielded by the TDP while the INC did not field a candidate as a mark of respect to the memory of Balayogi in the by-election to the Amalapuram constituency. Vijaya Kumari served as an MP for rest of the term.

It is significant to note that the BSP which made inroads into Andhra Pradesh did not contest these polls. Only the INC and the TDP were the major parties. It was thought that the presence of BSP in the polls would mark a shift from clientelism to competition on the part of SC political elite. But BSP's presence was rather erratic and it could not reach out to the masses in advocating its ideology.

Lok Sabha Elections 2004

In 2004 Lok Sabha elections the INC won from five SC reserved seats while the TDP secured one. The BSP contested unsuccessfully

26 seats and secured a vote share on just 1.42 per cent. The major parties – INC and TDP were strongly vying with each for power and the BSP did not make any impact in these polls. The RPI unsuccessfully contested one seat.

The INC fielded a new face from Amalapurama constituency. G.V. Haraha Kumar who was earlier NSUI leader at Andhra University, Visakhapatnam, was pitted against Dunna Janardhana Rao of the TDP. Rao was the Zilla Parishad Chairman. There was a tough competition for the TDP ticket of the Amalapuram constituency. This area is reputed to be stronghold of Ambedkarism. Yet there was craving for the TDP ticket, for in the era of coalition politics it was easy even for a regional party to occupy ministerial berths and top constitutional positions as illustrated in the case of G.M.C. Balayogi. As a result of anti-incumbency factor working against the TDP, for it was facing double anti-incumbency factor, and moreover the Assembly elections were being simultaneously held along with the Lok Sabha elections, the INC won the seat. Panabaka Lakshmi of the INC won from the Nellore constituency by defeating the BJP candidate. Chinta Mohan of the INC defeated the BJP candidate Venakataswamy from the Tirupathi constituency. From Nagarkurnool, Manda Jagannadham of the TDP defeated the INC candidate K.S. Ratnam. From Siddipet, Sarve Satyanarayana of the INC defeated K. Lingaiah of the TDP. From Peddapalli, the INC candidate G. Venkataswamy defeated Suguna of the TDP.

Though the BSP made reappearance, it was not of considerable impact. This time the INC emerged as a single majority party and it gathered its coalition partners to form the United Progressive Alliance (UPA) government led by Manmohan Singh. Now the Dalit political elite turned towards the INC for sops.

Lok Sabha Elections 2009

In the 2009 elections to Lok Sabha, the total number of constituencies remained 42 while the number of SC reserved constituencies rose to seven in proportion to the increase in SC population in the state after the delimitation of constituencies took place on the eve of the elections. The INC secured six seats while the TDP secured one. A noteworthy contestant of these elections is Sarve Satyanarayna, a Dalit Leader of INC, who won from the Malkajgiri general constituency. This illustrates that SCs competed with general candidates to seek ticket from general constituencies. But what is, above all, noteworthy is the victory of Satyanarayana from the general constituency. In all, the BSP contested 40 constituencies and forfeited deposits in all of them.

From the Peddapalli constituency, G. Venaktaswamy made way for his son G. Vivekanand who won on INC ticket. The INC candidate Manda Jagannadham won from the Nagarkurnool constituency. Warangal was reserved for SCs in the delimitation exercise. The INC candidate, Siricilla Rajaiah won from this constituency. From the Amalapuram constituency the INC candidate G.V. Harsha Kumar emerged victorious. He faced tough competition from the Praja Rajyam candidate Pothula Prameela Devi, the widow of P.V. Rao who spearheaded a movement opposing the classification of Scheduled Castes reservation. The TDP stood in the third place. Panbaka Lakshmi won on INC ticket from the Bapatla constituency earmarked for SCs following the delimitation exercise. The INC candidate Chinta Mohan won from the Tirupathi constituency. The TDP candidate N. Siva Prasad won from the Chittoor constituency.

There was a proposal of an alliance between the Praja Rajyam Party (PRP) floated by Telugu film star K. Chiranjeevi and the BSP. But it did not materialize as the BSP President Mayawati was furious over the State BSP President Nalla Surya Prakasa Rao confabulating with the PRP over the alliance. Subsequently, he was expelled from the Party. In the author's personal interaction with the expelled leader, it was argued that BSP and PRP combine in the state would have yielded positive results for both the parties. But Mayawati disliked the prospect of emergence of a new power centre in the form of K. Chiranjeevi. Though Kanshi Ram strived to expand the support base of BSP across the country, his successor Mayawati's prime concentration was Uttar Pradesh. Her active operation was confined to a single state. Though the BSP has the potential to emerge as an alternative to major political parties in several states, given its concept of Bahujan which encompasses the majority of members of the society, no serious effort was made in that direction. Nalla Surya Prakash also remarked that Mayawati is impervious to advice and takes an unreasonable length of time to grant audience even to the active members of the party.

With the advent of a new economic policy in 1991, money played a key role in politics. The author was privy to intelligence information that rich people took a plunge into politics and set new monetary standards to enter the electoral fray. Only political parties with the backing of industrialists could withstand the electoral contests. As a result, BSP without monetary backing could not retain deposits in Andhra Pradesh.

The thesis examines whether there has been a substantive transition from clientelism to competition on the part of SC political elite in the erstwhile Andhra Pradesh state which included the three regions of coastal Andhra, Rayalaseema and Telangana. The SC political elite who actively participated in the social movements tried to compete with other political parties in the initial phases of elections. They either won as independents or they represented non-Congress parties. But thanks to clientelistic overtures by the INC, the Dalit activists or leaders gradually turned their attention towards the Congress and kept contesting on its ticket. But the next generation of political elite from 1970s, voluntarily began to persuade the major political parties to accommodate them in their party organizational structure or to field them in elections. Here, the client was in search of a patron. At one stage the clients sensing the mood of electorate carefully chose that political party which was most likely to win the polls.

Assembly Elections

The first Assembly elections to the Madras State were held in 1951. Andhra being a part of Madras State went to polls in the same year. But after a separate state of Andhra was carved out of Madras State in 1953, the members representing Andhra region became representatives of the new state Assembly. In all, there were 19 double member constituencies reserved for SCs along with General candidates. Out of these, there were 12 non-Congress members. The SCF represented by Bojja Appala Swamy won from the Amalapuram constituency. The Communist Party won from six constituencies. Prominent among them was Guntur Bapanayya from the Divi constituency in Krishna district. He was active in the Dalit movement in the pre-independence era. Swarna Vemayya, another prominent Dalit Leader, won from Nellore constituency as an Independent candidate. The fact that non-Congress candidates dominated the elections in the reserved constituencies reflects people's support to the Dalit activism. But five years later, the equations began to change with the emergence of clientelism. The emerging political elite initiated negotiations with the most powerful party, the Indian National Congress which was riding high on India's liberation from British rule. As clientelistic politics began to percolate down to the electorate, they started preferring the Congress candidates to Dalit parties like the RPI. Moreover, such consequences stem from the system of joint electorate in the reserved constituencies.

The first elections to the Hyderabad Legislative Assembly were held in 1951. The state included parts of the present states of Maharashtra and Karnataka. In this election, though some of the leaders, active in the Dalit movement in the Telangana area entered the Assembly, the Indian National Congress won most of the seats reserved for SCs in double member constituencies. Arigay Rama Swamy, a prominent Dalit leader of the Dalit movement in Hyderabad, won on Congress ticket from Vikarabad constituency. The All India Scheduled Caste Federation (SCF) candidates – J.M. Rajamani Devi won from Siricilla constituency, Butti Raja Ram won from Jagityal constituency and B.M. Chander Rao won from Mahabubabad. Some SC members also won on the tickets of People's Democratic Front (PDF) and Socialist Party (SP). The liberation of Hyderabad from Nizam's rule wooed the electorate to favour INC candidates.

Andhra Assembly 1955

Assembly elections to the Andhra Legislature after the formation of Andhra State were held in 1955. Andhra Assembly had 167 seats out of which 27 were double-seat constituencies reserved for SCs. The INC has increased its figures substantially with clientelistic politics picking up momentum. Out of 27, the INC won 21 seats. Popular Dalit leaders, Bojja Appalala Swamy from Amalapuram and Battina Subba Rao from Burugupudi won as Independent candidates. While G. Nageswara Rao from Razole and Swarna Vemayya from Buchireddipalem won on the ticket of Communist Party. There was no presence of SCF in these Assembly elections. In the 1951 Assembly elections, the INC could win only seven out of 19 seats while non-Congress contestants emerged victorious in 12 seats. But a major shift was witnessed in the 1955 elections.

Assembly Elections in Telangana Region of AP

The Assembly elections to the Telangana Region of the newborn Andhra Pradesh State were held in 1957. Out of 18 constituencies reserved for SCs, the Indian National Congress won from 12 constituencies. The SCF represented by Antaiah won from Sangareddy constituency. Two members won as independents while three were elected on PDF ticket. The dominance of Congress riding high on India's freedom and liberation of Hyderabad from Nizam continued. Nevertheless, the SCF showed its presence in the Telangana region. It contested from two constituencies and won one. The percentage of votes it secured in these two constituencies was 17.11. In the Sirpur reserved constituency which was a double seat constituency, both the members elected were SCs though one belonged to the Congress and the other member, K. Rajamallu to the Praja Socialist Party (PSP). Butti Raja Ram who won on SCF ticket in 1951 elections from Jagityal constituency was won over by the Congress. This time he won on Congress ticket from Sultanbad constituency. Arige Rama Swamy jumped into the Congress having led the Dalit movement in Telangana in a bid of clientelism. He retained his Vikarabad seat in this election also. Despite Congress trying to court potential Dalit candidates to capitalize on their popularity, the Dalit leaders continued to win six reserved seats. The victory of SCF, though in a single seat is noteworthy, for the party contested purely on ideological grounds and was represented by prominent Dalit leaders who actively participated in Dalit emancipatory movements.

AP, Assembly Elections 1962

This is the first time after the formation of the state of Andhra Pradesh following the recommendation of the States Reorganization Commission and the Gentlemen's Agreement reached by the representatives of Andhra and Telangana, that elections were held simultaneously for both the regions of Andhra and Telangana. Polling was held for a total of 300 seats out of which 43 were reserved for SCs. The INC won from 32 constituencies. The Communists won nine seats while an independent candidate, G. Saidaiah won from Gajwel and one seat went to the Swatantra Party. The RPI contested in 16 seats (general and reserved) and could not secure even a single seat. The noteworthy contestants are J. Eashwari Bai from Yellareddy reserved constituency and Orepalli Venkata Subbaiah from Gudur reserved constituency. While Eashwari Bai secured a vote share of 40.97 per cent and stood second as against 50.03 per cent secured by the INC candidate, Venkata Subbaiah secured 15.27 per cent. Eashwari Bai secured a sizeable voting share heralding the emergence of a revolutionary and charismatic politician among Dalits.

K. Punnayya, a popular Dalit leader, who won from the Chipurupalli constituency on KLP ticket in 1955 was drawn to the INC in a clientelistic bid. This time he contested on INC ticket from Ponduru constituency and emerged victorious. Similarly, another Dalit leader, G. Suryanarayana who won from Gajapathinagaram constituency in 1955 on PSP ticket was won over to the INC. This time he contested on INC ticket from Ramathirtham and won.

As the clientelistic bid continued, popular Dalit leader, Bathina Subba Rao known for his dynamism and charity was won over to INC. Though he won as an independent in 1955, defeating the INC candidate from Burugupudi constituency, in this election he won on INC ticket from the same constituency. Popular Dalit leader Guntur Bapanayya won from Nidumolu constituency on CPI ticket. Swarna Vemayya who won from Buchireddypalem on CPI ticket retained his seat. The CPI candidate A. Krushnayya wrested the Venkatagiri seat from INC. Thavanam Chenchaiah, a popular Dalit leader won from Santanutalapadu on CPI ticket. It may be noted that some Dalit leaders who resisted the overtures of INC continued to win on CPI ticket due to their commitment to the Communist ideology, which is radically different from that of INC.

Dalit leader E. Basappa, who won as an Independent candidate from Makthal constituency in 1955 was wooed into INC in the 1962 elections. This time he won from Madoor constituency.

The luxury and privilege of Ministry, the advantages of being a ruling party legislator, etc. motivated the Dalit leaders to either voluntarily contact the INC or immediately respond to their overtures. Popular Dalit leaders who contested from non-Congress parties enjoyed an assured vote bank of Dalits and hence Congress courted such leaders to ensure its victory from reserved constituencies.

Popular Dalit leader, Gajwel Sadiah won as independent from Gajwel constituency earlier represented by INC candidate J.B.

Mutyala Rao. Dalit leader, Uppula Malsooru never yielded to the overture of INC. In the 1955 elections, he won from Suryapet constituency on PDF ticket. This time he won from the same constituency on CPI ticket. Arige Rama Swamy and Butti Rajaram continued their loyalty with INC and were the noteworthy candidates to have won on INC ticket.

AP, Assembly Elections 1967

In the Assembly elections held in 1967 for the AP State Legislative Assembly, the total number of seats were reduced to 287 and the SC reserved seats also reduced to 40. The Republican Party won from two constituencies. J. Easwari Bai won from Yellareddy constituency by securing a vote share of 47.12 per cent, while B.V. Ramanayya won from the Allavaram constituency by a vote share of 36.72 per cent. Orepalli Vekata Subbaih won as an independent candidate from Venkatagiri constituency. In the 1962 Assembly elections, he contested on RPI ticket from Gudur constituency and lost. Though there is a shift towards major political parties by the Dalit elite, the two victories of the Republican Party candidates proves that elite based on ideology were competing with major political parties. The INC won 25 seats; the Swatantra Party seven; the CPI-two; CPI (M)- one, and independents- three.

This time the INC's total had declined to 25 seats with the new entrant Swantantra Party wresting seven seats. Interestingly, Ealy Vadapalli who contested the second Lok Sabha election on SCF ticket and lost from Kakinada joined the INC and won from Tallarevu constituency. A close associate of Dr B.R. Ambedkar, he hosted him during his visit to the East Godavari district. He resisted the INC overtures for a long time but ultimately gave in. Swarna Vemayya continued his winning spree this time from Sarvepalli constituency on the same CPI ticket. P. Venkata Subbaiah won as an independent candidate from Sullurpet constituency. T.C. Mareppa won as an independent candidate from Kalyandurg. Once again in a clientelistic bid, Gajwel Sadiah who won as an independent candidate in 1962 elections was wooed into Congress and this time he won on Congress ticket from Gajwel constituency. It is noteworthy to observe how, popular Dalit leaders with independent standing have been gradually won over by the INC with every passing election. However, Uppula Malsoor retained his

Suryapet seat by winning on CPM ticket. He sailed with CPM after the split in Communist Party. B. Abraham won from Cheriyal constituency on CPI ticket. Despite the popularity of Congress, the Dalit leaders with high stature could win on Communist ticket resisting the clientelistic onslaught of the Congress. Contesting on Communist ticket meant that votes were sought from the electorate of all castes, not merely Dalits or the Backward castes. That is how the support base was widened.

AP, Assembly Elections 1972

In the elections to the state Legislative Assembly in 1972, totally 287 constituencies went to polls, out of which the SC constituencies were 40. Three SC candidates won as independents, while J. Easwari Bai won from Yellareddy, this time as a candidate of Sampurna Telangana Praja Samithi. Orella Subbaiah, formerly with RPI, this time won on INC ticketed from Venkatagiri constituency. The INC candidates won from 36 reserved constituencies. The RPI (Khobragade group) contested from nine constituencies unsuccessfully. Its candidate B.V. Ramanayya who contested from Allavaram reserved constituency secured 18.89 per cent votes. The clientelistic trend of SC elite towards the INC continued in these elections also.

The INC's tally shot up to 36 constituencies in a boost to clientelistic politics. However, Sali Venkat Rao won from Gopalapuram constituency as independent by defeating the INC candidate. Being a native of West Godavari district, the author closely observed the political developments in the district. Sali Venkat Rao was promoted by the Kamma gentry led by Alluri Bapineedu who was twice the Zilla Parishad Chairman by then, and by his industrialist brother Alluri Sarva Raya Chaudhari, who later became Member of Rajya Sabha. It was learnt by the author that the INC candidate, Taneti Veera Raghavulu failed to render favours to Bapineedu during the former's stint as Minister. Hence, Kammas being dominant caste in the constituency vowed to defeat Raghavulu. As the shift towards INC continued, P. Venkata Subbaiah who won as independent from Sullurpet constituency in the 1967 elections was wooed into INC and this time he won from the same constituency as INC candidate. O. Venkata Subbaiah who was with RPI and later won as independent candidate from Venkatagiri constituency in 1967 elections shifted to INC and retained his

Venkatagiri seat. Tirumalayya won as an independent from Vikarabad constituency which was held by Arige Rama Swamy consecutively till then.

AP, Assembly Elections 1978

Following delimitation of constituencies, the total number of constituencies rose to 294 while the SC reserved constituencies were reduced to 39 in the 1978 Assembly elections.

In these elections the AP electorate supported the charismatic Congress leader Indira Gandhi's faction after a split in INC. Hence, the Congress(I) candidates won from 29 constituencies and the INC won just two. The Janata Party won from seven constituencies. Guntur Bapanayya reappeared on the political scene by winning the Nidumolu reserved seat on CPI (M) ticket. Earlier, he won in 1962 on Communist Party ticket. Neethipudi Ganapathi Rao a prominent Communist leader who contested as an independent candidate from Kakinada in the Lok Sabha elections in 1957, won from the Nagaram constituency. Ganapathi Rao fought the oppressive dominant castes in East Godavari district with militant spirit. Though he won on sympathy factor, which worked in favour of Indira Gandhi as she was cornered by the old guard of the INC, he was denied ticket after he lost in the 1983 elections. Though he won from Nagarm constituency in 1989 and lost in 1994, he was repeatedly denied INC ticket due to the pressure from the local Kamma caste leader, Bolla Satyanarayana who belonged to the INC and influenced the selection of candidates for the reserved constituencies in Amalapuram division of East Godavari district. The author's personal interaction with the leader and the observation of his life from close quarters revealed the disadvantages of Joint Electorate System. The RPI contested one seat while the RPI(K) contested 14 seats unsuccessfully. The noteworthy contestants of RPI(K) were B.V. Ramanayya who secured a vote share of 34.63 and stood second, and J. Easwari Bai who contested from Jukkal constituency and stood second, securing a vote share of 32.77 per cent.

These elections held post-emergency, declared by the then Prime Minister Indira Gandhi saw the formation of Janata Party which was an amalgamation of Congress(O), Bharatiya Jana Sangh, Bharatiya Lok Dal and defectors from the Congress(R)[12] in the year 1977.

This election saw some of the disgruntled leaders of INC securing Janata Party tickets. Kothapalli Narasayya who won from Palakonda constituency in 1972 elections on INC ticket, this time won on Janata Party ticket from Etcharla constituency. P. Venkata Subbaiah from Sulurpet constituency got ensconced in INC. Interestingly V.B. Thirumalayya who won as an independent from Vicarabad constituency in 1972, this time was wooed into INC and he retained his Vicarabad seat.

Operating its clientelistic politics, the Congress was successful in winning over powerful Dalit leaders who won as independents, to its side. Such a pattern continued and Thirumalayya is a case in point in the 1978 election.

AP, Assembly Elections 1983

In the 1983 Assembly elections, the number of constituencies remained the same as in 1978. This time the Republican parties disappeared from the political scene. The Telugu Desam Party (TDP) with the cinematic fame of N.T. Rama Rao swept the polls in the state. The TDP secured 28 SC reserved seats while the INC secured only nine. The CPI won in two constituencies. With the advent, TDP began a new phase of clientelistic politics between the SCs and the TDP. While Congress(I) was relying on the image of Indira Gandhi who was riding on the wave of pro-poor welfare measures, N.T. Rama Rao was creating ripples in the state with his filmy dialogue delivery by replaying the mythological characters, this time off the screen. The Party fielded pliant candidates. There was no inner party democracy. The Party was run as per the whims and fancies of the party supremo.

Areti Kotaiah who won from Santanutalapadu on INC ticket in 1972 joined the TDP as he was denied Congress I ticket in 1978. T.C. Mareppa, a popular Dalit leader, who won from Kalyandurg constituency in 1967 elections as independent, this time joined the TDP and won once again from Kalyandurg. P. Mahendranath who won on INC ticket from Achampet constituency this time joined the TDP and won from the same constituency. Some Dalit leaders vacillated between the Congress I and the TDP. Those who were denied the Congress ticket did not hesitate to seek the TDP ticket. Clientelistic politics received a greater fillip with the advent of the TDP.

AP, Assembly Elections 1985

Mid-term polls for the AP Assembly were held in 1985 after Chief Minister N.T. Rama Rao recommended the dissolution of the House in order to seek fresh mandate. A split occurred in the TDP when Rama Rao was abroad. Owing to the lack of internal democracy within the Party, the disgruntled leaders remained dormant. Those who wished to vent their objections to Rama Rao's style of running the Party stood behind Nadendla Bhaskara Rao, the Finance Minister in the cabinet of N.T. Rama Rao who staked his claim to form the government as he claimed to have the requisite strength of MLAs. Subsequently, the Governor of AP Ramlal dismissed the NTR government and invited Bhaskara Rao to form the government. An aggrieved Rama Rao alleged that this drastic step was resorted to by the Governor on the direction of Indira Gandhi. He extensively toured the state pouring out his grievance to the people. Meanwhile, he managed to win over the requisite strength within a month and the Governor called for floor test. Bhaskara Rao resigned and Rama Rao was invited to form the government once again. He sought the dissolution of the House, which warranted mid-term elections. The total number of constituencies remained 294 and the SC reserved 39. Playing safe, Rama Rao entered into an electoral understanding with CPI, CPI(M), Janata Party and the BJP. Out of the 39 reserved seats, the INC could win only two seats. The CPI (M) and CPI won two seats each and the BJP and the Janata Party won one seat each. The rest of 31 seats were won by the TDP. The Republican Parties did not contest the polls.

N.T. Rama Rao took care not to field the candidates lacking credibility. Hence, a good number of new candidates were fielded. But it must be noted that the Congress and the TDP were vying with each other in running clientelistic politics in the state.

AP, Assembly Elections 1989

The total number of constituencies in the 1989 Assembly elections remained 294 and the SC reserved constituencies were 39 in number. The INC won 26 SC reserved seats while it supported independents in two constituencies. The TDP won seven seats. It entered into electoral understanding with the Communists and the BJP. The CPM(M) won three seats and the BJP won one seat. The BSP contested these Assembly elections from 79 constituencies unsuccessfully. But this was the first time in AP politics that a party led by Dalits contested so many seats. This also signals a change towards competition from clientelism on the part of a section of Dalit elite. The RPI contested one seat while the RPI(K) contested three seats unsuccessfully.

The Dalit political elite became well conversant with clientelistic politics. Though the BSP nominally contested 79 seats, the Dalit elite strived to make a political career either through the medium of INC or that of the TDP. Expediency dominated ideology. Clietelism took the centre stage. The Dalit elite competed overwhelmingly for tickets of both the leading parties. But the TDP looked for more pliant candidates. The Congress on the other hand fielded candidates like Neethipudi Ganapathi Rao who were vocal about Dalit welfare and who did not hesitate to question their own government on that count.

The organizational structure of the Congress had several crucial positions like the District Congress Committee (DCC) at the district level, the Pradesh Congress Committee (PCC) at the provincial level and the All India Congress Committee (AICC) at national level. Though the PCC played a decisive role in the selection of the candidates, the DCC has considerable influence on the selection of candidates. It is controlled by the dominant castes of the district. Such castes always looked for a pliant candidate. There are always instances where the central leadership of the Congress overrules even the PCC.

AP, Assembly Elections 1994

The total number of constituencies and the number of reserved constituencies remained the same as in the 1989 elections. The TDP swept the polls and formed the government. It is reflected even in the SC reserved constituencies. Having entered into electoral understanding with the Communists, the TDP won 29 seats out of 39. The CPI (M) won four seats while the CPI three. Independent candidate bagged the remaining one seat. The BSP contested 244 seats unsuccessfully. The only noteworthy contestant was Katti Padma Rao who contested from Bapatla unreserved constituency and stood second. He secured a vote share of 20.37 per cent. The BSP lost an opportunity to establish its support base, with Kanshi Ram turning down the proposal of TDP which offered the BSP 42 seats to strike an electoral understanding. The RPI contested in three constituencies while the RPI(K) contested in four. Both the parties could not make any positive impact on the electorate.

The TDP learnt from the 1989 Assembly elections that the Dalits form a strong vote bank of Congress and that it is necessary to divide the Dalits on caste lines to construct a vote bank for their party. Therefore, Chandrababu Naidu attempted to categorize the SC reservations in AP through a Government Order knowing full well that such an order would not stand judicial scrutiny. He intended to win over the Madigas by taking advantage of the traditional difference between the two major Dalit castes of AP – the Malas and the Madigas.

Masala Eranna who was with the Congress in 1978 and 1985 elections, this time contested on TDP ticket from Alur constituency. As clientelistic politics picked up momentum with the advent of TDP, those who were denied ticket in Congress often used to make a bid to join the TDP. In the Congress, it was open for ticket seekers to invoke multistage power centres to get a ticket. Hence, candidates started competing overwhelmingly. As time passed by, the criteria to select a candidate too began to change. In the Congress earlier, due consideration was accorded to those who participated directly or indirectly in the freedom movement. But since such a generation began to fade away with time, financial strength of the candidate began to gain ground as a prime criterion of the Congress. Hence, the Dalits who either made money by virtue of political power or those sponsored by the dominant castes vied with each other for Party tickets. The TDP thrived on the charisma of N.T. Rama Rao and was funded primarily by the rich Kammas who were looking for political power having attained affluence. Thus, the Party was keen on fielding pliant candidates who could easily be subjected to party discipline.

AP, Assembly Elections 1999

The number of constituencies remained unchanged. Out of the 39 SC reserved constituencies, the TDP secured 29 and the BJP won one seat in an electoral understanding with the TDP. The INC won eight seats and independent candidate won one seat. This time the TDP did not make electoral adjustments with the Communists. The BSP contested unsuccessfully 48 seats, the noteworthy contestant being Lakke Raja Rao who stood second from Paderu constituency of Visakhapatnam district. He secured a vote share of 23.47 per cent as against 28.25 secured by the winner. Though Kanshi Ram's campaigning and the people's response encouraged the BSP to contest in 244 constituencies in 1994, in this election there were not many applicants for the BSP ticket. The RPI unsuccessfully contested 8 seats while RPI(A) failed to make any impact on the lone seat it contested.

A crucial development took place in the TDP in 1995. The Party supremo N.T. Rama Rao was ousted from power by his son-in-law N. Chandrababu Naidu. Though Rama Rao was the President of the Party, it was funded by the rich Kammas. Ramoji Rao, a media baron who ran multiple businesses, and the other Kammas of his ilk persuaded Rama Rao to introduce new economic policy in the state on the lines of P.V. Narasimha Rao government, which began to take steps to liberalize the Indian economy. It is learnt that Rama Rao was not favourably disposed towards that proposal. The Kamma gentry were disappointed with the response of Rama Rao. At political level the family members of the Party chief were not happy as he was more gravitated towards his newly wedded wife Lakshmi Parvathi who they feared would claim his legacy. As she began to assume centre stage in the Party affairs, some of the loyalists of Rama Rao were also disenchanted with the new power centre. Hence, all the disgruntled players joined hands and supported Chandrababu Naidu, the son-in-law of Rama Rao. He was then the Finance Minister in Rama Rao's cabinet formed in 1994. Supported by the kin group of Rama Rao, Naidu displaced him with the support of majority of legislators. A dejected Rama Rao now left with a minor group of about 30 MLAs, passed away in 1996. A confident Naidu started to consolidate the gains he made by owning the original TDP. Rama Rao's widow, Lakshmi Parvathi continued with the residuary group as TDP-NTR, with the Party symbol Lion. Though she won in a by-election from Pathapatnam constituency in Srikakulam district, her Party which failed at the hustings in 1999 faded away into oblivion.

Chandrababu Naidu in order to construct an assured vote bank for his Party by winning over the Madigas among SCs, resorted to the policy of apportioning the SC reservation by dividing the SCs into four groups. This is explained in the later portions of this thesis in detail.

Naidu won the Assembly elections in 1999. By promoting SC politicians like G.M.C. Balayogi to the position of Lok Sabha Speaker and later by elevating Prathibha Bharati to the position of State Assembly Speaker, Naidu gave an unprecedented fillip to clientelistic politics in the state. The Dalit elite began to gravitate more towards the TDP to secure positions of power as Naidu proved it in the case of G.M.C. Balayogi who was rewarded for his unstinting loyalty towards the Party boss. It may be noted that Balayogi remained a silent spectator and was also a signatory to the cabinet decision to categorize SCs into four groups. After the Government Order to apportion SC reservations among various caste groups was quashed by Single Judge of AP High Court, Naidu adopted a resolution to divide the SC Reservation in the AP Assembly and sent it for the assent of the Governor who referred it to the President of India. Subsequently, the M.P. of Nagarkurnool constituency, Manda Jagannadham met President Naraynan to persuade the latter to give his assent to the Bill. Narayanan sought the opinion of Balayogi the then Speaker of Lok Sabha and he responded in the affirmative which prompted Narayanan to give his assent.

Naidu also claimed in many informal contexts as observed by the author, that he was instrumental in promoting K.R. Narayanan to the position of President of India. Despite Naidu's bid to divide SCs in the name of proportional representation in reservations, Dalit elite competed for the TDP ticket in the elections. This development proves that the SC candidates did not count much on the support of SC electorate of the constituency, but were attracted to positions of power.

AP, Assembly Elections 2004

The numerical status of the constituencies – unreserved or reserved remained unchanged in the 2004 Assembly elections to the AP State Legislature. Out of the 39 SC reserved seats, the INC secured 24 and the TDP seven. While the CPI (M) secured two seats, the Telangana Rashtra Samith (TRS) secured six seats. The BSP contested in 160 constituencies and won the Paderu constituency reserved for Scheduled Tribes. Its candidate Lakke Raja Rao who stood second in the previous Assembly polls, emerged victorious this time. The BSP had improved its vote share from 0.98 per cent in 1999 to 2.21 per cent in the 2004 elections. The RPI(K) contested from five constituencies and all its candidates forfeited their deposits. So was the case with three RPI candidates and the lone candidate of RPI(A).

Lakke Raja Rao who finished a close second in the 1999 Assembly elections from Paderu constituency, this time scored a victory from the same constituency. He was supported by the Dalit activists of Visakha Steel Plant, Andhra University and some active members of the Ambedkar Memorial Society, Visakhapatnam. Some of them extended financial assistance while some rigorously campaigned in the constituency.

Gollapalli Surya Rao who was with the TDP in 1985 elections, was denied a ticket in 1989 and hence, tried vigorously to secure the INC ticket from Allavaram constituency in vain. He contested against G.M.C. Balayogi of the TDP, on INC ticket in 1999 in the Lok Sabha elections from Amalapuram constituency and lost. He contested on INC ticket from Allavaram constituency in 2004 Assembly elections and won. The Dalit political elite shifted parties only to get into positions of power.

AP, Assembly Elections 2009

In the Assembly elections of 2009, while the total number of constituencies remained 294, the number of SC constituencies jumped from 39 to 48 following the delimitation of constituencies. The INC which was invited to form the government secured 32 of the 48 SC reserved seats; the TDP won from 13 constituencies; the TRS from two and the CPI from one constituency. The BSP which contested 270 seats forfeited deposits in all the seats. Its share of votes was 1.14 per cent. The RPI contested from five constituencies; the RPI(A) from eleven and the RPI(K) from two constituencies. The candidates belonging to all the three parties lost their deposits.

The Republican parties issued tickets to candidates from reserved as well as general constituencies. But the contest had become so trivial that most of the candidates were non-serious and filed their nomination to gain some identity in the active politics. Excepting candidates like B.V. Ramanayya and Easwari Bai, others could not make any impact on the politics of AP. Easwari Bai snubbed Minister Thimma Reddy on the floor of the house when he tried to defend the prime accused in the murder of a Dalit boy Kotesu of Kanchikacherla in Krishna district.

There has been a shift in the perception of a section of Dalit elite who wished to strengthen the BSP and attain political power on the lines of Mayawati, who worked out a political strategy to rope in upper castes into the BSP while retaining the Chief Ministership with herself. Nalla Surya Prakash labouriously prepared the ground to rope in Kapus into the BSP by convincing film star K. Chiranjeevi of the benefits accruing to Kapus by joining the BSP. However, Mayawati who feared the emergence of Chiranjeevi as a power centre, turned down the offer. Otherwise, the transition from clientelism to competition on the part of Scheduled Caste elite would have been achieved by now.

The Congress as well as the TDP continued their clientelistic understanding with the Dalits. Having observed the Dalits taking a tilt towards the BSP in the 1994 elections, Chandrababu Naidu the TDP President not only tried to divide the Dalits in order to prevent them from emerging as a formidable force, but lured them by promoting some Dalit leaders of the TDP to attain high positions like GMC Balayogi becoming the Speaker of Lok Sabha and K. Pratibha Bharati being chosen as the Speaker of AP Legislative Assembly. After she was declared elected in 1999 as Speaker, Yanamala Ramakrishnudu former speaker and Minister in Chandrababu's cabinet, while praising the credentials of Pratibha Bharati, repeatedly referred to her Dalit status. He stated that it is a landmark development in the history of the state that a Dalit woman has attained such an exalted position. This was the strategy of Chandrababu Naidu to harp on the concessions granted to Dalit politicians of his party.

These elections were marked by flow of money. Money and pliancy became prime considerations for a political party to consider the candidature of the applicants. Political Parties and their sponsors came forward to fund the elections of only subservient candidates. Government employees also evinced interest to contest the elections. Dokka Manikya Vara Prasada Rao and Audimulapu Suresh who were government employees were elected to the 2009 Assembly. Prasada Rao made his entry in 2004 Assembly elections from Tadikonda constituency.

More than ideology, money and liquor were used to target the lower class voters who were predominantly Dalits. It is instructive to note that majority of the upper class and a section of middle class do not exercise their franchise. Those who cast their vote standing in long queue lines for hours are the lower classes who are mostly Dalits and other Backward Classes who look for immediate gains in the form of liquor and money. This characteristic of Indian politics has made the elections very expensive.

The Rise of Damodaram Sanjeeviah in AP Politics

While the Constitution guaranteed political reservations to the Dalits, the selection of candidates to contest the elections has been the prerogative of the dominant caste leaders representing various political parties. Though pliant candidates were chosen to contest from the reserved constituencies, some first generation learners or educated Dalits tried their hand at politics and achieved positions of prominence. One such politician was Damodaram Sanjeeviah, a Dalit from Pedapadu hamlet which is five miles away from Kurnool town in Andhra Pradesh. Sanjeeviah lost his father at a young age and the family was plunged into poverty. But his elder brother Chinnaih took up the responsibility of educating Sanjeeviah and resolutely supported him to reach remarkable levels in higher education. He studied in his native village up to fourth standard and later joined the American Baptist Mission School and thereafter Kurnool Municipal High School at Kurnool. He passed his SSLC in 1938 and stood first in the district. He studied Intermediate at the Government ceded District College at Anantapur. He opted for the MPC group as he was fond of Mathematics. He passed his BA Mathematics from the same college in 1942. He secured Law Degree from Madras Law College and enrolled himself in the Madras Bar as an advocate in 1950.

K.V. Vema Reddy of the Pradesh Congress Committee was searching for a young Dalit representative. At that time one K.B. Narasappa suggested the name of Sanjeeviah and almost forced him to accept the position in Congress Committee though he was reluctant to join politics. The Indian Constituent Assembly which was elected to draft the Indian Constitution became the Provisional Parliament after the Constitution was adopted on 26 January 1950. Subsequently, some of the members of the Provisional Parliament who held membership in the State Assemblies were asked to resign from one position and retain the other. One such member was Nagappa who belonged to Scheduled Caste. He resigned from Provisional Parliament and retained his Assembly seat. This vacated seat in Parliament was earmarked for SCs and hence the Indian National Congress was looking for a suitable SC member. A committee comprising Kumaraswamy Raja, Chief Minister of Madras, Bezawada Gopala Reddy (one of the Cabinet Ministers) and other members was constituted to select the candidate for the vacant reserved seat. Bezawada Gopala Reddy looked after the selection of candidates for the entire Andhra region. As such, he selected Sanjeeviah and the Chief Minister approved the selection. After being elected to the Provisional Parliament, Sanjeeviah became member of the Parliamentary Committee of the Home Department and toured various industrial centres across the country and submitted a detailed report to the Parliament. In the first general election held in 1952, Sanjeeviah contested on Congress ticket from the double member constituency of Yemmiganur-Pattikonda for the reserved Assembly seat and won. C. Raja Gopalachari became Chief Minister of the Composite Madras state as a choice of the Congress High command on 20 April 1952. Sanjeeviah at the age of 31 years became Minister in the cabinet of Rajaji. Communal representation necessitated Rajaji to select an able and educated Dalit as his cabinet colleague.

In October 1953, separate Andhra State was carved out of Telugu speaking areas of the composite Madras state. T. Prakasam was made the Chief Minister and Neelam Sanjeeva Reddy the Deputy Chief Minister. Sanjeeviah was included in the cabinet as the representative of the SCs. He held the portfolios of Health, Harijan Welfare, Rehabilitation, Planning and Affairs of ex-soldiers. In November 1954, the Prakasam government fell after the opposition moved a no-confidence motion on the issue of prohibition. The Assembly was dissolved and President's rule was imposed in Andhra. Mid-term elections were held for the Assembly in 1955 and the Congress, Praja Party and Krishik Lok Party formed a pre-poll alliance to defeat the Communists. Sanjeeviah was elected from the Yemmiganur reserved constituency. Bezawada Gopala Reddy became the Chief Minister and Neelam Sanjeeva Reddy the Deputy Chief Minister. Sanjeeviah held the portfolios of Transport and

Commercial Taxes in the Ministry. As he started to become a seasoned Minister capable of handling key portfolios effectively, Chief Minister Gopala Reddy was all praise for him.

The States Reorganization Commission recommended conditionally the merger of the Telugu speaking areas of Hyderabad state i.e. the Telangana region with Andhra State to form Andhra Pradesh on 1 November 1956. There was a stiff competition between Bezawada Gopala Reddy and Neelam Sanjeeva Reddy for the Chief Ministership of the newly formed State. Sanjeeviah threw in his weight behind Sanjeeva Reddy. Secret parleys and confabulations were held at the residence of Sanjeeviah in support of Sanjeeva Reddy. With Sanjeeva Reddy being anointed as the Chief Minister of Andhra Pradesh, Sanjeeviah joined his ministry as Minister for Local Self Government and Labour.

Towards the end of 1959, Chief Minister Sanjeeva Reddy was offered the post of President, All India Congress Committee. Confabulations began on who would take over the mantle of Chief Ministership. It was speculated in political circles that either Kasu Brhamananda Reddy or Alluri Satyanarayana Raju, close followers of Sanjiva Reddy, would lead the government in the state. But Sanjiva Reddy was not favourably disposed towards Satyanarayana Raju. He thought that Raju would nullify his influence in the state once he takes over as Chief Minister. At the same time, he did not overtly support the candidature of Kasu Brahmananda Reddy. The Telangana leader, K.V. Ranga Reddy though did not contend for the position initially, later declared that denial of Chief Ministership to a candidate from Telangana would be a grave political mistake. In such indecisive atmosphere the Congress leaders – Konda Laxman, V.B. Raju, A.C. Subba Reddy, P.V.G. Raju, Nukala Ramachandra Reddy and others confabulated at the residence of Konda Laxman. They expressed their opposition towards Brahmananda Reddy and proposed the name of Sanjeeviah to whose candidature Sanjiva Reddy was not averse. But as Satyanarayana Raju began to campaign vigourously for himself, a contest seemed inevitable. Meanwhile, K.V. Ranaga Reddy rushed to Sanjeeva Reddy to explain that in the event of a contest, the chances of himself or Brahmananda Reddy being elected are thin and Satyarnarayana Raju's prospects are bright. Hence, the convenient way out would be to honourably accept the candidature of the one whom

Satyanrayana Raju liked. Hence, Ranga Reddy and Sanjiva Reddy agreed for the candidature of Sanjivayya rather than Pattabhi Rama Rao – the choice of Satyanarayana Raju. Consequently, Sanjiva Reddy telephoned Satynanarayana Raju and conveyed his willingness for the choice of Sanjivayya. Thus came to an end, the contention for leadership of the state with Sanjiva Reddy proposing Sanjivayya for Chief Ministership, and the rest accepting his candidature as a compromise candidate. Sanjivayya proved to be a non-controversial candidate acceptable to all. He was unanimously elected as the leader of Congress Legislature Party of Andhra Pradesh on 10 January 1960 at the age of 39.

A serious complaint against the composition of Sanjivayya's Ministry was that the SCs and STs were not given representation in the Ministry in proportion to their strength in the Assembly. This criticism came from Dalit leaders like Vemula Kurmaiah, Krishnaiah, B. Appala Swamy and Anantaiah. Though, Sanjiva Reddy accepted Sanjivayya as Chief Minister to stifle the claims of Alluru Satyanarayana Raju for the key position, he was determined to keep Sanjivayya's administration fragile, as a formidable Sanjivayya may prove difficult for Sanjiva Reddy to regain the position of Chief Minister any time in future. He often commented disdainfully that it is no great achievement to mount a horse but one should have the capability to hold its reins.

Satyanarayana Raju and A.C. Subba Reddy, ministers in the cabinet took undue advantage of their proximity to the Chief Minister. Their unrestrained conduct often irked Sanjivayya and even undermined his stature as Chief Minster. Subba Reddy contested for the position of the member, Pradesh Congress Committee much against the wishes of the Chief Minister who openly took exception to it. In response, Subba Reddy went to the extent of making derogatory remarks against the caste of Chief Minister. An exasperated Sanjivayya divested Subba Reddy of all his portfolios. Thereupon, the Congress party was divided into two factions, one led by the Chief Minister and the other by Subba Reddy. Sanjiva Reddy the AICC president, whose agenda was to weaken the leadership of Sanjivayya, supported the group of Subba Reddy, which consisted among others of two prominent leaders, Brahmananda Reddy and V.B. Raju. This group came to be known as 'Unity Front' while the Chief Minster's group came to be identified as 'Ministerial Group'. The Chief Minster was subjected to deep distress over the resignation of Subba Reddy. In order to retain Subba Reddy as Minster, Sanjiva Reddy entertained an appeal by the former to delay the process as long as possible. Accordingly, Subba Reddy sent his resignation to the Congress Parliamentary Board (CPB), to forward it to the Governor if it was willing to do so. At last, the CPB took a decision to give a freehand to the Chief Minster to deal with the contentious issue. Soon, the Chief Minster forwarded the resignation to the Governor.

Sanjiva Reddy was not to remain unruffled and he continued to meddle with AP politics. Citing technical lapses in Pradesh Congress committee elections, he sought to reconduct them to wield control of the provincial organization. Factionalism came to the fore in the Municipal Corporation Elections of Hyderabad after the merger of the twin cities of Secunderabad and Hyderabad. An exasperated Chief Minster expressed his deep anguish over the style of functioning of the Congress President.

The twenty-seven months of Sanjivayya's rule as Chief Minister were fraught with disunity and discord presided over by the AICC president, Neelam Sanjiva Reddy. Sanjivayya weathered such challenges and strived his best within his strength to give the people a welfare oriented governance. 'He took a landmark decision to accord reservations to the Backward Castes of the state. To him goes the credit of empathizing with the lives of the Backward Caste people, he himself being a Dalit, to introduce reservations in government employment and in government run educational institutions'.

In the General Elections held on 19 February 1962, Sanjivayya led the Congress to victory with the party securing 175 out of 300 seats. He was, however, instructed by the Congress Central leadership to keep off the contest of Chief Ministership. In this election Sanjivayya contested from Kodmur – reserved constituency and won. The stage was set for Sanjiva Reddy to become the Chief Minister of the state once again. Heeding to the instruction of Nehru, Sanjivayya opted out of the contest for Chief Ministership. But an unusual development in Indian politics is that Nehru advised Sanjiva Reddy to include Sanjivayya and his friends into his cabinet. Reddy offered Ministership to Sanjivayya. But the latter refused to accept it because his friend Alluru Satyanarayana Raju was denied the same opportunity. This advice of Nehru speaks a great deal about the treatment meted out to Sanjivayya by the key leaders of Congress. Normally, a candidate who occupies the exalted position of Chief Minister does not accept a ministerial position after stepping down as Chief Minister. But Nehru's advice for inclusion of Sanjivayya in Sanjeevar Reddy's cabinet reveals that Sanjivayya was made a Chief Minister only as a stopgap arrangement. He was elevated to that position only to make way for Sanjeeva Reddy as and when he desired to become the Chief Minister. Any other candidate, it was suspected would get entrenched into that position and sealed the opportunity of Sanjeeva Reddy.

Sanjivayya was unanimously elected as Congress president in the AICC meeting held on 6–7 June 1962. He became the first SC individual to hold a lofty organizational position in Indian politics. Sanjiva Reddy was successful in regaining his position as Chief Minister after an interlude of two years by displacing Sanjivayya, yet could not bear the latter's elevation to the topmost organizational position. He commented that it was humiliating to note that people who had never seen Mahatma Gandhi occupy high posts. After a stint of nineteen months as the AICC president, Sanjivayya made way for K. Kamaraj who was elected president on 6 January 1964. But soon Sanjivayya was appointed Minister for Labour on 22 January 1964 in the Central cabinet at the age of 43. Having served in that capacity in the cabinets of Jawaharlal Nehru and Lal Bahadur Sastri, he was offered the portfolio of Industries in the cabinet of Indira Gandhi in 1966. In the General Elections held in 1967, Sanjivayya contested from Kurnool Lok Sabha constituency and was defeated. The local Congress leaders were waiting for an opportunity to crush the prospects of Sanjivayya and finally they succeeded in defeating him. The Reddys of the constituency were determined to defeat him at the behest of Sanjiva Reddy. Sanjivayya who met with a road accident earlier on was bedridden at Kurnool General Hospital and could not campaign.

After the split in Congress party, Sanjivayya sailed with Congress(I) led by Indira Gandhi. On 18 February 1970 Sanjivayya joined Indira Gandhi's cabinet as Minister for Labour and continued up to 18 March 1971 till he became the AICC president for the second time. On 29 March 1970, he was elected to Rajya Sabha from Andhra Pradesh. He could win only in the fifth round of counting with great difficulty. On 7 May 1972 an ailing Sanjivayya passed away in New Delhi at the age of 51.

Sanjivayya's rise in Indian politics is attributed to providential circumstances. His educational qualifications and his practice as advocate won him a place in the Pradesh Congress Committee as the party was looking for an educated Dalit. He could become the member of the Provisional Parliament because the position was earmarked for SCs. Thereafter, he was elected to the Madras Legislative Assembly from a reserved constituency.

Though his hard work and serious engagement with the portfolio and non-controversial style of functioning won him place in the ministries, he was chosen to a high position as a representative of Dalits. His elevation to the position of Chief Minister was not a privilege conferred on a Dalit. It was because Sanjiva Reddy after being chosen as AICC President, preferred a weak candidate without a group of followers among MLAs, as Chief Minister. Sanjivayya was his aptest choice as he was, in the estimate of Sanjiva Reddy vulnerable enough to be easily displaced once Sanjiva Reddy chose to return to the state politics.

He was chosen as AICC President as a compensation for not contesting for Chief Minister's post, though he led the Congress party to victory in the 1962 General Elections to the State Assembly. As he was a flexible politician, he could be easily shifted from Ministerial post to an organizational position and vice-versa to suit the convenience of the party. It is thus inferred that the rise of Sanjivayya in regional and national politics does not signify the parity attained by Dalits with dominant castes in Indian politics. While the policy of political reservations allowed him to contest the elections, he was later used as a tool to accommodate the vested interests of dominant caste politicians like Neelam Sanjiva Reddy. But still the Congress leaders claim the credit of elevating a Dalit to the glorious position of Chief Minister as a matter of rhetoric.

The Bahujan Samaj Party (BSP) factor in Andhra Pradesh

Though the All India Scheduled Caste Federation and the Republican Party of India attempted to prove the strength of Dalits, gradually the Congress and later the TDP operated clientelistic politics and won over all prominent Dalit leaders who earlier made a mark for themselves through their ideology with the inspiration of famous Dalit leaders like Ambedkar. However, they were wooed by the Congress. Frontline Dalit leaders like Vemula Kurmayya, B.S. Murthy, Ealy Vadapally had all joined the Congress. Orepalli Venkatasubbaiah of the RPI who later contested and won as an independent candidate also joined the Congress. But in later years the BSP showed promising signs of making an impact on the electorate of AP, especially Dalits, but strategic flaws led to its failure.

The BSP which made inroads into AP in early 1990s failed to strike roots, for it could not replicate the Uttar Pradesh (UP) model in AP. On the eve of 1994 Assembly elections, Kanshi Ram was riding high on the success of the UP experiment and could arouse political ambition among the Dalit activists and politicians. He worked to win over leaders like Katti Padmarao, K.G. Satya Murty, etc., working in different organizations to his side. The BSP rallies organized in Hyderabad, Visakhapatnam and Nalgonda in January and February, 1994 drew sizeable crowds.

In UP the Samajwadi Party (SP) which has a strong support base of Backward Castes (BCs) allied with the BSP to face the tide of Hindutva in 1993. The BCs, SCs and the minorities united to take on the upper caste Hindutva forces. The unified front of lower caste groups supported by the Muslim minorities succeeded in attaining political power. The unifying factor is the anti-Hindutva stance taken by the lower castes and minorities.

Unlike in UP, the BCs in AP were not prepared to work under the leadership of the ex-untouchables. Mobilization against upper castes was not plausible in Andhra Pradesh, because the leading castes of the major parties did not belong to the upper varnas. The Reddys and Kammas are the Sat Sudra castes whose rise in politics of AP is attributed to the financial gains they made following the Green Revolution. These Sudra castes became dominant castes in their regions and could easily dominate the political landscape of AP. The Congress party came to be dominated by the Reddys who successfully seized the prime positions of the organizational structure from the Brahmins. On the other hand, the Kammas also the beneficiaries of the Green Revolution dominated the Communist parties in the State till the TDP was founded in 1983.

These Sat Sudra castes did not occupy ritually a high position in the Hindu social structure and thus could accommodate the backward Sudra castes in their organizational structure. Thus, there were no conducive factors for polarization in AP on the lines of UP where the Brahmanical spirit led the Hindutva forces could polarize the society into upper castes and lower castes supported by the Muslim minorities. Therefore, BSP could not make a substantive impact in the electoral politics of AP.

Moreover, the BCs who make a sizeable portion of the electorate found more of natural affinity with the Sat Sudra Kamma and Reddy castes than with the SC elite who are ritually below their rank and were treated as outcastes. The Backward Castes unity often appears to be showcased to demand concessions on par with the SCs. Though there are most backward castes in AP like the fishermen, washermen, barbers, etc. associated with defiling professions, the relatively advanced castes like Velamas, Gowdas, Yadavas, etc. continue to enjoy the reservations and keep afloat the slogan of Backward Castes unity with an eye on concessions from the state. But in their social perception, they continue to claim ritual superiority over the SCs.

While the attacks on SCs by the BCs are reported from various places of the state, the BC leaders demand 'sub plan' (special financial allocations) for BCs and also an Act on the lines of SC and ST (Prevention of Atrocities) Act 1989 for the protection of BCs.

BSP was dominated by the leaders of Mala caste which is a Scheduled Caste and the Madigas (the other sizeable caste among the SCs of AP) did not join it, for the party in north is led by Chamars, their corresponding caste in northern India. As such, the Madigas are not prepared to work under the leadership of Malas. Madigas on most occasions played second fiddle to Malas in politics. Having been deprived of a preeminent position in the organizational structure of the BSP, they launched a movement demanding classification or redistribution of reservations as per the strength of the various SCs by dividing them into groups.

Earlier, Manda Krishna Madiga (original name Elia) was disillusioned by the Naxal movement when he was beaten by the Sudra Naxals who objected to his forcing a Sudra moneylender to apologize to a Madiga borrower whose rickshaw was confiscated by the lender and was beaten up in a praja court (People's Court). Krishna Madiga gave up Naxalism and embraced Ambedkarism and joined the BSP. Before that, he sought an audience with K.G.

Satyamurthy, also known as Shivasagar, who himself renounced Naxalism. When Elia approached him he was scantily addressed as Krishna. Henceforth, Elia identified himself as Krishna. Though he is not entitled to Scheduled Caste status, being a Christian, he later spearheaded a nonviolent revolution to subclassify the SC reservations in the state as per the population of various SCs. The Dalit Christians in Andhra Pradesh are placed in Backward Castes-C category.

Krishna vigourously campaigned for BSP in the 1994 General Elections to the AP State Legislative Assembly. Nevertheless, he was not considered for any prominent position in the party. The same was the case with the other Madiga aspirants of the BSP. Manda Krishna later left the BSP and launched a movement for classification of SC reservations in the State under the banner Madiga Reservation Porata Samiti (MRPS)

In the run up to the 1994 Assembly elections, the Congress party held a public meeting in Hyderabad, which was attended by less than a lakh people. The TDP in order to demonstrate its strength organized a public meeting in the name of 'Prajagarjana' or people's roar at Hyderabad, which was attended by more than ten lakh people.

Kanshi Ram

The BSP president, Kanshi Ram's political roots were traced to the Republican Party of India (RPI).[14] Kanshi Ram hailed from Khawaspur village of Ropar district in Punjab. He belonged to a lower middle class Sikh family which converted from Chamar caste. Kanshi Ram in an interview to French political scientist, Christophe Jaffrelot said that in the Sikh community Dalits do not share the same status as upper-caste Sikhs but at the same time do not suffer discrimination and oppression which Dalits are subjected to in Hindu society. He added that the teachings of the Sikh Gurus were more egalitarian and that the converted Chamars had scope for upward mobility. It was during his engagement at Kirkee munitions factory of the Defence Research Development Organization (DRDO) as Laboratory Assistant that he saw first-hand the social oppression and economic exploitation suffered by the Scheduled Castes of Maharashtra, such as Mahars and Mangs. Thus, he had a belated realization about the stigma of his caste. The two works of

Ambedkar namely, *Annihilation of Caste* and *What Gandhi and the Congress Have Done to the Untouchables* influenced him the most. He later came across the ideology of Jotirao Phule, the nineteenth century social reformer from Maharashtra, who fought against the oppression of lower and untouchable castes. Phule while launching the Satyashodak movement in the Bombay Presidency in 1873, first spoke of the need to mobilize the 'Bahujan Samaj' i.e. the majority of the people outside the pale of upper castes. Kanshi Ram quit his job and in mid-sixties joined the RPI, a Dalit organization claiming historical links to Ambedkar's Scheduled Caste Federation (SCF). He resented the endemic factionalism within RPI and also found RPI exclusivist in its approach by limiting its reach to mostly Buddhist Mahars.

Kanshi Ram gave a call for a public meeting at Hyderabad in 1994 on the eve of General Elections to the Assembly. About three lakh people attended the meeting. The meeting was exceptional because while the ruling Congress and the principal opposition, the TDP mobilized people to attend the meeting; it was mostly a voluntary participation with regard to the meeting of Kanshi Ram. It was also attended by the erstwhile RPI cadre and some of the surrendered Naxalites. The meeting especially attracted rural youth, middle class employed section and party activists from Telangana and Coastal Andhra districts.[15] This meeting sent dominant political parties into jitters. This meeting was able to stir the conscience of the BCs and SCs with regard to their complacency. The predominant presence of Backward classes signaled their demand for greater political representation in the forthcoming elections, for the UP experiment meant political power to the Backward classes. Kanshi Ram's slogan of *Vote Hamara Raj Thumara, Nahin Chelega, Ab se Nahin Chelega* – which means 'How come the votes are ours and power is yours, this will not continue hereafter', captured the imagination of the subaltern sections.

Atrocities against Dailts especially the two incidents at Karamchedu and Chunduru impelled the Dalit masses to look for an alternative political power which in view of the majority would be the BSP. In the year 1985, in Karamchedu village in Prakasam District, some Kammas executing a well planned massacre killed six Dalits and injured many more displaying the muscle of the dominant castes against any kind of defiance by the Dalits. The victims of violence who left the village had been reluctant to return to the village. In fact, they preferred to stay back at Chirala town. In a similar incident in Chunduru village in Guntur district, nine people belonging to the Mala caste were killed and their bodies were packed in gunny bags and were thrown into canals in and around the village.[16] Though the Indian Constitution guaranteed certain rights and concessions to the Scheduled Castes, the tradition bound social structure was not prepared to accommodate the Constitutionally prescribed rights of the hitherto excluded groups. Hence, any sign of assertiveness by the Dalits was ruthlessly thwarted by the dominant castes.

The Dalits formed the traditional support base of the Congress because of populist and patronage politics of Indira Gandhi. The Chundur event taking place during the Congress rule involving Reddys who own Congress and the tepid reaction of the Government disillusioned the Dalits about the real character of the Congress, catalysed them to look for a political identity. The Dalits of Chundur returned to their village after the violence and built a memorial for their martyrs. These two incidents catalysed the change in perception of Dalits vis-à-vis dominant castes.

In Telangana, the agrarian struggles and the Left student movement radicalized the Dalit youth, leading to their disgust with the dominant discourse and the political state of affairs. The CPI (ML) as a part of its anti-feudal movement organized the victims of bonded labour, i.e. Dalits. The emergence and spread of Dalit organizations like Dalit Kala Mandali and Dalit Writers, Artists and Intellectuals United Forum (DWAIUF), and also the Ambedkarite organizations propelled the politicization of the Dalit intelligentsia in the rural areas of Telangana. They spread the anti-caste message of Ambedkar in the northern Telangana districts of Warangal, Karimnagar and Nizamabad. Such groups with ideological orientation had been gravitating towards the BSP. Though the Dalits of Coastal Andhra and Telangana turned towards the BSP as a suitable political alternative, the milieu in which their political objectives became crystallized was different. The dominant upper caste violence against the Dalits in Coastal Andhra spurred them to come together to look for a political platform which would not only protect them but also empower them. But in Telangana the movement was built around ideology inspired by the thought of

Ambedkar. The DWAIUF took up the task of creating artists, writers and poets among the Dalit bahujans to carry forward the movement of caste annihilation. The DWAIUF covered a good deal of ground work like conducting workshops at Mandal headquarters involving young Dalits to identify their talent and train them to improve their potentialities. This organization was instrumental in catalysing the Dalits to produce subaltern literature on an unprecedented scale and also construct an ideology which would form the basis for their movement. The approach of this movement differed from the traditional Ambedkarite articulation of Coastal Andhra which centred around reservation and share in political power, in that, it focused on systemic political economy within the Marxist contours.[17]

With such factors favouring the BSP, a meeting which proved to be success was conducted on 30 October 1994 at Gymkhana grounds at Hyderabad. Moved by the overwhelming attendance to the meeting of Kanshi Ram, N.T. Rama Rao proposed an electoral alliance with the BSP in the State. Chandrababu Naidu, the TDP politburo member sent an emissary – N. Yatiraja Rao, Legislator from Chennur constituency to Kanshi Ram with an offer that TDP would enter into an electoral alliance with BSP by conceding it 42 Assembly seats. This offer came to Kanshi Ram when he was addressing a public meeting at Godavari Khani. When some party members evinced interest in the proposal, Ram remarked that such members wish to become Legislators effortlessly and are thus encouraging the alliance. Kanshi Ram, however, held consultations with important functionaries of the party over the proposal. This proposal was vehemently opposed by Bojja Tarakam, Dr P. Sundaraiah and B.S.A. Swamy. Tarakam, in particular, was critical of the move because of the atrocities committed by some people of Kamma caste against Dalits at Karamchedu village in Prakasam district. Since the TDP was led by Kammas, some BSP members were averse to an alliance with Kammas. However, prominent among those who favoured the alliance were Katti Padmarao, Dr M. Gopinadh and Dr K. Chiranjeevi. Kanshi Ram finally resisted such overtures. It would have been a watershed in the AP politics had BSP accepted the proposal of the TDP president. The huge response to Kanshi Ram's public meetings panicked the major political parties. An alliance with the TDP would have fetched the BSP at least some 20 seats. But the BSP local leaders ignored the ground realities. Ideology prevailed over pragmatism. The BSP in 1994 Assembly elections could not win even a single seat in the State.

The other disadvantageous factors were the BSPs limitations in its organizational structure, particularly with regard to leadership projection and ideological specificity which would show its distinctiveness from other dominant political parties despite the favourable ground situation, where there was general disenchantment with the Congress and TDP rule. The success of Kanshi Ram's experiment in UP has turned the Dalit bahujans euphoric in the state. But his style of operation was autocratic. The vernacular press which never saw the entry of BSP in a positive light, started to depict BSP as an outside party, by time and again focusing on organizational vulnerabilities. No one was projected as a state leader. Kanshi Ram behaved like the 'be all and end all' of the BSP. The state leadership in the organizational structure was represented by the Malas of Coastal Andhra. Madigas, another major Dalit caste and the OBCs were conspicuous by their absence. The Malas of Coastal Andhra by virtue of educational avenues created by the Christian missionaries and also of the policy of reservation, and the ruling class extending patronage and their cooption after independence have been way ahead of the Madigas of Telangana. Hence, the Mala elite are visible in bureaucracy, academia and politics of AP.[18] Thus, the dominance of Malas in the BSP's organizational structure has upset the Madigas.

The vernacular press has systematically established that BSP is a party of SCs and also raised doubts about its success in AP in the absence of a force like Samajwadi Party. Abolition of Patel Patwari system by N.T. Rama Rao in the Telangana region during his tenure as Chief Minister of the State, creation of Mandals while restructuring the Panchayat Raj system, prepared grounds for emergence of middle class from the Backward Castes like Yadavas, Goudas, Munnuru Kapu, Padmashali, etc. and the TDPs strategies to win over the Backward Castes worked in its favour in the 1994 elections.[19]

Though the BSP contested the Assembly elections in 1989, it could not make any impact on the AP electorate, for the Dalits formed the traditional vote bank of the Congress reflecting clientelistic politics. N.T. Rama Rao riding on his filmic image could upset the voting equations by influencing even the Dalits.

Nevertheless, Congress regained power in 1989. The Karmachedu event disillusioned the Dailts about the hegemonic attitude of the empowered Kammas, who could not tolerate Dalit assertiveness. The murder of V.M. Ranga, a popular Congress Legislator of Vijayawada belonging to the Kapu caste tilted the Kapu support in favour of Congress on the eve of 1989 elections to the AP Assembly. Hence, ideological impact of the BSP in 1989 was limited.

In 2008, the news of Telugu film star K. Chiranjeevi floating a new political party was widespread. The author's personal interaction with Nalla Surya Prakash revealed that the latter, the President of BSP State unit, sensing the prospect of Chiranjeevi's entry into politics launched a tour of Godavari districts where the people of Kapu caste to which Chiranjeevi belongs are numerically preponderant. He held rallies showing posters and cut-outs with the pictures of Ambedkar and Sri Krishna Devaraya, who is believed to have belonged to Kapu caste. The message was that the Kapus would come to power by joining the BSP which has strong ground level cadre of Dalit bahujans. And by floating a party of their own, they cannot compete with the rich Kammas who own a regional party, the TDP. This message moved the Kapus, and Chiranjeevi invited Surya Prakash for talks. The BSP state President could convince the film star of the accruing success if he joined the BSP. Chiranjeevi invited Mayawati, the BSP national President, for a lunch through Surya Prakash. But Mayawati not only turned down the invitation but in a public meeting held at Hyderabad openly stated that film stars should be confined to the film field and they are unfit for politics. She summoned Surya Prakash to Delhi and explained to him that if BSP secures a good number of seats in the Lok Sabha elections in AP under the leadership of Chiranjeevi, the leaders of either UPA or NDA would directly contact Chiranjeevi and not the Party President. This would open a new and parallel power centre of the BSP in AP. Hence, the alliance did not materialize. This was another opportunity the BSP failed to seize to strengthen its base in AP. Mayawati given her autocratic style of functioning did not pay heed to the aspirations of the local cadres of the party.

Though the BSP tried to lead the transition of SC political elite from clientelism to competition with its 'Dalit Bahujan' ideology, due to inadequacies in its strategy, and its Central leadership weighing all opportunities vis-à-vis Uttar Pradesh could not rise to the occasion to attain political power in the State.

Political Parties Consideration of SC Candidates for Reserved Seats

Political parties normally confine the SC candidates to reserved seats only with exceptions like Sarve Satyanarayana contesting and winning from Malkajgiri Lok Sabha constituency in 2009 Lok Sabha elections on INC ticket. In 2014 elections to Lok Sabha, while 84 seats were reserved for SCs, there is no bar on them to contest the 412 general seats across the country. In fact, the Constituency Assembly debates and the deliberations of the Delimitation Commission in 2008 clearly expect the parties not to restrict the SCs or STs to reserved constituencies. However, out of the 6,711 candidates who contested from 412 seats, 1,027 were SC candidates. These candidates were overwhelmingly independents with less than half being fielded by various political parties. BSP gave tickets to 134 SC candidates from general constituencies. But in UP where BSP has a strong base, not even a single seat is allotted to an SC candidate from general seats. The BJP and Congress, the two major national parties gave tickets to only three SC candidates in the 2014 Lok Sabha elections. In Tamil Nadu the two major Dravidian parties, DMK and AIDMK did not allot even a single ticket to SC candidates from general seat. Even during Mayawati era as BSP Supremo they were also following the same tactics. She does not allow any SC/ST candidate to contest in General Seats, particularly in UP. 'Winnability' being the main criterion in granting the party ticket to the candidate, the SC candidates have been out of the consideration of political parties.[20]

Politics of Co-optation

Politics of co-optation has been a distinct characteristic of Indian democracy. The major political parties led by upper caste politicians could easily shake the ideological foundations of lower caste parties and co-opt a minor dissenting group or a strong leader of the lower caste parties. The hierarchical structure of Hindu society 'lent itself to the implementation of a clientelistic network'.[21]

Jotirao Phule's Satyashodhak Samaj (Society for the Search of Truth) which was founded in 1873 to unite the lower castes and untouchables merged with the Congress in 1930s to defend its interests.[22] Phule belonged to the caste of Malis who traditionally cultivated fruits and vegetables. His family supplied flowers to the court of Peshwas. These flowers were grown on thirty-five acres of land granted to them by the rulers. Jotirao studied in a school in Poona (now Pune) run by Scottish missionaries. Here, he mixed with students of all hues including untouchables. In his twenties he started a school for girls of lower castes.[23] He opened a school in 1853 which admitted untouchables. Over a period of time his Satyashodhak Samaj became a more Maratha dominated organization and after his death in 1890 lost its direction and ultimately merged with Congress.[24]

After the Second Round Table Conference, the Hindu Mahasabha tried to counter Ambedkar by co-opting other untouchable leaders. This was manifested in the alliance formed between S.M. Moonje of the Mahasabha and G.A. Gavai, an influential untouchable leader from the Vidarbha region. Gavai was appointed to the Legislative Council of the Bombay Presidency in 1920. In 1929, the Simon Commission consulted him in his capacity as President of the Depressed Classes Association of Nagpur. Gavai then spoke in favour of separate electorate for 'untouchables', but in 1931 he did a volte-face by speaking against separate electorate. Moonje used Gavai against Ambedkar to break a common stand by the depressed classes leaders. In this clientelistic bargain, Gavai was appointed to the Working Committee of the Hindu Mahasabha and was promised a party ticket for the forthcoming elections.[25]

Ambedkar attended the Round Table Conferences accompanied by Rao Bahadur Rettemalle Srinivasan – a Dalit member of the Legislative Council of the Madras Presidency. After the Second Round Table Conference, Moonje tried to weaken Ambedkar's stand of separate electorate by pitting him against Gavai who was the General Secretary of the All India Depressed Classes Association which was created by the Congress party. Gavai was used as middleman between Moonje and Rao Bahadur M.C. Rajah, who was the Association's president and represented 'untouchables' in the Imperial Legislative Council since 1927. Though Ambedkar was named Vice-President of the body, he never evinced interest in the Association. The idea of the Congress was to confer less significant positions on Ambedkar and marginalize him in the organization. In

1930, Ambedkar founded his own organization called All India Depressed Classes Congress. The Rajah-Moonje pact was concluded in March 1932 which settled for Reserved seats in a joint electorate as against Ambedkar's demand for separate electorate. Rajah wrote to the British Prime Minister to ignore the demand of Ambedkar for separate electorate.[26] Rajah who supported Gandhi in 1932, was disillusioned by the politics of Congress especially under Rajagopalachary in 1937 Madras State, and joined the SCF in 1942. In 1935 the Congress created another organization called 'All India Depressed Classes League which was headed by Babu Jagjivan Ram of Bihar.[27] This was a ploy to prove that Ambedkar was not the sole representative of the depressed classes.

Ambedkar founded the Independent Labour Party (ILP) in August 1936. This was to widen his social support base. Ambedkar sought to emerge as a leader of the toiling masses. In the 1937 elections in Bombay Presidency, the ILP fielded seventeen candidates - thirteen in the constituencies reserved for Scheduled Castes, where it won in eleven constituencies and four upper caste candidates in the general constituencies where the party won in three constituencies. Despite an attempt to include all the labour class into its fold, Dalits constituted the majority of the party cadres and support base, and the lower caste people of the party continued to consider themselves superior to the untouchables. As the experiment did not yield the anticipated result, Ambedkar disbanded the ILP and founded the Scheduled Castes Federation (SCF) in July 1942. The SCF fared badly in 1945–46 elections, winning only two seats in the provincial Assemblies - one in Bengal and the other in Central Provinces and Berar. In the 1951–52 elections, the SCF won two seats in Lok Sabha - one in Hyderabad and the other in the Bombay presidency. SCF for the first time won representations in the Assemblies of Madras, Hyderabad, the State of Mysore, PEPSU (Patiala and East Punjab States Union) and Himachal Pradesh.[28] Nevertheless, a political party with Dalit-centric ideology could not translate the votes into seats. Hence, a political party with a universalistic appeal rather than a particularistic focus was the need of the hour for Ambedkar.

Ambedkar with an intention to forming alliances with other social and political sectors, began negotiations with socialist parties and also Ram Manohar Lohia. Though he did not live to see the formation of Republican Party of India (RPI), the party was the end product of his objective to broaden the social base. RPI was formed in October 1957. Before that the SCF allied with Samyukta Maharashtra Samiti which was for redrawing the provincial boundaries on linguistic lines in November 1956. Such an alliance proved advantageous for SCF. In the February 1957 elections held after the death of Ambedkar, the SCF won four seats in the Lok Sabha in Bombay province and fifteen seats in the Legislative Assembly of provinces mostly in Bombay.[29]

Congress always used co-optation as instrument against the Dalit parties or its prominent leaders. P.N. Rajbhoj was the first to join the Congress after the death of Ambedkar before the formation of Republican Party of India (RPI). He was elected to Rajya Sabha in 1957. After the formation of RPI, R.D. Bhandare – the leader of RPIs Bombay branch joined the Congress. He always defied Gaekwad's leadership and suggested the merger of RPI with Congress. In Uttar Pradesh, B.P. Maurya, the main leader of RPI crossed over to Congress after the collapse of RPI in 1969 elections. In exchange he was given a ministerial berth by Indira Gandhi in her government. Congress constantly encouraged defections from RPI.

In 1959, the personal difference between Gaikwad and Kamble resulted in split of RPI with Kamble forming Durushta RPI. Later, Durushta RPI merged with Congress. The second split in RPI occurred in 1969 after Khobargade walked out of RPI led by Gaekwad, to form RPI(K). The split occurred because R.S. Gavai was chosen over Khobagade as a candidate for the Upper House in Maharashtra. Gavai succeeded Gaekwad a little later as the President of the party. By 1970s, Bhayyasaheb Ambedkar, the son of Ambedkar floated his own RPI naming it as RPI (Ambedkar). Hence, by 1970, there were four RPIs in Maharashtra. Jagjivan Ram drew a good number of Ambedkarites from RPI to Congress. The four RPIs collaborated with Indira Gandhi in 1977 elections. Yaswanth Rao or Bhayyasaheb Ambedkar passed away in 1978. His son, Prakash Ambedkar tried to unite all the factions of RPI. Ramdas Athawale quit from RPI Ambedkar and joined the Congress.

In 1996, all the RPI groups converged under the leadership of Prakash Ambedkar. They contested the 1996 elections but not even a single seat was won. But two years later, in the 12th General Elections, RPI won four seats all in non-reserved constituencies in alliance with Congress and Samajwadi Party. In 1999 with the effect of political recidivism, faction fighting once again came to the fore. There emerged three Dalit parties one led by Athawale allied with Sharad Pawar's Nationalist Congress Party; the other led by Prakash Ambedkar remained allied with Congress and the third group was led by R.S. Gavai. In 1999 and 2004 elections the RPI factions won only one seat each time.[31] In 2009 elections to Lok Sabha the factions of RPI drew a blank.

Major political parties have always vied with each other to co-opt prominent Dalit leaders to woo the Dalit voters to their side. Co-optation of a Dalit leader or a faction meant wooing Dalit voters not only in reserved constituencies but also in general constituencies. Ganta Arun Kumar a close associate of Ambedkar in Andhra was a product of the charity of Sri Ramjee Rao's hostel for Depressed Classes at Bundar. When the Dalit students of that hostel participated in Quit India Movement, they were arrested. Ramjee Rao sought the intervention of Ganta Arun Kumar who successfully persuaded the authorities to release the Dalit students without booking cases against them. Arun Kumar promised Ambedkar that he would remain in SCF despite the attempts of Congress to co-opt him. He remained in SCF and thereafter in RPI. He was the state president of RPI till his last breath without succumbing to the politics of clientelism adopted by Congress and other major parties.

Notes

1. Balmiki Prasad Singh, *The Indian National Congress and Cultural Renaissance,* Allied Publishers, New Delhi, 2007, pp.64–66.
2. Eleanor Zelliot, 'Congress and the Untouchables, 1917-1950' in Richard Sisson and Stanley Wolpert (eds) *Congress and Indian Nationalism: The Pre-Independence Era,* Berkeley, University of California Press, 1988 –197 pp. 182.
3. Balmiki Prasad Singh, No.1, Ibid.
4. Christophe Jaffrelot, *Dr Ambedkar and Untouchability: Analysing and Fighting Caste,* C.Hurst and Co Ltd., London, 2005, pp. 80–84.
5. Rajasvi M.I., *Mayawati: Hope of Dalits and Faith of Bahujan Society,* Manoj Publications, Delhi, 2011.
6. P.V. Ratnam, *Socio-Political Philosophy of Dr B.R. Ambedkar,* Ambedkar-Lohia Socialist Centre, Hyderabad, 2005, p.145.
7. M.S. Rana, *India Votes: Lok Sabha and Vidhan Sabha Elections,* Sarup and Sons, New Delhi, 2006 p. 20.

8. http://indiankanoon.org/doc/277646/ accessed on 14.03.2014.
9. Thummapudi Bharati, *A History of Telugu Dalit Literature*, Kalpaz Publications, Delhi, 2008, p. 95.
10. *The Hindu*, 11 February 2014.
11. http://indiankanoon.org/doc/17159/ accessed on 14.03.2014.
12. S.C. Bhatt and Gopal K. Bhargava, *Land and People of Indian States and Union Territories,* Kalpaz Publications, Delhi, 2006, p. 172.
13. G. Venkat Rajaram, *Damodaram Sanjivayya and His Times,* Hyderabad, Media House Publications, Hyderabad, 2001.
14. Vivek Kumar, 2006, *India's Roaring Revolution: Dalit Assertion and New Horizons,* Gagandeep Publications, Delhi, p. 115.
15. Ajoy Bose, *Behenji: A Political Biography of Mayawati,* Penguin Books, New Delhi, 2008, pp.
16. K. Srnivasulu, 'BSP and Caste Politics', in *Economic and Political Weekly,* 1 October 1994, Sameeksha Trust, Mumbai, pp. 2583–2586.
17. Ibid. p. 2583.
18. Ibid.
19. Ibid., p. 2585.
20. Ibid.
21. *The Hindu*, 23 November, 2014
22. Christophe Jaffrelot, No. 4, p. 159
23. Ibid., p. 17.
24. Ramachandra Guha, *Makers of Modern India,* Penguin Books, New Delhi, 2012, pp. 75–78.
25. Christophe Jaffrelot, No.4, pp. 16–17.
26. Ibid., p. 58.
27. Ibid., pp. 56–59.
28. Ibid., p. 89.
29. Ibid., pp. 84–85.
30. Ibid., pp. 74–90
31. Ibid., pp. 153–155.

CHAPTER 5

Dalit Elite Response to Atrocities against Dalits

Elite Formation

The traditional Hindu society is based on the Varna system and the society was divided into four orders: (i) Brahmins, the priestly Varna; (ii) Kshatriyas, the warrior Varna; (iii) Vaishyas, whose occupation was trade; and (iv) Sudras, whose occupation was service to the preceding three Varnas. Outside this Varna framework were placed the avarnas also known as chandals or untouchables.[1] These untouchables have been oppressed by the Hindu society for centuries together. The untouchables are a socially alienated lot.

With the advent of British rule in India, the British made deep impact on the politics of the country as well as the society. Various factors like introduction of Western education, communication facilities like Railways, Posts and Telegraphs and the propaganda by Christian missionaries, social reform movements started by Raja Ram Mohan Roy, Dayananda Saraswathi, and non-Brahmin movement started by Jyotirao Phule of Poona who began to advocate the very un-Hindu idea of 'asserting the worth of man irrespective of caste'[2] catalysed the social change in the Indian society.

Jyotirao Phule challenged the Brahminical authority first by opening a school for non-Brahmins in Poona (now Pune) in 1848 and three years later established a school for untouchables. This was the first school in India for untouchables.[3]

Hindu reformers wanted to offset both Christian missionaries and Islamic influence among the lower castes. After the 'mutiny' of 1857, the British attitude changed towards both Hindus and Muslims. There was also self-assertion among the non-Brahmins against the Brahmanical domination. All these factors helped the lower classes to become conscious of their social existence. With that awareness, small sections of untouchables got encouraged to get formal education. Several Indian princes, particularly of Baroda, Mysore (now Mysuru) and Travancore (now Tiruvananthapuram) showed interest in this matter both under the influence of Hindu reformism and of their British advisors. The maharaja of Baroda established a school for untouchables in 1883,[4] and it was the scholarship he offered that enabled Dr Ambedkar to go to Columbia university in New York in 1913.

For the first time, the untouchables were receiving education, a privilege that had been denied to them by the Hindu society for centuries. Dr Ambedkar, a product of modern Western education, realized the nature of exploitation and oppression of his kinsmen in different spheres of life and started fighting against the oppressive system.

Dr Ambedkar, for the first time appeared on Indian political scene in 1919, when he was called to testify before the 'South Borough Committee'. The Legislative Council of Bombay Presidency was proposed to consist of 100 members. Dr Ambedkar suggested that the untouchables be allowed nine representatives, eight for their percentage of the population and one from among the nine to be elected by them to the Imperial Legislative Council.

But, Dr Ambedkar's pleas went in vain.[5] The Committee ignoring Ambedkar and Gawai, and some other caste Hindus who urged direct representation of the depressed classes, gave them one nominated representative in the Bombay Legislative Assembly.

The first man selected as representative was D.D. Gholap,[6] a Mahar from Satara who had been incharge of Dr Ambedkar's paper *Mook Nayak*. This was the first political representation given to untouchables by the British. Later, due to Ambedkar's efforts and struggles, the untouchables got 'separate electorates'. in 1932 which was announced as 'Communal Award' by Ramsay Macdonald, the then Prime Minister of Britain.

According to the Communal Award, the depressed classes were to have a number of special seats assigned to them for a period of 20 years. Only depressed classes could vote for these seats although they were entitled to vote for the general seat. This was a victory for Ambedkar. At this juncture, Gandhi rejected the Award and undertook 'fast-unto-death'. Consequently after sustained negotiations, Ambedkar and Gandhi reached an accord known as 'Poona Pact'. According to this Award, Ambedkar had given up the 'Communal Award' and accepted in its place a system of a 'Joint Electorate' with the caste Hindu majority.

Endorsing this agreement, the British government passed the 1935 Government of India Act. Thus, the untouchables for the first time got political reservations to contest elections in reserved seats. Thus emerged the political elites of the Scheduled Castes in Indian society. The emergence of political elite in India from among the SCs is a historical development and culmination of resolute efforts by social reformers, especially by Dr B.R. Ambedkar who mobilized SCs across the country and applied Constitutional methods seeking social mobility. It must be noted that the formation of SC political elite in India is attributed to the mandatory Constitutional provisions and was not due to attitudinal change among the caste Hindus that paved the way to the former's political participation. Their attitude about SCs continued to be governed by the Hindu Institutes of Law. An attitude of social distance from the SCs got ingrained in the psyche of the caste Hindus. Hence arises the necessity of the policy of protective discrimination. The political reservations to the Dalits, emanating from the Constitution, were surrounded by certain limitations at the ground level, the consequences of which were elaborately discussed in the fourth chapter of this thesis. The political elite thus formed as a choice of the dominant castes mostly functioned as tools in the hands of their political masters. Thus, despite the considerable presence of Dalits in the political power structure, atrocities continued to be perpetrated against them, particularly in the rural side of the state. The dominant castes take it for granted that the Dalit elected representatives would not intervene on behalf of the victims, for they cannot get re-elected without dominant castes' support. Moreover, their political career hinges on the caste Hindu patronage.

With the enforcement of the Constitution of India on 26 January 1950, the caste system lost its quasi-legal basis. Equality of all citizens before law was envisaged. Article 330 of the Constitution guarantees the reservation of seats in Lok Sabha for Scheduled Castes and Scheduled Tribes. Article 332 guarantees reservation of seats to SCs and STs in State Legislative Assemblies. The Constitution also guarantees the reservation for SCs and STs in education and employment. Article 335 of the Constitution lays down thus: 'The claims of the members of the Scheduled Castes and Scheduled Tribes shall be taken into consideration, consistent with the maintenance of efficiency of administration, in the making of appointments to services and posts in connection with the affairs of the Union or of a State'.[7]

Dalits for the first time entered into the political power structure by virtue of law, a privilege they were denied for ages. Political reservations thus engendered the emergence of SC political elite.

Elite Politics

Political reservations provided a strong ground for the emergence of elite among SCs right from Panchayat level to that of Parliament. Clientelistic politics gave further boost to the emergence of political elite. Inevitably the intermediary castes – Reddys and Kammas control the major political parties in AP. Before the emergence of TDP, Congress dominated the politics of the state. The educated Dalits given the facility of reservations in employment, Local Self Government and the Legislative bodies at the provincial and central level came forward to occupy the political space accruing to them through law. The political elite were of two types. One type insisted on ideology and inclination towards parties established by Dalits like the SCF, RPI and now the BSP. The other type of elite remained the clients of major political parties controlled by the dominant castes. Maintaining a political party meant incurring heavy expenditure. As such, the Dalit political parties banking mainly on ideology could not flourish in the state. On the other hand, political reservations always kept the political space open for Dalits to contest the elections. Hence, it became the prerogative of the dominant castes of the region controlling a political party to pick up the candidates to contest on their party tickets. The dominant caste leaders became sponsors of electioneering. Thus, in order to control the candidates post-election, they always preferred docile and pliant candidates. Thus emerged the dominant castes controlled elite in the politics of AP. In the process of clientelistic operation, the second type of elite revolved round the dominant caste political leaders. Under the gaze of dominant caste leaders, these elite could not focus on the Dalit welfare, for they ought to be responsive to the varied needs of all the people of the constituency in the system of Joint Electorate. In certain contexts, extending favours to their brethren meant going against the interests of the non-SC groups of the constituency. Thus, the Dalit legislators remained in a systemic trap, in so far as their obligations to their fellow SCs are concerned.

For these elite, obliging the dominant castes meant enjoying their continuous patronage. Electoral politics have assumed such proportions that money rather than ideology or personality became a key component to consider the candidature of the aspirant. Under such circumstances the safe option for Dalit politicians or aspirants for political positions is to revolve round the dominant caste leaders.

An examination of the educational qualification of the 48 SC MLAs of the 2009 Legislative Assembly shows that after more than sixty years of independence and despite the availability of qualified Dalits, the political parties have picked up 10 candidates who did not cross Intermediate level of education. Of them, four candidates just passed SSC. This clearly shows that the dominant castes look for pliant candidates who are subservient to their political mentors. Even the qualified candidates ought to be subservient in order to attract the attention of party leaders. Subservience is the major qualification required on the part of the Dalits to attain political positions.

Educational Qualifications of SC Members of AP Legislative Assembly, 2009

S. No.	*Name*	*Constituency*	*Party Affiliation*	*Qualification*
1	Nalla Odelu	Chennur	TRS	BA
2	Gunda Mallesh	Bellampally	CPI	HSC
3	Hanumanth Shinde	Jukkal	TDP	BE
4	Koppula Eashwar	Dharmapuri	TRS	BA
5	Suddala Devaiah	Choppadandi	TDP	BA
6	Arepalli Mohan	Manakondur	INC	M.Com, LLB
7	C. Damodar Rajanarsimha	Andole	INC	BE
8	J. Geeta	Zahirabad	INC	MBBS

Cont'd...

Cont'd...

9	K.S. Ratnam	Chevella	TDP	SSC
10	G. Prasad Kumar	Vicarabad	INC	BA
11	P. Shankar Rao	Secunderabad Cantt.	INC	MBBS
12	Abraham V.M.	Alampur	INC	MBBS
13	P. Ramulu	Achampet	TDP	BA
14	Chirumarthy Lingaiah	Nakrekal	INC	SSC
15	Mothkupalli Narsimhulu	Thungathurthy	TDP	BL
16	Thatikonda Rajaiah	Ghanpur (Station)	INC	MBBS
17	Kondeti Sridhar	Wardhanapet	INC	SSC
18	Mallu Bhatti Vikramarka	Madhira	INC	ML
19	Sandra Venkata Veeraiah	Sathupalli	TDP	Inter
20	Kondru Murali Mohan	Rajam	INC	MBA
21	Savarapu Jayamani	Parvathipuram	INC	Inter
22	Golla Babu Rao	Payakaraopeta	INC	LLB
23	Pinipe Viswarupu	Amalapuram	INC	B.Sc, B.Ed.
24	Rapaka Vara Prasada Rao	Razole	INC	BA
25	Pamul Rajeswari Devi	P.Gannavaram	INC	SSC
26	T.V. Rama Rao	Kovvur	TDP	B.Com
27	Taneti Vanita	Gopalapuram	TDP	M.Sc.
28	Maddala Rajesh Kumar	Chintalapudi	INC	M.Tech.
29	Dirisam Padma Jyothi	Tiruvuru	INC	B.Sc., B.Ed.
30	D.Y. Das	Pamarru	INC	Polytechnic
31	Tangirala Prabhakara Rao	Nandigama	TDP	LLB
32	Dokka Manikya Vara Prasada Rao	Tadikonda	INC	LLM
33	Ananda Babu Nakka	Vemuru	TDP	BL
34	Mekathota Sucharita	Prathipadu	INC	MA
35	Audimulapu Suresh	Yerragondapalem	INC	Ph.D
36	B.N. Vijay Kumar	Santhanuthalapadu	INC	BE.
37	Gurrala Venkata Seshu	Kondapai	INC	M.Com
38	Balli Durga Prasada Rao	Gudur	TDP	LLB
39	Parasa Venkata Ratnaiah	Sullurpeta	TDP	Ph.D
40	Kamalamma P.M.	Badvel	INC	M.Sc
41	Koramutla Srinivasulu	Kodur	INC	BL
42	Labbi Venkataswamy	Nandikotkur	INC	Inter
43	Parigela Murali Krishna	Kodmur	INC	MCA
44	Sake Sailajanath	Singanamala	INC	MBBS
45	K. Sudhakar	Madakasira	INC	M.Phil.
46	H. Hemalatha	Satyavedu	TDP	MA.
47	Gummadi Kuthuhalamma	Gangadhara Nellore	INC	MBBS
48	P. Ravi	Puthalapattu	INC	MBBS

The Number of Legislators with Specific Educational Qualification:

PG	*Graduates*	*Law*	*Medical*	*Engineering*	*SSC*	*Inter*	*M Phil.*	*Ph.D*	*Polytechnic*
6	9	8	7	4	4	6	1	2	1

Note: Information provided in the tables is gleaned from Election Commission of India website www.eci.nic.in

Another key factor which determines the selection of candidates is the financial strength. Political parties which are either unable to give election fund or are disinclined to give fund to the candidates, prefer candidates with rich monetary resources. If the Dalit aspirants for political space are not rich enough to compete for the party ticket, they surrender to the rich non-SC political leaders of the constituency seeking their physical and financial support. There were very few politicians who could withstand all the challenges to occupy political positions. J. Easwari Bai who could win the Assembly elections either on RPI or STP ticket, was originally a migrant from Maharashtra, who belonged to the Mahar caste. Her husband belonged to Poona and they were financially well-off. While contesting the elections from various constituencies, the author learnt that there was disquiet among the local leaders that a migrant who does not belong to their local caste was seeking election, thereby depriving them of an opportunity.

C. Damodara Rajanarasimha who represents the Andole constituency in Medak district does not belong to the Madiga caste. His father C. Rajanarasimha was a migrant from Karnataka and their family belonged to Mochi caste, native to Karnataka. This caste is not native to Andhra Pradesh. Yet, being in financially better position than the local Dalits, they could easily outsmart them to claim reserved positions. Damodara Rajanarasimha claims to be a Madiga by caste only to mobilize the Madiga support and also to use the leverages gained by Manda Krishna Madiga in course of his nearly two decades old social movement demanding apportioning of SC reservations as per the proportion of their population by dividing them into groups. Krishna Madiga constructed a distinct identity for the Madigas through his prolonged struggle which still continues.

Such misrepresentations of identity as in the case of either Easwari Bai or Damodara Rajanarasimha were widely debated by some local leaders and such information was often brought to the notice of the author. When the author started to delve into such misrepresentation of facts by Dalit politicians, J. Geeta Reddy the daughter of Easwari Bai and Minster in the INC cabinets formed in 2004 and 2009 got the author, a high ranking police official, transferred to a less significant position as a strong warning against delving into such issues. Similarly, Damodara Rajanarsimha on another occasion after knowing about the discerning attitude of the author about the caste status of the Legislator got him transferred to a less significant position on a complaint that he is pro-Telangana Rastra Samithi (TRS) and failed to deal sternly with the protesters while on duty. But the author used mild force to disperse the protesters to avoid strong-arm methods which the situation did not warrant. As such the higher authorities are expected to ascertain the facts through the state intelligence wing. But Rajanarasimha exerted undue pressure on the administration, ignoring the advice of Nandi Yellaiah, Member of Parliament, to the contrary, to get the author who belongs to Scheduled Caste transferred only to please the party bosses, in a clientelistic submission.

Kadiam Sri Hari enjoyed Ministerial positions in N.T. Ramarao and Chandrababu Naidu governments since 1994 to 2004, winning from the Station Ghanpur SC reserved constituency. His party colleagues questioned his Dalit claims as he joined the TRS Party. He earlier claimed to belong to Madiga caste and vociferously supported the SC subclassification of reservation. Later he issued a statement that he belongs to Baindla caste and that he is not a Madiga.[8] Mothkupalli Narsimhulu the TDP leader of Telangana stated that both his parents belonged to Padmasali caste which is listed as Backaward Caste and just because Srihari's family enjoyed the patronage of a SC Baindla caste man, the caste does not change his caste status and hence it amounts to misuse of SC reservation.[9]

Concentrating on misuse of SC political reservation, the author also complained in vain about the caste status of Koneru Ranga Rao who was contesting from SC reserved constituency, claiming to be a member of SC, though his father was a Kamma by caste and his mother belonged to SC. As per the Supreme Court judgment in *Sobha Hymavathi vs Setty Gangadhara Swamy and others* case,[10] 2005, the individual owns the caste of his/her father in an intercaste marriage if the father belonged to non-SC/ST and the mother belonged to SC/ST. Non-SCs and non-STs, manipulating the caste status to contest the elections on the ticket of leading political parties deprives the genuine candidates of their legitimate opportunities.

Being patronized by the dominant caste leaders, the Dalits remain subservient to them. Their attention is drawn more by the non-Dalits rather than Dalits. Their future career depends on the furtherance of patronage by the non-Dalits. Hence, they are responsive to the dominant caste electorate who are more conscious about their benefits, having been in a better position compared with the Dalit electorate who can be pleased with minor sops.

The Republican Party which contested the elections in AP could not accommodate itself in the system of Joint Electorate. For pragmatic reasons the Dalits themselves did not have the inclination to apply for its ticket with few exceptions like B.V. Ramanayya of East Godavari district and J. Easwari Bai in Telangana area. The SC elite remained mute spectators to many developments which actually necessitated their intervention.

Despite atrocities taking place against Dalits from time to time across the state, Kusuma Krishna Murty, Member of Loksabah from Amalapuram constituency was picked up by Prime Minister Indira Gandhi as a member of Indian delegation to the United Nations in 1981 to harp on the welfare measures undertaken by Congress for the uplift of Dalits, and to emphasize that Dalits are safe under the Congress rule in India. Krishna Murty readily obliged his party president and the Prime Minister. This is how the political parties take advantage of the SC representatives and the SC elite readily oblige them in a clientelistic obligation.

N. Chandrababu Naidu during his stint as AP Chief Minister from 1995 to 2004 sought to build an assured Dalit vote bank by encouraging the Madigas to demand apportioning of SC reservations to various Scheduled Castes. Many top brass politicians of the upper caste pitted Madigas against Malas and vice versa to suppress the demands of the Dalits. If a Dalit leader belonging to Mala caste sought a major favour with the Chief Minister, he would cite the Madigas demand for the same favour and vice versa. The author had learnt this from Dalit MLAs during the second stint of Kotla Vijaya Bhaskar Reddy as Chief Minister. Thus, a serious divide developed between Malas and Madigas during Vijaya Bhaskara Reddy's tenure as Chief Minster. Taking advantage of this, Chandrababu Naidu strategized to pit the Madigas against the Malas to divide the SC vote and form a new vote bank of Madigas for the TDP. He encouraged Manda Krishna Madiga to undertake a *Padayatra* or walkathon from Naidu's native village, Naravaripalli to Hyderabad to herald the divide between Malas and Madigas. But it is instructive to note that Naidu categorized the SCs into four groups through a Government Order (GO) without respect to the due process of Law.

He appointed Justice (retd) Ramachandra Raju Commission to study the demand for apportioning of SC reservations in the state. He held cabinet meetings to discuss this issue. But all through the proceedings and developments, the Mala legislators and ministers who were implicitly against any such proposal remained silent without voicing even a word of protest. This is the result of the politics of clientelism. Naidu in executing the division with a mere Government Order knew full well that such an arrangement is possible only through a Constitutional amendment and that before initiating such process, it is imperative to consult the National Commission for Scheduled Castes.

Despite protests and movements by the Malas publicly opposing the GO on SC categorization, the MLAs remained silent fearing action from Naidu in case he is criticized for acting unilaterally. The flashpoint of the movement was East Godavari district where the Dalits, mostly Malas who claimed the nomenclature of Adi-Andhra were placed in group 'D' with a mere one per cent of reservation out of the total 15 per cent. G.M.C. Balayogi who represented Amalapuram constituency in Lok Sabha and who was the Legislator of Mummidivaram SC-reserved constituency remained either silent or evasive on a development of far-reaching consequences. In the thick of such protests, elections were held for Lok Sabha; Balayogi was asked by the TDP President Chandrababu Naidu to contest from the Amalapuram constituency in the Lok Sabha elections. Balayogi obliged his party President and was elected to Lok Sabha. The local dominant castes ensured his victory, for the TDP was attempting to break the unity of the Dalits. Moreover, the economically backward Dalits could be easily wooed by money. It is only the middle class Dalits who react and work to inflict defeat on the party which is detrimental to their interest. But the limitation is that a good number of them do not participate in voting which would otherwise influence the outcome of the election.

TDP secured 16 seats in the elections and the NDA which was invited to form the government was looking for the support from any quarter, to sustain the government. Chandrababu Naidu was wooed by the BJP to either extend outside support or abstain from voting during the floor test in Lok Sabah in exchange for allotting the Speaker's post to the TDP. Chandrababu as a part of clientelistic politics chose Balayogi for the position. Balayogi earned the distinction to be the first Speaker of Lok Sabha from the Scheduled Castes. In order to assuage the ruffled feelings of Malas, Chandrababu extended them a privilege by promoting Balayogi to a high profile position. Had Balayogi opposed Chandrababu's decision to categorize SC reservations in the state, he would not have been favoured to attain such an exalted position in Indian politics.

Chandrababu later elevated K. Pratibha Bharati, to the position of Speaker of AP Assembly from 1999 to 2004. This was a move to placate the agitating Malas over the issue of categorization of SC reservation which Naidu kept alive having already created a vote bank of Madigas. The Madiga leader, Krishna Madiga enjoyed such leverages with the TDP that he played an important role in fielding Madiga candidates from the reserved constituencies where Madigas are numerically preponderant. Though the Supreme Court struck down the SC categorization on the grounds that state government is not empowered to change the policy of SC/ST reservations which emanate from Indian Constitution, Chandrababu was successful to a large extent to drive a wedge between Malas and Madigas and construct a vote bank of Madigas in favour of the TDP. This is how the SCs played themselves into the hands of dominant caste party leaders displaying clientelism. The pliant candidates were identified to be fielded in the elections and for such candidates political power was more important than ideology. Moreover, they did not rely on SC voters among the electorate.

Elite Response to Dalit Issues and Atrocities

Assertiveness and social articulation of the Dalits became intolerable to the dominant castes. The Dalit movements inculcated consciousness of rights and safeguards. Adi-Andhra movement predates the Harijan upliftment and has been instrumental in enlightening them. Ambedkar's leadership contested the hegemonic nationalist ideology propounded by the upper caste intelligentsia.[11] Some of the post-independence incidents on Dalits illustrate how hegemony of non-Dalit castes prevailed over Dalits.

With the advent of Green Revolution in 1970s in Andhra Pradesh, the intermediary castes, particularly the Kammas gained unprecedented financial strength. The introduction of Chinese TN1 rice seed in 1980s increased the agricultural surplus in coastal Andhra significantly.[12] The Andhra Pradesh Land Reforms (Ceiling on Agriculture Holdings) Act passed in 1973[13] through a series of initiatives such as abolition of intermediaries, tenancy reforms, ceiling legislation and so on had the important effect of strengthening the peasant caste. Thus, the Kammas, being a peasant caste concentrated in the Krishna and Guntur districts, began to make substantial gains out of Green Revolution and the AP land reforms legislation. Over a period of time they consolidated their gains. They diversified their investments and migrated to Telangana and certain areas of Karnataka such as Raichur, Gangavati, etc. and purchased land which was relatively cheaper. They could thus make fortune over a period of time.

Having attained economic strength they were looking for political power. The Congress was dominated by the Reddys, another intermediate caste. The Kammas entered the Communist party for political space. But Communists were hardly in a position to form government given the popularity of Congress party gained over India's liberation from the British rule and the charisma of Jawaharlal Nehru and his charismatic daughter Indira Gandhi. Moreover, the enterprising Kammas did not fit into the Communist mould though there were some of them committed to the Communist ideology. They could hence not fulfil their political ambitions within the Communist parties. They saw an inconsistency between their financial strength and political status. This gap was filled up with the advent of Telugu Desam Party (TDP) founded by N.T. Rama Rao, a famous Telugu film star who was Kamma by caste. Their long cherished ambition was fulfilled with the TDP, founded by their caste man N.T. Rama Rao coming to power in the State in 1983 in its maiden attempt at the hustings. Having attained political power, they began to resist the Dalit assertiveness. Their oppressive attitude was evident in some incidents to be discussed in the later part of this work.

Despite Constitutional safeguards in favour of Dalits, atrocities continue to be perpetrated against them from time to time. It is instructive to note that it is these legal rights and privileges which invited the ire of upper castes, especially the dominant castes of the area in question. These upper castes could not tolerate changes in social structure, imposed from above by the Constitution, which have the potential to equate the status of Dalits with theirs. Hence, they resisted any progressive initiative by the Dalits. B.R. Ambedkar on 25 November 1949, while addressing the Constituent Assembly observed thus:

> I feel, however good a Constitution may be it is sure to turn out bad because those who are called to work it, happen to be a bad lot. However bad a Constitution may be, it may turn out to be good if those who are called to work it happen to be a good lot.[14]

Atrocities continued on Dalits in independent India. Freedom to the nation did not mean freedom to the Dalits. Though the caste Hindus attained freedom from the British rule, the Dalits did not attain freedom from the discriminatory tradition espoused by the caste Hindus. Thus, the social reforms had to be imposed from above in the form of Constitutional guarantees, for the reforms could not gain social acceptability. The upward social mobility of Dalits which is a departure from tradition, provoked the non-Dalits whose mindset remained traditional despite the changes in the law facilitating the uplift of the Dalits.

Any attempt on the part of Dalits to utilize the privileges and concessions accruing to them legally was reckoned by the dominant castes as contempt of the traditional order. Many incidents have gone unreported. With regard to atrocities on Dalits it is not only the upper castes who perpetrate them but even the intermediary castes do not spare the Dalits. Even those castes who enjoy reservations on the claim of being Backward Castes, perpetrate violence against Dalits. So to put it in bare terms, the Scheduled Castes are targets of all castes in the Hindu caste framework. Such incidents have been occurring since independence, for there is no social acceptability to the reforms which stem from the Constitution. Some of the incidents illustrate the observation.

The law which safeguards the Dalits and facilitates their uplift was put in place since the Constitution was enforced from 26 January 1950. Yet the caste Hindus' journey with tradition continued. In two villages Haribanda and Makannapuram in Sompet Taluk of Srikakulam district, Dalits were attacked thrice by caste Hindus in April-May, 1950, the reason being that the Dalits on the so-called Harijan Day drew water from the common well. The government in fact declared the 30th of every month as Harijan Day. The District Collectors were instructed to bring together Dalits and savarnas to organize inter-community activities. But on the fateful day after the conclusion of celebrations, Dalits were attacked for violating the social norm. The terrified Dalits fled the village. The attempts of the government to foster the commingling of Dalits with other caste Hindus did not bear fruit.

In the year 1950 in Appikatla village of Guntur district, Dalit agricultural labourers were attacked by upper caste rich peasants over an otherwise trivial issue. They were driven out of the village. The issue was brought to the notice of B.S. Murthy, Minister in the Madras state government. He took up the issue and ordered for building a colony for the Dalits in the outskirts of Bapatla town near Lam Farms on the Guntur-Bapatla-Chirala Road. The colony was named by the Dailts as Murthy Rakshana Nagar, popularly known as M.R. Nagar.

In Kusukurru village of Krishna district, a well educated Dalit couple participating in a marriage procession was dragged out of their car and beaten up. Though the Dalits on one hand have been waging a struggle for their just rights, and the law to protect them was in place, there has been a strong resistance by the non-Dalits against the former's attempts of mobility. In Kalvacharla village in West Godavari district, a Dalit woman Nagalamma was tortured by the brother of a village officer for drinking water from a public well.[15] Efforts of Dalits to join the mainstream of the society by invoking Constitutional guarantees were strongly resisted by the caste Hindus, revealing the influence of tradition which is deeply ingrained in their psyche.

Post-1956, after the formation of Andhra Pradesh, in Sambavaram village in Kurnool district, one Dalit was killed and 16 others were injured as the caste Hindus attacked them for undertaking construction of a community hall in a Dalit locality. A couple of haystacks were also burnt.[16] Claim of any privilege was replied with violence to the extent of killing the Dalits. The intent to kill depicted the deep seated animosity against the Dalits. It was also to prevent further claims by terrifying them.

Incidents Recorded in 1960–61

In a village in Hyderabad district, the caste Hindus drove nearly 200 cattle for grazing into the fields owned by Dalits, which were ready for harvest as a signal of intimidation and also to resist their prosperity. In a village called Khondalpalli in Cuddapah district, some houses of Dalits were burnt and completely destroyed because a Dalit cut grass in the field of a caste Hindu. In Gundapalli village of Cuddapah district, 47 houses of Dalits were burnt by caste Hindus because a buffalo owned by Dalits was seen grazing in the field belonging to the caste Hindus.[17] It is instructive to note that the non-SCs, either the so-called twice born castes or the Sudra casts condemned the SCs to permanent ostracism. They could not tolerate tradition being superseded by law.

The Report of the Commission for SC/ST, 1964

In some of the villages of Anantapur district, Dalit students were made to sit separately in the schools run in temples and *Dahrmasalas.* It must be noted that the concept of untouchability emanates from adherence to religious tenets which are valid or not. Hence, running schools in temples for Dalits meant temple entry by untouchables which was unacceptable. In another incident in the same district, a Dalit Sarpanch and two other Dalits were killed as they drew water from the village tank for the purpose of drinking. In Govindpeta village of Nizamabad district, a Dalit woman was beaten to death for suspected robbery. It was taken for granted that Dalits being economically backward would resort to stealing to satisfy their needs. Moreover, they were too weak to resist such violent attacks. The caste Hindus thereby also fulfilled their hegemonic urge. It must also be noted that during attacks on Dalits, their fellow Dalits do not come to their rescue for they are financially dependent on the caste Hindus for their survival. In another village in East Godavari district, one person was killed and six others were grievously injured when caste Hindus attacked the Dalits who wanted to enter a temple.[18]

In 1958, two Dalit youths who visited Nimmakur village in Krishna district were tortured for seven hours, tied in a gunny bag and thrown into Bandar canal suspecting them to be thieves as they stood on a house which belonged to a Kamma landlord, to catch the glimpse of their favourite film star, N.T. Rama Rao. They, in fact, walked for several miles to see him. Caste Hindus did not want the aesthetic faculties of Dalits to develop. They were not prepared to accept Dalits' cultural parity with them. When Dalit agricultural labourers in Ramannapalli village in Cuddapah district demanded increase in their wages, 500 armed caste Hindus raided a Dalit colony and indiscriminately attacked Dalit men, women, and children. In the attack they burnt all the 109 households. In China Ogirala village of Krishna district, one Dalit was murdered and twenty more were severely injured by the caste Hindu landlords because government wastelands were allotted to 108 Dalit families. In another village in Kurnool district, 30 huts belonging to Dalits were demolished by upper caste landlords as Dalits were allotted 711.73 acres of land for the purpose of house construction.[19] The caste Hindu landlords perpetrated atrocities against Dalits with impunity. It is instructive to note that the law enforcing officials are non-SCs or even if they are SCs by virtue of reservation policy, they were controlled by non-SC higher-ups. Moreover, the economic power of the landed gentry enabled them to control the resources of the village including the politicians and officials. They held their stranglehold over the governing structure.

The Iillay Perumal Committee on Untouchability reported several instances of untouchability in various parts of Andhra Pradesh. Some of them are the following:

In Padmagalai village in Anantapur district, SCs were not allowed to walk through the village on footwear. In Anantapur, the SCs were not allowed to sit in a cart when it passes through the streets inhabited by caste Hindus. In Vijayawada, the SCs were not allowed to sit in boats along with caste Hindus. In Kaumbaripalem village in West Godavari district the SCs were not allowed to fetch water from the public drinking water wells. In Jankampet village of Nizamabad district, separate glasses were kept for SCs in tea shops. The glasses were to be cleaned by the SCs themselves before and after use. This practice still continues in some remote villages across the state. In Bangaripalyam of Chittor district, SCs were not served in plates in hotels. The SC children are not allowed to sit with children belonging to other communities in Cheekatim Anipally, in Anantapur district.[20]

It is instructive to note in this context that between 1960 and 1962, Damodaram Sanjeevayya, a Dalit leader from Kurnool district, was the Chief Minister of the state. The Dalit political representatives rarely reacted to such violent incidents as their personal interests dominated the safety of their brethren whose very existence gave the leaders a Constitutional concession. But trapped in clientelistic politics, they were either helpless to come to the rescue of the victim or they feared their own safety. Having attained exalted position in the state, Sanjeevayya went on to occupy the highest organizational position in the Congress – the President of AICC. He was also the Central Minister in the Cabinets of Jawaharlal Nehru and Indira Gandhi. Yet he pursued clientelistic politics and operated within the boundaries set by the Congress top brass.

One incident in Krishna district rocked the AP Assembly. Attention of the House was drawn to the killing of a young Dalit. In a place called Kanchikacherla in Krishna district one Arikatla Kotesu,[21] a Dalit youth, used to eke out his livelihood by working as a coolie. On 24 February 1968, he was passing through the village of Kanchikacherla when two upper caste men suspecting him of stealing some utensils of their household brought him to a tobacco barn. They tied him with a rope, poured kerosene on the body, lighted a match and set fire to his clothes. Kotesu managed to run away and contacted a private doctor who advised him to go to the Government hospital or to a police station. At about 5.30 p.m. he went to the police station at Kanchikacherla where his statement was recorded. He was thereafter admitted to the Government hospital where his dying declaration was recorded at about 9.30 the next day morning. He succumbed to his injuries in the afternoon of the 26th. The burn injuries on the palms of one of the offenders convinced the Court that the accused tried to put out the fire and in the process received burn injuries. Thus, the Supreme Court confirmed the judgment of the High Court convicting the accused. This issue came up for discussion in the AP Assembly. Minister Peddireddy Thimma Reddy tried to downplay the incident of Kotesu's murder. J. Easwari Bai, the Republican Party legislator lambasted the Minster brandishing her footwear at him for his uncharitable and arrogant remarks offending the SCs in defence of the accused.

On 5 January 1983, four Dalits were killed and 80 families were rendered homeless following an attack by upper caste TDP supporters at Padirikuppam village in Chittoor district. Their properties and livestock were also completely burnt. The incident happened on the polling day of the 1983 Assembly elections. N.T. Rama Rao, the TDP president, was contesting from Tirupati which is just 60 km away from the village. The TDP workers or the Kamma gentry of the village thought that the Dalits voted for Congress en masse. Hence, they let their fury on the poor and helpless Dalits. Rama Rao after becoming Chief Minister ordered a judicial inquiry by a retired High Court Judge of AP Y. Venkateswara Rao.[22] The report of inquiry has not been placed in the public domain.

On 17 July 1985, six Dalits were killed and three Dalit women were raped in a mass attack by hundreds of forward caste men of the Kamma caste in Karamchedu village of Prakasam district. Madigas who are a Scheduled Caste, constituted a strong force in Karmchedu. Kammas were a dominant caste of the village. Having cultivated the fertile lands of the area, they tried their hand even at the film field. Daggubati Rama Naidu a noted film producer hails from this village. Since they owned vast swathes of land in the village they had the final say in all the affairs of the village. They often misbehaved with the Dalit girls. Any resistance on the part of the Dalits was met by a strong offence. Any kind of a resistance to the Kamma hegemony from any non-Kamma quarter was least tolerated by them. Ten years before the carnage occurred, the *Upparas,* a backward caste of the village, rebelled against the Kammas for the latter's frequent interference in their internal matters and also for being dictatorial in conduct. In response to this, the Kammas frequently raided the *Uppara* locality. They even raided the Mala locality. But the Madigapalle came to the rescue of Malas. The fact that Madigas are strong enough to physically resist the Kammas and were successful in defending the other communities against the Kamma assault, provoked the dominant caste further. Hence, they were waiting to strike the Madigas at an opportune movement. Madigas were warriors and they were adept in *Karrasamu*, a martial art practised with a cane. The Madiga youth always intervened on behalf of helpless people, especially women when they were harassed by Kammas.

After the formation of TDP, the Kammas of Karamchedu village joined the party en bloc while the Dalits remained with the Congress. Daggubati Chenchuramaiah sought the Paruchur ticket of the TDP for his son, Daggubati Venkateswara Rao who is also the son-in-law of Rama Rao. Chenchuramaiah campaigned for his son's victory. In course of his campaign he visited Madigapalle in Karamchedu village and sought the support of Madigas. In fact, he commanded them for their support. Madigas who were independent of any influence on such matters did not give any assurance to Chenchuramaiah. They said that they would have to think about it. On the polling day the TDP agents clashed with the Madigas and even tried to prevent them from voting. But the Madigas resolutely stood their ground. As Kammas were looking for a source of ignition, the awaited moment came. One day, two Kamma youth took their buffaloes to the water tank at Madigapalle, and were feeding them with cattle drink in buckets. A Madiga boy objected to it because they were polluting the drinking water whereupon they attacked him. Meanwhile a Madiga woman who reached the tank to collect water came to the rescue of the boy under attack. When the Kamma youth turned their attention on the woman, she raised the vessel against them in defence. This incident provoked them. As they reported the matter to their elders, they could not tolerate a Madiga woman raising her hand against their men. This reason was enough for the Kammas to launch an attack on the Madigas. As they knew that their strength would not match that of Madigas of the village, they mobilized Kammas of seven surrounding villages and launched an organized attack on Madigapalle in the morning of 17 July 1985. About 300 Kammas armed with deadly weapons created mayhem at Madiga locality.[23]

About four hundred families fled the village. They rigged up a rehabilitation camp some eight km away from Chirala and began to fight for justice with the help of Dalit leaders. N.T. Rama Rao, the then Chief Minister and the President of the TDP, delayed taking action on the 'Kamma' caste offenders. Moreover, the village Karamchedu happened to be the native place of his son-in-law, Daggubati Venkateswara. About 200 Dalit women then staged a protest in front of his Hyderabad residence pressing for the arrest of the accused and also to provide amenities to their new colony near Chirala which they named as Vijayanagar colony. They were led by Guduru Seethamahalakshmi, also known as rationalist Lakshmi, who braved the police threats and the protest continued till Rama Rao appeared before them to consider their demand. The Dalits boycotted the inquiry Commission of Retired Judge D.P. Desai with a belief that he was coming with preconceived notions. Earlier two Judges turned the job away.[24]

Katti Padmarao, a college lecturer and Dalit leader, spearheaded the movement for justice to Dalits. The Dalits refused to return to Karamchedu and they bought eight acres of land with funds raised by the 'Karmachedu Victims Relief Committee' to build homes for themselves. In a movement free of politicians, the Dalits demanded the government land near the camping site to build a new colony and also government jobs. To avoid criticism about his pro-Kamma leanings, Rama Rao agreed to the proposals.[25]

The Karamchedu incident created a furore in the Assembly. But the Dalit legislators of the ruling TDP could not pressurize the government for a rigorous pursuit of the case. The legislators enjoying the 'Kamma' patronage could not demand the immediate punitive action against the assailants of the same caste. Hence, it was the AP Dalit Mahasabha led by Katti Padmarao which took up the cause of Dalits who were violently chased out of the village by the Kamma assailants. The reaction by the Dalit legislators was limited. The TDP Dalit legislators in particular could not have sacrificed their political career by espousing the cause of the victims.

After a protracted legal battle for 23 years, the Supreme Court awarded life imprisonment to the prime accused and three years of imprisonment to 30 others. Conviction of 159 accused by a trial court at Ongole had been set aside by the AP High Court. Though Special Leave Petition was filed in Supreme Court in 1998, the final verdict came only ten years later.[26]

Close on the heels of Karamchedu incident, landlords belonging to the TDP set fire to 30 houses of Dalits in Avdhapur-Medak district on 17 January 1986.[27] On 15 July 1987, a major incident of rioting occurred against Malas, perpetrated by the upper caste Kammas at Neerukonda village in Guntur district. This incident has parallels with that of Karmchedu. Neerukonda situated a few km away from the Mangalagiri town was a Kamma dominated village, both in terms of numerical preponderance and land ownership. The Kammas consisted of about 200 families, while the

Mala families were about 150 in number. There were about forty 'Golla' (Yadava) families in the village. The bulk of the land in the village was owned by Kammas while the Malas constituted majority of the agrarian labour force working in the tobacco and paddy fields owned by Kammas for low wages. The lower than minimum wages were also not paid promptly. For instance, for grading tobacco, the wages were paid only after the product was marketed, which means the Dalits had to wait for nearly six months for the payment. Women working in paddy fields complained that they were paid only after the crop is marketed, which means they were forced to wait for at least three months to receive the payment. This onerous gap forced the Dalits to borrow money from the rich landlords demanding high interest. One cause of Kamma rancour was Dalits conducting a marriage procession in the village. The Kammas objected to this and an agreement was reached to confine such processions to Dalit locality. Another but deeper cause of Kamma rancour was the assertiveness of Malas. For instance, they fielded their own candidate in the local elections in 1981, sending a signal to Kammas that they are not prepared to toe the line of the dominant caste. The TDP coming to power after the 1983 Assembly elections further boosted the strength of Kammas. The party candidate from Mangalagiri constituency was M.S.S. Koteswara Rao, a Kamma from Neerukonda village. While the Kammas intimidated the Malas to vote for the TDP, the Malas stood their ground being the traditional vote bank of the Congress. The Kammas conducted occasional raids on Mala locality and beat up the Dalits randomly. In the 1985 mid-term elections to the AP Assembly, Koteswara Rao was fielded again as TDP candidate pitted against Jamuna, a famous film actress of yesteryears, contesting on Congress ticket. On account of Jamuna, the Congress paid great attention on this seat. The TDP deemed it as a prestige to win the seat and Koteswara Rao emerged victorious and was gifted with ministerial berth in Rama Rao's cabinet. The Kammas deemed this development as immunity to their wild acts. Unable to bear the Dalit assertion and inclination towards the Congress, and inspired by the Karamchedu violence, the Kammas organized an assault on Malas as a show of strength. Hundreds of armed Kamma youth attacked Malas. Four Malas were killed along with one man of the Golla caste. Following this incident the Malas left Neerukonda and settled in a colony at Mangalagiri.[28] The Kammas taking full advantage of TDP's patronage conducted themselves brutally.

In Gudiada village in Vizianagaram district, on 15 July 1987 one Dalit labourer was killed in a dispute over a small patch of tank bed land by a mob of backward caste farmers led by a forward Kshatriya caste Congress Party leader. In Chirala town of Prakasham district on 13 August 1987, a key witness in the Karamchedu murder case was killed by Karamchedu killers. In Bandilapalli village, four Dalits were beaten and stabbed to death in an attack by a group of forward caste men on 27 November 1987. At Kodavatikallu village on 2 February 1988, a Dalit labourer was murdered by a landlord. On 19 January 1989, a Dalit *upasarpanch* of Beernakallu village of Nellore district was killed by a TDP landlord. The killing of representatives of the local self-government reveals the friction between the constitutional guarantees to the subaltern groups and the traditional power structure. In Gokarajupalli village, on 16 January 1989 a Dalit labourer was killed by landlords. In Tanguturu of Prakasham district on 3 March 1989, a Dalit woman was raped and burnt to death by a forward caste TDP men. In Jabbargudem village in Ranga Reddy district on 27 April 1989, one Dalit was killed in a mass attack by the followers of a TDP landlord. In Pippara village of West Godavari district on 4 June 1989, one Dalit was killed in a mass attack by forward caste men led by village *upasarpanch*. In Kanchikacherla – Krishna district on 19 March 1990, a Dalit farm servant was killed by youth of a landlord's family. In Gutlapadu – West Godavari on 19 May 1990, two Dalits were killed in a mass attack by forward caste men. In Kothapulavandlapalli – Ananthapur district on 6 June 1990, a Dalit was burnt alive by forward caste men. On 28 November 1990, in Chillakallu village in Krishna district a Dalit Sub-Inspector of police shot himself dead due to casteist harassment by the Circle Inspector. This incident reveals that even government employees are not free from persecution by the upper caste bosses. In Moodurallapalli village in Kurnool district on 18 March 1991, a Dalit labourer was beaten and stabbed to death by a mob of forward caste men. In Timmasamudram village of Prakasam district in January 1991, Dalits were driven out of the village in an attack by Kammas. When the Dalits of the village launched a movement seeking land for the tiller, a band of Kammas attacked them by hurling bombs in the presence of police. Most of these incidents reported during the TDP regime either had the involvement of Kammas or the support of the Kammas.[29]

In Chundur, Guntur district on 6 August 1991, eight Dalits were killed several others grievously injured in a mass assault by Reddys men not only from Chundur but from the adjoining villages. Some of the Dalits went missing and were not traceable even after many years since the incident. The Malas of Chunduru, were predominantly agricultural labourers. But few years before the violent incident, the new generation of Dalit youth which had been concentrating on educational facilities sponsored by the state could secure government jobs around the village. Having developed awareness of education and rights, the morale of Dalits rose high and their dressing and food patterns changed. The youth especially, began to move confidently in the streets. They no longer were prepared to emulate the subservience of their elders toward the upper castes. These developments have perturbed the upper caste Reddys whose dominance was getting eroded with the Dalits gradually moving toward financial independence through government jobs and schemes. The Reddy rancour grew day by day against the Malas over their progress in education and economy. Meanwhile, a Mala youth who was employed elsewhere visited his native place Chunduru and was one day watching a movie in a local film theatre. Stretching himself in the seat he allegedly touched the Reddy youth in the front seat with his foot. The Reddy youth reacted with rage and a scuffle ensued. This incident snowballed into a major controversy as the Reddys were awaiting an opportunity to unleash their fury on the Malas. They mobilized their fellowmen from Modukuru, Dindipalem and Valiveru villages and launched a brutal attack on the Dalits. Eight people were axed to death and their bodies were packed in gunny bags and were thrown in canals in and around Chunduru. Seven of those killed were Malas while one Angalakuduru Rajamohan Gandhi was a Madiga. Several others were grievously injured.[30] This incident rocked the State Assembly as the attackers belonged to the Reddy caste, displaying hegemony during the Congress government. With this it is evident that the persons belonging to the caste of Chief Minister felt that they enjoyed immunity even from criminal activities. Later, Ram Vilas Paswan, a national Dalit leader visited Chunduru and addressed a meeting at Vijayawada. He warned the hegemonic castes of a nationwide Dalit revolution, if they continue to perpetrate atrocities.

Even as the wounds of Chundur remained fresh, another incident took place in Gokarajupalli village in the neighbouring Krishna district on 3 August 1991 where a Dalit labourer was killed by forward caste men.[31]

The Trial court in Chunduru Dalit massacre case convicted 56 accused in 2007. However, in April 2014 the AP High Court struck down the conviction. Following mass agitations across the state by Dalits especially from Visakhapatnam led by Vaska Raghavendra Rao of the Ambedkar Memorial Society, apart from Bojja Tarakam and others at Hyderabad, the Government of Andhra Pradesh filed a Special Leave Petition in the Supreme Court in June 2014. The Supreme Court in July heard the petition and stayed the High Court verdict.[32]

In a village called Pottilanka[33] in East Godavari district, the dominant caste Kapus beat up one Ambadi Rajaratnam as he allegedly misbehaved with a Kapu girl near a hotel on the highway on 20 June 2008. He was beaten again severely after he visited the same hotel for breakfast on the following day. Anticipating the reaction of SCs on the incident, nearly a hundred Kapus raided the SC locality with lethal weapons and attacked the helpless Dalits. Palli Veerapandu died with his skull broken and Vemula Yesu was grievously injured and whoever came to the rescue of those under attack also received injuries. The police did not register case against the Kapus till 26 of June, though false cases were foisted against Dalits to downplay the violence perpetrated by the dominant caste. For any political party to win in East Godavari district, the support of Kapus is vital. Hence, the Congress government headed by Y.S. Rajasekhara Reddy did not espouse the cause of Dalits in this event. The case slowly was hushed up. No Dalit legislator reacted to the incident in adequate measure excepting issuing some statements in support of victims, and against the offenders in a display of bravado. Antagonism with Kapus meant sealing once own political career. It is incompatible to note that the Kapu caste which practises open discrimination against Dalits and does not hesitate to perpetrate atrocities against them is sought to be included in the Backward Castes list.

In 1996, Thota Trimurtulu an independent MLA of Kapu caste representing the Ramachandrapuram constituency in East Godavari district got two Dalit youths forcibly tonsured at his residence for their alleged uncomplimentary remarks against Kapu women. Though, the Dalit organizations agitated against the government to take action against the MLA, the political elite remained silent except condemning the incident through newspapers. No issue was raised against him in pubic when the same MLA abused the Dalit women in unparliamentarily language when he descended on Namavaram village in East Godavari district to forcibly take with him a Dalit youth who allegedly attacked someone who complained to the MLA. This incident took place in May 2013.[34] But no legislator felt the need to pursue the issue of the abducted youth.

The political elite do not respond meaningfully to the atrocities on SCs. The Karamchedu incident occurred during the TDP rule where the power was concentrated in the hands of Kammas. The Chunduru massacre of Dalits took place when the Congress was in power, dominated by the Reddys. On these occasions it was only the Dalit organizations which protested the violence perpetrated on their brethren and pressured the government to arrest the guilty and pay compensation to the victims. The SC legislators and Parliamentarians did not take decisive steps against the violence.

On 12 June 2012 in Laxmipet, violence against the Malas by Turpu Kapus killed five Dalits and 19 people had their skulls broken. It is a resettled village of those displaced by the 'Madduvalsa' irrigation project. The original village got submerged by the project and hence a new settlement was shown by the government. The two major castes of the village are Turpu Kapu and Mala. Though the Turpu Kapus are listed as Backward Castes, they are economically and politically a dominant caste in the north coastal districts of Andhra Pradesh. The other major caste 'Malas' are a Scheduled Caste and are landless agricultural labourers. Kapus, being owners of land with well constructed houses, were given compensation for their property. Additionally, they were given government jobs. The landless Malas received a token amount as compensation for their small huts or houses. They were not given even a single government job.

In the resettled village both the communities were provided house sites and their houses were constructed in each other's vicinity with only a small road dividing their line of houses. After the completion of the irrigation project, about 250 acres of surplus land remained. It was assured that even if the tank reaches maximum limit of water level it would not submerge the aforesaid surplus land. Though legally it was no more their land, the villagers began to cultivate the land. The Kapus started to cultivate about 190 acres and the Dalits the remaining 60 acres. The owners of the 60 acres of land cultivated by Dalits settled at faraway places having received compensation. Neither the government, nor the Kapus initially objected to the Dalits cultivating it. But after Botsa Satyanarayana, a Turpu Kapu became the Provincial Congress Committee President with authority over party affairs across the state, at a time when INC was the ruling party, wielded enormous power and clout. The rise of Chiranjeevi in politics after he joined the INC and became a member of Rajya Sabha, also arrogated the people of Turpu Kapu caste. Ensured of protection at the top echelons of administration the Turpu Kapus at Laxmipeta village threatened the Malas to stop cultivation and vacate the land. The Malas refused to vacate the land as they claimed to be paying lease amount to the erstwhile owners of the land though it was not required. To terrify the reluctant Malas the Turpu Kapus attacked them with country bombs and other lethal weapons, killing five persons and injuring many.[35]

Laxmipeta falls in Rajam Assembly constituency which is reserved for SCs and represented by Kondru Murali Mohan who is also a Minister in the ruling dispensation. He did not react adequately in support of the victims. Notably, he did not visit the village to express his solidarity with the sufferers. On the other hand it is learnt that he advised the Malas to vacate the land for the Turpu Kapus, for they constitute the dominant caste in the constituency of Murali, and any serious action against them would jeopardize the political career of the sitting MLA. Remarkably, the violence against SCs took place at a time when all the local administrative functionaries in charge of law and order – the police inspector, the Dy. Superintendent of Police (DSP) and the Mandal Revenue Officer were all SCs.[36]

The female DSP who was bold and forthright was interviewed by the author. She was the Sub-Divisional Police Officer at Palakonda, and Laxmipet fell within the jurisdiction of Palakonda. Having learnt in March 2012 that the Turpu Kapus are planning an offensive against the Malas at Laxmipet, she took some of the potential offenders into preventive custody and got a police picket posted at the village. As long as the police picket remained, the law and order in the village remained stable. But on 12 June 2012, the picket was removed at the behest of higher authorities in the administration citing that it was redundant as the situation in the village was calm, and moreover, the police personnel were required for some other pressing purpose. But the Malas during the author's visit to the village in February 2015 confided in him that the picket was removed to facilitate violence against them. Post-violence, complaints were lodged against the offenders by the Malas and also the Dalit activists who reached the village in solidarity with the victims of violence. Since cases were to be booked under The Scheduled Castes and Scheduled Tribes Act (Prevention of Atrocities) Act, 1989, the DSP is the investigating officer as per the Act. As the DSP undertook the investigation and began to identify the accused, she received phone calls from an unexpected quarter. It was Kondru Murali Mohan Rao a Cabinet Minister holding the portfolio of Medical Education in the cabinet of N. Kiran Kumar Reddy, the then Chief Minister of erstwhile Andhra Pradesh. He categorically told her not to register case against any of the Turpu Kapus. But as she persisted with her investigation, the Minister went on making phone calls threatening to get her suspended. Since the officer did not relent, he got her transferred from Palakonda.

Investigation of Laxmipet case was completed in record time and the trial began within two and a half years. As the Deputy Inspector General of Police in the AP Crime Investigation Department (CID), the author took necessary care during investigation and trial. He attended every session of the special court till he was transferred to Legal Metrology Department, to boost the morale of the victims who complained of intimidation by the caste people of the accused. The author also acknowledges the cooperation extended by Dwaraka Tirumala Rao, IPS, Additional Director General of Police, CID in the course of investigation.

In the system of Joint Electorate in reserved constituencies, the non-Dalits constitute the majority and the dominant castes of the constituency have a decisive say in the electoral prospects of the candidates. Hence, the SC candidates who embarked upon a political career could not afford to antagonize the non-Dalits. They can antagonize the non-Dalits only by sealing their own fate or ending their career. Thus, the SC elite who are committed to the welfare of their Dalit brethren cannot prosper in politics. The dominant caste leaders of the reserved constituency try to field pliant candidates among the SCs to wield control of the constituency. The SC politicians on the other hand, oblige the non-Dalits to improve their electoral prospects. Thus, the firebrand leaders among SCs could not repeat their success stories due to rejection by the non-SCs.

The instances of Backward Castes (BCs) attacking the Dalits still continues despite the BCs enjoying reservations and demanding the privileges on par with the SCs. Dalits who attained pivotal positions in politics have also not been spared. An attempt was made to assault Mayawati on 2 June 1995 by the BC followers of Mulayam Singh Yadav. Panic-stricken Mayawati made frantic calls to the then Prime Minister P.V. Narasimaha Rao, Vajpayee and Advani to rescue her from the state guest house where she locked herself up to save her life. The then Governor Motilal Vohra had to send his personal security to the rescue of Mayawati.[37]

Dalit Mahasabha (APDM) presided by Katti Padma Rao led the protest movements against the atrocities on Dalits at Kamachdu and Chunduru villages. Padmarao's attempts to enter the Legislature under the banner of BSP failed. Having led the Karmchedu and Chunduru agitations, he was identified with the cause of SCs. Hence, non-SCs would not cast their vote in his favour. Though he entered electoral politics as a key functionary of the BSP, he could not win the elections.

Manda Krishna Madiga spearheaded a campaign for classification of SC reservation on the banner of Madiga Reservation Porata Samiti (MRPS). He was partially successful in his mission for the Chandrababu Naidu led TDP government classified the SCs into four groups first through a Government Order and later through an Assembly resolution. It was struck down by the Supreme Court in 2004, mostly based on procedural lapses and the constitutional limitations of the state government to enact such legislation. Nevertheless, the movements served many latent functions. The Madigas could construct a distinct identity for themselves. Many of them suffixed the caste name 'Madiga' to their names on the lines of Manda Krishna Madiga. They became an influential pressure group and began to demand their share in 'Nominated Posts' of the state government, the positions of Vice-Chancellors in Universities and such other privileges.

P.V. Rao who led the Mala caste group opposed the classification of SC reservation. He mobilized the Malas across the state and waged a legal battle against the State Government in the High Court and the Supreme Court. It must be noted that the Mala legislators during the TDP rule did not oppose the process of SC classification fearing loss of patronage by the TDP.

In 2004, during the tenure of Y.S. Rajasekhar Reddy as Chief Minister of Andhra Pradesh, the AP Assembly adopted a resolution seeking an introduction of Bill in the Parliament for subclassification of SCs for the purpose of reservations. In 2005, Manda Krishna Madiga undertook *Padayatra* or a journey on foot for 1,500 km from Bangalore (now Bengaluru) to Hyderabad pressurizing Rajasekhara Reddy to lead a delegation to New Delhi to prevail upon the UPA government to amend the constitution to fulfil their demand.[38]

The Union Government appointed the Justice (retd) Usha Mehra Commission to study all aspects of the demand for SC classification and submit a report. The Commission submitted its report in 2008, favouring classification of SCs for judicious redistribution of reservations. It sought the amendment of Article 341 of the Constitution. Before embarking on introduction of a Bill in the Parliament, the Union government sought the views of National Commission for Scheduled Castes (NCSC) on the Usha Mehra Commission report. The NCSC disapproved of such a move as it would be unconstitutional and would not stand judicial scrutiny. This view of the NCSC restrained the Union Government from further proceeding with the proposal to amend the Constitution.[39]

Only interest groups were found espousing the cause of their brethren rather than the political elite. Thus, the limitations of the SC political elite in reacting against the atrocities committed on their brethren or to take up their legitimate demands with the government are laid bare. For them it is a systemic trap wherein they struggle to negotiate between their political career and the cause of their people and despite an inclination to oblige their people cannot do so, for it would cost them their political career.

Notes

1. B.R. Ambedkar, *The Untouchables*, Bheem Patrika Publications, Jalandhar, 1948, Preface.
2. G.S. Ghurye, *Caste and Race*, cited in Harold Issac's *India's Ex-Untouchable*, Asia Publishing House, Bombay, 1965, p. 43.
3. Dhananjay Kheer, *Life and Mission of Dr Ambedkar*, Popular Prakasan, Bombay, 1971, Preface.
4. H.R. Issac, *India's Ex-Untouchables*, Asia Publishing House, Bombay, 1965, p. 44.
5. E. Zelliot, 'Learning the Use of Political Means', in, *Caste in Indian Politics*, Rajani Kothari (ed), Orient Longman Ltd., Delhi (1970), p. 41.
6. Ibid.
7. D.D. Basu, *Introduction to the Constitution of India*, Prentice Hall of India Pvt. Ltd., New Delhi (1980), p. 346–47.
8. *Andhra Jyothi*, 30.01.2015.
9. *Andhra Jyothi*, 29.01.2015.
10. http://indiankanoon.org/doc/1380261/ accessed on 05.03.2014
11. A. Satyanarayana, *Dalits and Upper Castes: Essays in Social History*, Kanishka Publishers, New Delhi, 2005, p. 206.
12. Biao Xiang, *Global Body Shopping: An Indian Labour System in the Information Technology Industry*, Princeton University Press, New Jersey, 2007, p. 32.
13. http://ebookily.net/pdf/andhra-pradesh-land-reforms-ceiling-on-agricultural-holdings-26549727.html.
14. N. Mishra (ed), Introduction, in *Socio-economic and Political Vision of Dr B.R. Ambedkar*, Concept Publishing Company Pvt. Ltd., New Delhi, 2010, p. 25.
15. A. Satyanarayana, No. 9, pp. 207–209.
16. Ibid., p. 209.
17. Ibid.
18. Ibid.
19. Ibid., p. 210.
20. Sanjay Paswan and Pramansi Jaideva (eds), *Encyclopedia of Dalits in India: Struggle for Self Liberation*, Vol. 2, Kalpaz Publications, Delhi, 2004, p. 124.

21. http://indiankanoon.org/doc/1320900/Accessed on December 23, 2013
22. *India Today*, 15 February 1983.
23. Katti Padmarao, History of Karamchedu and What Actually Happened? http://roundtableindia.co.in/index.php?option=com_content&view=article&id=3450:history-of-karamchedu-and-what-actually-happened-&catid=118:thought&Itemid=131, accessed on 05.03.2014.
24. *India Today*, 31 July 1987 and interview with Guduru Seetamahalakshmi.
25. Ibid.
26. *Times of India*, 20 December 2008.
27. K. Srinivasulu, *Caste, Class and Social Articulation in Andhra Pradesh: Mapping Differential Regional Trajectories*, Overseas Development Institute, London, 2002, p. 43.
28. Ramesh Chandra, *Minority: Social and Political Conflict*, Isha Books, Delhi, 2004, pp. 123–124.
29. K. Srinivasulu, No. 25, p. 43 and Interview with Nookathoti Babu Rao, General Secretary, Dalita Mahasabha.
30. Thummapudi Bharati, *A History of Telugu Dalit Literature*, Kalpaz Publications, Delhi, 2008, pp. 98–106.
31. K. Srinivasulu, No. 25, p. 43.
32. *The Hindu*, 30 July 2014.
33. *The Hindu*, 2 July 2008.
34. *The Hindu*, 30 May 2013.
35. Bojja Tarakam, Laxmipeta: Deadly Combination of Caste and Political Power, *Economic and Political Weekly*, Vol. XLVII, No. 28, 14 July 2012, Web Exclusive
36. Hyderabad Political Economy Group, 'Laxmipet Dalit Killings', in *Economic and Political Weekly*, Vol. XLVII, No. 47 and 48, 1 December 2012, Sameeksha Trust, Mumbai, pp. 26–28.
37. Kalyani Shankar, *Pandora's Daughters*, Bloomsbury Publishing India Pvt. Ltd., New Delhi, 2013, pp. 95–96
38. *India Today*, 27 June 2005.
39. *The New Indian Express*, 15 December 2008.

CHAPTER 6

Summary and Conclusion

This thesis studied the political orientation of Scheduled Caste (SC) elite by taking into account the electoral statistics of SC reserved Assembly and Parliamentary constituencies in the erstwhile state of Andhra Pradesh till the General Elections of 2009 for Lok Sabha and State Legislative Assembly. It examined whether the political elite oriented their activities towards clientelism or whether there were instances or tendencies, which drove them towards competition with other political parties.

The concept of clientelism was elaborately dealt with in the first chapter. The main strand of clientelism i.e. political clientelism and its various dimensions were discussed. A suitable dimension was applied to study the Indian electoral politics with reference to SC political elite. The objectives of the research work were discussed along with methodology. The methodological tool of 'content analysis' was applied along with the material gathered from primary and secondary sources.

As the research framework is anchored in the concept of 'caste', the second chapter deals with caste in Indian society. The origin of Varna or caste is studied according to various theoretical formulations along with the indological perspective. The genesis of untouchability was taken up, for the concept of affirmative action for SCs is rooted in the practice of untouchability by the 'Savarna Hindus'. Ambedkar's theory of 'Broken Men' to trace the genesis of untouchability was focused at. The British perceptions of untouchability under their governance and their way of dealing with it; the role of Christian missionaries; the reform movements in shaping the perceptions of untouchability and also in the emancipation of the untouchables have been examined. Contributions of B.R. Ambedkar in the transformation of untouchables and 'Reservations' and 'Distributive Justice' have been dealt with. The last section of this chapter analyses 'reservations' as an electoral plank/tool to attract votes from the backward classes and also from those who lay claim to backward caste status. The constitutionality of such claim and the experiments by political parties to outmanoeuvre each other to grab political power were discussed in this chapter. The third chapter on Dalit movements in colonial Andhra and Telangana forms the backdrop for the growth of Dalit movements in the state. It explores the origin, spirit and course of the Dalit movements in the two main regions of AP, namely the Andhra region which was under the British rule and Telangana which was a part of Princely state under the rule of Nizam of Hyderabad. It begins with history of AP under Sathavahanas and other rulers to study the influence of caste in the normative patterns of the society. The efforts of the social reformers, Hindu saints at national level and the reformers at the regional level were studied. It also lists out the non-Dalit reformers who generously contributed to the emancipation of Dalits. The chapter then embarked on Dalit movements in colonial Andhra and Telangana with Bhagya Reddy Varma, a leader of depressed classes of Telangana virtually leading the movement in both the regions. It throws light on the course of the movement, which gradually lost its vigour with the Indian National Congress (INC) admitting some of the prominent leaders in the process of political clientelism.

The role of Dalit literature in building up the movement has been examined. The literature comprised contributions from Dalit and non-Dalit writers. Literature, silently and vividly and often provocatively, portrayed the exploitation of Dalits by the caste Hindus. It sensitized the Dalits about their rights and the injustice meted out to them by the archaic Institutes of Law, which were claimed to be sanctimonious and inviolable only to perpetuate the hegemony of the superior castes. Literature encouraged the Dalits to acquire education to become conscious of their exploitation. While some non-Dalit writers set the tone for Dalit writers to produce literature by exposing injustice done to Dalits, a batch of non-Dalit writers tried to focus on the benefits for Dalits if they joined hands with peasant castes – N.G. Ranga's 'Harijana Nayakudu' is a case in point.

The fourth chapter 'Andhra Pradesh Dalit Electoral Politics: Dalit Participation' deals with the efforts of the Dalit leaders, especially B.R. Ambedkar to carve out a political constituency for Dalits across the country by founding a political party in competition with other major political parties. It signaled his will to withstand the force of the INC, which was not only spearheading the Indian freedom movement but also was riding high on the claim of securing freedom for India from the British rule. The electoral performances of the All India Scheduled Caste Federation (SCF) and the Republican Party of India (RPI) have been studied.

This chapter identified a pattern in the Dalit electoral politics since independence. It was observed that prominent Dalit leaders who were active in the Adi Andhra movement, began winning the elections to either Lok Sabha or the state Legislative Assembly either as independents or on the ticket of Communist parties or the Dalit parties like the SCF or later the RPI. The INC in the clientelistic process co-opted the leaders gradually and awarded ministerial or other vital positions in the power structure to give them the taste of political power. Thus convinced of it, powerful Dalit leaders gradually made their entry into the INC. It was also observed that some prominent leaders of the Adi Andhra movement who could not win elections as contestants of Dalit parties, could secure major share of the Dalit vote. Such candidates like Ealy Vadapalli of the SCF in East Godavari district were co-opted by the INC. Contesting on INC ticket, they could win the elections. Thus, the INC was able to woo the potential Dalit leaders into its fold by showering on them the benefits of political power.

After the co-optation of powerful Dalit leaders into the INC became complete, then began the internal competition among SC political elite within the contours of clientelism. The founding of Telugu Desam Party (TDP) gave a fillip to the clientelistic politics in the state. The political parties in order to construct for themselves assured vote banks, resorted to various tactics. The TDP for instance, embarked upon the tactic of subclassification of SC reservation in Andhra Pradesh by dividing them into four groups despite knowing full well that the Order would not stand judicial scrutiny. It is instructive to note that 'Adi Andhra', a euphemistic term coined against the pejorative terms of Mala and Madiga, was conferred a specific caste status. It was seen as different from Malas and Madigas, though in reality the Dalits of AP use it only to free their caste names from the stigma of untouchability. Adi Andhra is a term coined as a protest against the Aryan hegemony, as the concept of 'caste' was reckoned as an Aryan import. Irrespective of historical facts the TDP government went ahead with subclassification by showing Adi Andhras as a separate caste group. Though the Supreme Court quashed the order of the AP government, the TDP succeeded in driving a wedge between the two prominent SCs in the state in a bid to build a vote bank of Madigas. While this process was underway, the prominent Mala leaders of the TDP remained silent spectators, for any revolt would amount to loss of rewards they have been enjoying in the clientelistic bargain.

A change in the political orientation of the SC elite was witnessed when the Bahujan Samaj Party (BSP) made inroads into the AP politics. Kanshiram, the BSP Chief addressed a series of public meetings across the state and attracted mammoth crowds at every venue. The combination of SC, ST and BC votes was expected to alter the political equations of the state. Thus, the BSP threw a formidable challenge marking a shift in the Dalit electoral politics from clientelism to competition. The mood of the Dalit electorate seemed upbeat and shook the confidence of the TDP which was to bounce back to power on the anti-incumbency factor in the elections. N.T. Ramarao the TDP president sought an electoral alliance with BSP and offered the party 42 Assembly seats. But the offer was turned down by Kanshi Ram as there was resistance from the party cadres, who maintained that since the Kammas perpetrated atrocities on Dalits at Karamchedu, Neerukonda, Padirikuppam and other places, such a move would amount to surrender to the enemy and send wrong signals of political expediency to the Dalit electorate of the state.

Though the entry of BSP into the state politics marked the transition of SC political elite from clientelism to competition, the electoral outcome of 1994 Assembly elections was not encouraging, as the party failed to open its account in the state by securing just 1.32 per cent[1] of the total vote share. Nevertheless, it continues to contest the general elections, though it has not consolidated its support base. The party failed to convert sympathy and moral support into votes. Though educated Dalits concur with the ideology of the party, they only try to jump on the bandwagon of the INC or the TDP during elections. The Dalit leaders in order not to lose the patronage of the ruling party, often speak in abjectly servile terms. Once Pulaparthy Narayana Murthy, a TDP legislator of P. Gannavaram constituency in East Godavari district engaged himself in an argument with the Dalit youth who wanted all Dalits to toe the line of BSP and that their status is that of slaves in other political parties. Narayana Murthy claimed with pride, more so in the presence of media that he is a humble servant of Chandrababu Naidu and would serve him in all subservience throughout his life, thus openly declaring his loyalty and ensuring continuous patronage. Once M. Mareppa, an SC legislator and Minister in the INC cabinet of Rajasekhara Reddy (2004–2009), hailed Reddy as Jesus Christ. Ravela Kishore Babu, Minister in the cabinet of Chandrababau Naidu (June 2014 – till date) hailed Naidu as his God, for bestowing upon him the ministerial portfolio. Thus, to ensure the patronage of the party bosses, the Dalit politicians resort to sycophancy of sorts.

One noteworthy development took place in the 2004 Assembly elections where Lakke Rajarao of the BSP who finished a close second in the 1999 Assembly elections won from the Paderu (ST) constituency. In the process of political clientelism, it was found that the Dalit political elite shifted to major parties only to remain in power. The chapter also deals with the rise of Damodaram Sanjeevayya in state politics. He was made Chief Minister in 1960, as a stopgap arrangement to re-anoint Neelam Sanjeeva Reddy as Chief Minister of AP in 1962. Thus, he was used as a safe political tool to protect the vested interests of Sanjeeva Reddy.

Chandra Bhan Prasad notes that though Dalits almost reached the threshold of vital positions, their prospects were thwarted by the rest. He observes that Jagjivan Ram was promoted by the INC to counter the growing popularity of B.R. Ambedkar who was emerging as a Dalit icon. Though Ambedkar resigned as Law Minister protesting the non-cooperation of INC in pushing through the Hindu Code Bill, Jagjivan Ram remained silent as he was a client of INC. But after joining the Janata Party post-emergency, he was a contender for Prime Ministership. His prospects were thwarted by Charan Singh of upper Shudra caste. Thus, a Dalit lost an opportunity to become the Prime Minister of the country, for the role of a client has its own limitations. As an appeasement move, Ram Dhan was to be made the Chief Minister of UP after Janata Party won the UP State Assembly elections. But Charan Singh insisted on a democratic method of electing the leader of the ruling party and manoeuvred through the Shudra lobby to make Ram Naresh Yadav the Chief Minister.[2] Such incidents reflect the limits of SC politicians within a clientelistic framework.

Meera Kumar, the daughter of Jagjivan Ram, proved to be a product of clientelistic politics. Her career illustrates that the Dalit intelligentsia despite the second generation advantages (her father being the first generation politician) could not emerge out of the thralldom of clientelism. She supported the subclassification of SC reservation in AP without calculating the fallout of it if implemented at national level. Being a national level Dalit leader, she encouraged identity politics of Madigas, toeing the line of Chandrababau Naidu.

During the National Democratic Alliance (NDA) rule, which was supported by the TDP, an international conference was held at Durban, South Africa against racial discrimination in 2001. The BJP led government was against raising the issue of caste discrimination in India on par with racial discrimination. Instructively no party including the Dalit representatives of the various political parties questioned the government's stand. It was only BSP, which openly criticized the stand taken by the NDA government.[3] Such episodes illustrate the restricted space of Dalits in the politics of clientelism.

Clientelistic politics promote ruling class doctrine and the Dalits who get indoctrinated, abjectly accept the doctrine[4] as if it is the result of social or political evolution which is inevitable. Such dominant class view is never subjected to critical thinking by the Dalits, as the view envelopes the psyche of majority of the people especially with the support by the media.

The last chapter 'Dalit Conflict and Dalit Elite Response' deals with elite formation, elite politics and elite response to the Dalit issues and atrocities. It presents the qualifications of the SC legislators of the Assembly constituted in 2009. A good number of them did not cross intermediate. This illustrates that the party bosses prefer subservience to efficiency. Since subservience is inbuilt in undereducated candidates, they are more preferred for the party ticket. The SC elite politics in AP operated within the contours of clientelism as the patrons succeeded in accommodating the clients to high profile positions. For instance, G.M.C. Balayogi being made Speaker of Lok Sabha stood as a temptation for many more clients to embrace politics of clientelism.

The atrocities on Dalits have been discussed since independence, despite Dalit political representatives being in place. It is inferred that trapped in the politics of Joint Electorate, the Dalit political representatives failed to rise to the occasion to come to the rescue of the victims of atrocities as they depended on the votes of the perpetrators of violence. Hence, despite the Dalit representatives entering the highest law making bodies, the perpetrators of atrocities understand that the former for the furtherance of their political career depend on non-Dalit votes. Thus occurred a series of violent incidents on Dalits at Padirikuppam, Neerukonda, Karamchedu, Chunduru and Laxmipeta in recent history. Fearing loss of political patronage, the Dalit representatives could not raise their voice against the regime, which was slow to act against the accused. All the while, the Dalit activists spearheaded the movements pressurizing the government to act against the perpetrators of atrocities.

The SC legislators remained silent when the funds of the Special Component Plan meant for their welfare were diverted with impunity by the State Government. The Kiran Kumar Reddy led INC government in the state of AP enacted a law on 2 December 2012 to spend the earmarked funds for the welfare of SCs and STs.[5]

B.R. Ambedkar cautioned the Dalit political leaders about the dangers of clientelism while addressing a public meeting at Agra on 18 March 1956. He said:

> If somebody invites you to his palace, you may go willingly. But you must not go there by putting your own hut on fire. If that king quarrels with you some day and drives you out of his palace, where will you go? If you want to sell out yourselves you may do so but not at the cost of destroying your organization. I do not fear any dangers from others, but I fear danger from our own people.[6]

In the same meeting, Ambedkar added:

> With great difficulty, I have brought the caravan where it stands today. Let the caravan march on and further on, despite the hurdles, pitfalls and difficulties that may come in its way. They must rise to the occasion, if they want to live an honourable and respectable life. If my people, my lieutenants are not able to take the caravan ahead, they should leave it where it stands today, but must not under any circumstances, allow the caravan to lag behind.[7]

He said thus, due to the apprehension of the damaging role of clientelistic politics.

However, despite being trapped in clientelistic politics, the Dalit politicians cutting across party lines strived to obtain some concession for the Dalits. There was a collective demand on the part of Dalit Members of Parliament (MPs) to confer Bharat Ratna, the highest civilian award of the nation on B.R. Ambedkar. This materialized during the tenure of V.P. Singh as the Prime Minister at the behest of his cabinet colleague Ram Vilas Paswan along with the Dalit MPs. Another such instance is the long pending demand of stringent punitive action against the perpetrators of atrocities on Dalits. This collective demand of the MPs once again spearheaded by Ram Vilas Paswan resulted in the SC/ST (POA) Act 1989. This Act was a dire necessity for the protection of SCs because the Protection of Civil Rights Act-1955 (PCR Act) totally failed to protect them. The SC/ST (POA) 1989 Rules 1995 was passed by Parliament for the effective implementation of the Act. Similarly, the Dalit MPs fought in unison for promotion of Dalits in central services in all departments, excepting in All India Services like IAS, IPS and IFS. As the SC/ST (POA)Act 1989 proved to be ineffective, a draft Bill was introduced by the UPA government in the last session of Parliament in 2014 on the collective demand of Dalit MPs irrespective of the party. Now the NDA government sent the Bill for a Select Committee to examine and submit a more comprehensive and effective draft to the Parliament.

There are other instances where collective efforts yielded fruit viz. declaring 14 April the birthday of B.R. Ambedkar as a holiday, installing the portrait of Ambedkar in the Central Hall of Parliament, instituting Dr Ambedkar Foundation to further the ideology of Ambedkar by launching schemes in the fields of education, medical aid, sanitation, etc. Also the National Commission for SCs and STs was set up with the collective efforts of the MPs.

Impediments to Competition

Inspired by the Adi Andhra Movement, the Dalits voters stood by their leaders of Dalit parties in the initial stages. But as clientelistic politics gained impetus, the patrons began to resort to novel methods of subjugating the Dalit electorate to construct assured vote banks. The author observed in his field studies that vote banks are built not only by promising and delivering certain sops but also by intimidating the Dalit voters. It is not always true that the Dalits vote for non-Dalit led political parties after receiving temporary benefits like cash, cheap liquor, etc. It must be noted that there always persists a threat to their lives if they do not vote en masse to the party which paid them or intimidated them. The atrocity perpetrated against Dalits at Padirikuppam in Chittoor district is a case in point. Hence, violence is one of the critical factors which keeps the Dalit electorate under the fear of violence. The fear restrains the electorate to progress towards any kind of enlightenment.

Rigging and booth capturing are also methods adopted by the political parties especially in the polling booths where Dalits predominate, to usurp their voting rights. Another recent phenomenon is the change of polling booths where Dalits preponderate. The author witnessed in course of his field observations that due to the uninformed change of polling booth poor Dalits especially senior citizens unable to walk up to the new booth give up casting their vote. This gives an opportunity for the dominant parties to illegally cast the votes of the Dalits who could not turn up for voting. These are some of the ways and methods adopted by the dominant political parties led by upper castes to usurp the franchise of Dalits and thereby prevent any progress or enlightenment in their thinking which would otherwise develop in them the competitive spirt.

The thesis having examined the transition of SC political elite from clientelism to competition has keenly dealt with various phases of Adi Andhra movement, which infused a revolutionary spirit among its leadership and cadres against the caste Hindu hegemony, which dictated the course of Indian society and polity. The Adi Andhra movement supplemented by its Dalit literature was able to build a strong current of opinion, that a radical shift is necessary to win the rights for the deprived. Though initially the Dalits scored some victories on SCF or RPI tickets, clientelism has set in with INC initiating moves to expand its support base by wooing the Dalits. Thus, the ideology got considerably diluted and the clientelism gained momentum. Though Congress remained the patron until the advent of TDP, the latter's entry gave a fillip to clientelistic politics. The Dalit leaders vied with each other and oscillated between the Congress and the TDP. The clientelistic politics were in full swing until the advent of BSP. The entry of BSP into AP created a flutter in the AP politics with the TDP offering to have an electoral understanding with the former. Nevertheless, it was a temporary phenomenon and once again clientelism received a boost with Dalits vying for the tickets of Prajarajyam Party launched by film star K. Chiranjeevi.

Though competition with entrenched political parties in the midst of rampant clientelism is not easy, there are instances where the BSP stood a close second. The Dalit intelligentsia after observing the social engineering and the methods followed by Mayawati in UP to don the mantle of power, have intensified their efforts to build the BSP movement. The movements by Dalit parties in Andhra Pradesh remained urban-centric and the ideology of Ambedkar could not be effectively propagated in the villages of the state where majority of the electorate lives.

The 'Ambedkar movement' is confined to few urban pockets and there have been numerous divisions among the Ambedkarites. The BAMCEF or the All India 'Backward and Minority Communities Employees Federation' launched by Kanshi Ram also stands divided as 'Kanshi Ram' BAMCEF and 'Khaparde' BAMCEF. While these are the weaknesses in the Dalit political movement, only a unified Dalit force can take on the entrenched political parties of the state by following the line of Kanshi Ram, Mayawati and R.K. Chaudary MLA who build the party brick by brick in UP. However, the social and political conditions in AP are different from those in UP and need to be addressed specifically by adopting alternative and foolproof strategies to make the Dalit's transition from clientelism to competition. This is an era where clientelistic politics is operated vigorously and the Dalit leaders are won over like saleable commodities. Hence, it needs more than a mere strategy to build a strong Dalit party against the entrenched parties.

B.R. Ambedkar said:

> Political democracy cannot last unless there lies at the base of it social democracy. What does social democracy mean? It means a way of life, which recognizes liberty, equality and fraternity as the principles of life.[8]

Thus, for political democracy to be meaningful, it should be built on the foundations of social democracy. Unless policies are formulated and tuned in the direction of social democracy, skewed democracy would continue to give way to clientelistic politics.

Instead of striving for social democracy, some of the Dalit leaders, encouraged by identity politics, are playing into the hands of dominant caste politicians. Venkaiah Naidu, a Central Minister, goaded by RSS top brass is encouraging subclassification of SC reservations at national level. The Supreme Court in November, 2004, struck down the micro-classification of SC reservations stating that such an Act by Government of erstwhile Andhra Pradesh as unconstitutional. The then Chief Minister, Chandrababau Naidu saw a clear political advantage in micro-classification of SC reservation. It was to carve out a vote bank out of the Madigas. However, in the successor state of Andhra Pradesh after separation of Telangana, Malas constitute a majority among SCs and Naidu has been showing a tilt towards Malas by bestowing up on them some key positions such as Chairmen of SC Finance Commission and SC and ST Commission. But the move of Venkaiah Nadu would send wrong signals to the Malas on the intent of Chandrababu and jeopardize his electoral prospects.

As long as Dalit leaders play into the hands of hegemonic castes, clientelism of SCs would continue and social democracy would remain a distant dream.

Notes

1. http://eci.nic.in/eci_main/StatisticalReports/SE_1994/Statistical Report-AP94.pdf accessed on 23.01.2015.

2. Chandra Bhan Prasad, *Dalit Diary: 1999-2003,* Navayana Publishing, Pondicherry, 2004, pp. 133–135.
3. Ibid., pp. 139–141.
4. Ibid., pp. 160–162.
5. *The Hindu*, Hyderabad, 3 December 2012.
6. Lella Karunyakara, *Modernisation of Buddhism: Contributions of Ambedkar and Dalai Lama XIV,* Gyan Publishing House, New Delhi, 2002, p. 237.
7. Bindeshwar Pathak, 'Relevance of Dr Ambedkar in Present Day Context' in S.N. Mishra (ed) *Socio-economic and Political Vision of Dr Ambedkar,* Concept Publishing House, New Delhi, 2010, p. 236.
8. *Outlook,* http://www.outlookindia.com/article/The-Grammar-Of-Anarchy/289235 accessed on 18 February, 2015.

Appendix

SC Members of the First Andhra Legislative Assembly Constituted on 1.10.1953

S. No.	*Name*	*Constituency*	*Party Affiliation*
1	Gunnayya, Pothula	Cheepurupalli	Congress
2	Narayana Kavali	Srikakulam	KLP
3	Suryanarayana Gantlana	Vizianagaram	PSP
4	Venkata Rao Saka	Kakinada	Communist
5	Appalaswami Bojja	Amalapuram	SCF
6	Nageswara Rao Gangi	Razole	Communist
7	Syamasundara Rao Padala	Narasapur	Communist
8	Rajeswara Rao Mallepudi	Kovvur	KMPP
9	Rama Rao Gungi	Gudivada	Communist
10	Bapanayya Guntur	Divi	Communist
11	Malakondayya Kasukurthi	Ongole	Communist
12	Vemaiah Swarna	Nellore	Independent
13	Shanmugham, Kamatham	Kandukur	Congress
14	Sanjivayya Damodaram	Kurnool	Congress
15	Venkatasubbayya Pala	Rajampet	Congress
16	Santhappa, K.	Kalyandurg	Congress
17	Mallayya T.	Adoni	Congress
18	Srungaram	Chittoor	KLP
19	Doraikannu M.	Tiruttani	Congress

Note: Information provided in the tables is gleaned from Election Commission of India website www.eci.nic.in

SC Members of the Second Andhra Legislative Assembly Constituted in 1955

S. No.	*Name*	*Constituency*	*Party Affiliation*
1	Gunnayya, Pothula	Pathapatnam	Congress
2	Rajayya, Boyina	Salur	Congress
3	Punnayya, Kottapalli	Cheepurupalli	KLP
4	Suryanarayana, Gantlana	Gajapathinagaram	PSP
5	Pothuraju, Mutyala	Narsipatnam	Congress
6	Subba Rao, Battina	Burugupudi	Independent
7	Kamayya, Reddi	Pallipalem	Congress
8	Appala Swamy, Bojja	Amalapuram	Independent
9	Nageswara Rao, Gangi	Razole	Communist
10	Veeraraghavulu, Taneti	Kovvur	Congress
11	Srinivasa Rao, Namburi	Tadepalligudem	Congress
12	Perumallu, Dasari	Palacole	Congress
13	Kurmayya, Vemula	Gudivada	Congress
14	Rajeswara Rao, Mallipudi	Divi	Congress
15	Jiyyar Dass, Talluri	Ongole	Congress
16	Vemayya, Swarna	Buchireddipalaem	Communist
17	Shanmugam, Kamatam	Venkatagiri	Congress
18	Munuswami, Merlapaka	Gudur	Congress
19	Singaraiah, Patra	Kalahasti	Congress
20	Doraikannu M.	Tiruttani	Congress
21	Rathnam	Punganur	Congress
22	Parthasarathi, Potharaju	Rajampet	Congress
23	Rukmini Devi, B.	Hindupur	Congress
24	Santhappa, K.	Dharmavaram	Congress
25	Rajaram, M.	Gooty	Congress
26	Sanjivayya, Damodaram	Yemmiganur	Congress
27	Lingam, N.K.	Nandikotkur	Congress

SC Members Elected from Telangana Area of AP Assembly- 1957

S. No.	*Name*	*Constituency*	*Party Affiliation*
1	Naganna, K.	Kalwakurti	Congress
2	Basappa, E.	Makthal	Independent
3	Mahendranath, Puttapaga	Nagarkurnool	Congress
4	Sumitra Devi	Jubilee Hills	Congress
5	Rama Rao, V.	Shahabad	Congress
6	Ramaswamy, Arige	Vikarabad	Congress
7	Antiah	Sangareddy	SCF
8	Muthyala Rao, J.B.	Gajwel	Congress
9	Sadalakshmi, T.N.	Kamareddi	Congress
10	Venkata Swamy, G.	Sirpur	Congress
11	Rajaram, B.	Sultanabad	Congress
12	Narsiah, Karalla	Sirsilla	PDF
13	Ramulu, Gadipalli	Huzurabad	Independent
14	Rama Lingam, Goka	Janagaon	Congress
15	Sailu, Manda	Parkal	Congress
16	Peddanna, Namavarapu	Khammam	PDF
17	Malsoor, Uppala	Suryapet	PDF
18	Laxmiah, M.	Devarakonda	Congress

SC Members of AP Assembly, 1962

S. No.	*Name*	*Constituency*	*Party Affiliation*
1	Pothula Gunnayya	Kothuru	INC
2	Kotapalli Punnaiah	Ponduru	INC
3	Gantlana Suryanarayana	Ramathirtham	INC
4	Mande Pitchiah	Payakraopeta	CPI
5	Bathina Subba Rao	Burugupudi	INC
6	Ganti Kamayya	Tallarevu	INC
7.	Chikile Gangisetty	Allavaram	INC
8	Geddam Mahalakshmi	Razole	INC
9	Paddala Syamasundara Rao	Achanta	CPI
10	Taneti Veera Raghavulu	Gopalapuram	INC
11	Revulagadda Yesupadam	Chintalapudi	INC
12	Ganji Rama Rao	Gudivada	CPI
13	Guntur Bapanayya	Nidumolu	CPI
14	Thavanam Chenchaiah	Santhanuthalapadu	CPI
15	Swarna Vemayya	Buchireddypalem	CPI
16	Allam Krushnaiah	Venkatagiri	CPI
17	Merlapaka Munuswamy	Gudur	INC
18	Patra Singaraiah	Yerpedu	INC
19	Tambura Balakrushnaiah	Satyavedu	INC
20	Kusini Nanjappa	Palamner	INC
21	N. Penchaliah	Kodur	Swatantra
22	B.Rukmini Devi	Madakasira	INC
23	Hindi Narasappa	Kalyandurg	INC
24	Damodaram Sanjeevayya	Kodumur	INC
25	Sitri Jaya Raju	Allagadda	INC
26	K. Naganna	Achampet	INC
27	Elleri Basappa	Madoor	INC
28	P. Mahendranath	Nagarkurnool	INC
29	Sumitra Devi	Hyderabad East	INC
30	V. Rama Rao	Chevella	INC
31	A. Ramaswamy	Vicarabad	INC
32	C. Rajanarasimha	Sadasivpet	INC
33	Gajwel Sadaiah	Gajwel	Independent
34	T.N. Sada Lakshmi	Yellareddy	INC
35	Kodati Rajamallu	Chinnur	INC

Cont'd...

...Cont'd

36	Butti Rajaram	Peddapalli	INC
37	Bandari Janakiram	Nerella	INC
38	Gaddipalli Ramulu	Huzurabad	INC
39	Goka Ramalingam	Jangoan	INC
40	Rauthu Narasimha Ramaiah	Parakal	INC
41	Kathula Santaiah	Palair	INC
42	Uppula Malchooru	Suryapet	CPI
43	Yelmineti Peddaiah	Devarakonda	CPI

SC Members of AP Assembly, 1967

S. No.	*Name*	*Constituency*	*Party Affiliation*
1	Pothula Gunnayya	Patapatnam	INC
2	J. Joji	Palakonda	Swatantra
3	G.Suryanarayana	Payakraopeta	INC
4	B. Subba Rao	Kadiam	INC
5	Ealy Vadapally	Tallarevu	INC
6	B.V. Ramanayya	Allavaram	RPI
7.	Geddam Mahalakshmi	Nagaram	INC
8	D. Perumallu	Achanta	INC
9	T.V. Raghavulu	Gopalauram	INC
10	Vemula Kurmayya	Tiruvuru	INC
11	Someswara Rao Kanumuri	Nidumolu	INC
12	Swarna Vemayya	Sarveplli	CPI
13	P. Venkata Subbaiah	Sullurpet	Independent
14	O. Venkata Subbaiah	Venkatagiri	Independent
15	K. Munuswamy	Satyavedu	Swatantra
16	V. Munisamappa	Vepanjeri	INC
17	M. Munuswamy	Bangarupaleom	INC
18	T.C. Rajan	Palamner	Swatantra
19	N. Penchaliah	Kodur	Swatantra
20	M.B.R. Rao	Madakasira	Swatantra
21	T.C. Mareppa	Kalyandurg	Independent
22	G. Govinda Das	Alur	Swatantra
23	P.R. Rao	Kodumur	Swatantra
24	P. Mahendranath	Achampet	INC
25	K. Naganna	Shadnagar	INC
26	Arige Ramaswamy	Vicarabad	INC
27	V.R. Rao	Secunderabad Cantt.	INC
28	S. Devi	Medchal	INC
29	G. Saidaiah	Gajwel	INC
30	C.R. Narasimha	Andole	INC
31	J. Easwari Bai	Yellareddy	RPI
32	K. Rajamallu	Chinnur	INC
33	G. Rajamallu	Mydaram	INC
34	B. Rajaram	Nusthulapur	INC
35	G. Bhoopathi	Nerella	INC
36	B. Abraham	Cheriyal	CPI
37	R.N. Ramaiah	Hasanparthy	INC
38	K. Santalaiah	Palair	INC
39	U. Malsoor	Suryapet	CPM
40	V.K. Ram	Ramannapet	INC

SC Members of AP Assembly, 1972

S. No.	*Name*	*Constituency*	*Party Affiliation*
1	Sukka Pagadalu	Patapatnam	INC
2	Kottapalli Narasiah	Palakonda	INC
3	Gantlana Suryanarayana	Payakraopeta	INC
4	B. Subba Rao	Kadiam	INC
5	Sadanala Sattiraju	Tallarevu	INC
6	Sri Vishnu Prasada Rao Moka	Allavaram	INC
7.	Geddam Mahalakshmi	Nagaram	INC
8	Gottimukkla Venkanna	Achanta	INC
9	Sali Venkata Rao	Gopalauram	Independent
10	Kota Ramaiah	Tiruvuru	INC
11	Kanumuri Someswara Rao	Nidumolu	INC
12	Areti Kotaiah	Santanuthalapadu	INC
13	Mangalagiri Nanadas	Sarvepalli	INC
14	Pitla Venkatasubbaiah	Sullurpet	INC
15	Orepalli Venkatasubbaiah	Venkatagiri	INC
16	C. Dass	Satyavedu	INC
17	V. Munuswamy	Vapanjeri	INC
18	M. Munuswamy	Bangarupaleom	INC
19	Gunti Sriramulu	Kodur	INC
20	M. Yellappa	Madakasira	INC
21	M. Lakshmi Devi	Kalyanadurg	INC
22	P. Rajaratna Rao	Alur	INC
23	D. Muniswamy	Kodmur	INC
24	P. Mahendranath	Achampet	INC
25	N.V. Jagannadham	Shadnagar	INC
26	Tirumalayya	Vicarabad	Independent
27	V. Mankamma	Secunderabad Cantt	INC
28	Sumitra Devi	Medchal	INC
29	Gajwel Sadaiah	Gajwel	INC
30	C. Rajanarasimha	Andole	INC
31	J. Easwari Bai	Yellareddy	STS
32	Kodati Rajamallu	Chinnur	INC
33	G. Easwar	Mydram	INC
34	Premlata Devi	Nusthalapur	INC
35	G. Bhoopathi	Nerella	INC
36	Pambala Katama Lingaiah	Cheriyal	INC
37	Routu Narasimha Ramaiah	Hasanparthy	INC
38	K. Santalaiah	Palair	INC
39	Yedla Gopaiah	Suryapet	INC
40	Vaddepalli Kasi Ram	Ramannapet	INC

SC Members of AP Assembly, 1978

S. No.	*Name*	*Constituency*	*Party Affiliation*
1	Kambala Rajaratnam	Palakonda	Janata (JNP)
2	Kothapalli Narsaiah	Etcherla	JNP
3	Maruti Adeyya	Payakaraopeta	INC (I)
4	Moka Sri Vishnu Prasada Rao	Mummidivaram	INC (I)
5	Devarapalli Venkatapathy	Allavaram	INC (I)
6	Ganapathi Rao Neethipudi	Nagaram	INC (I)
7.	Kota Dhana Raju	Achanta	INC (I)
8	Dasari Sarojini Devi	Gopalapuram	INC (I)
9	Vakkalagadda Adamu	Tiruvuru	INC (I)
10	Guntur Bapanayya	Nidumolu	CPM
11	Amrutha Rao T.	Tadikonda	INC (I)
12	Vema Yellaiah	Santhanuthalapadu	INC (I)
13	Patra Prakasa Rao	Gudur	INC (I)
14	Pitla Venkata Subbaiah	Sulurpet	INC (I)
15	C. Doss	Satyavedu	INC (I)
16	B. Arumugam	Vepanjeri	JNP
17	A. Ratnam	Palmner	INC (I)
18	Nidiganti Venkatasubbaiah	Kodur	JNP
19	Hindi Narasappa	Kalyandurg	JNP
20	B. Rukmani Devi	Singanamala	JNP
21	Masala Eranna	Alur	INC (I)
22	D. Munuswamy	Kodumur	INC
23	R.M. Manohar	Achampet	INC (I)
24	B. Kistaiah	Shadnagar	INC (I)
25	V.B. Tirumalayya	Vicarabad	INC (I)
26	Sumitra Devi	Ibrahimpatnam	INC (I)
27	B. Machinder Rao	Secunderabad Cant.	JNP
28	Gajwel Sadaiah	Gajwel	INC (I)
29	C. Rajanarasimha	Andole	INC
30	Gangaram	Jukkal	INC (I)
31	Dasari Narsaiah	Asifabad	INC (I)
32	C. Narayana	Chinnur	INC (I)
33	G. Eashwar	Mydaram	INC (I)
34	Pati Rajam	Narella	INC (I)
35	Goka Rama Swamy	Ghanpur	INC (I)
36	Sammaiah Bochu	Parakal	INC (I)
37	Hassaunu Potta Pinjara	Palair	INC (I)
38	Annamulupuri Paradamulu	Suryapet	INC (I)
39	Salluri Pochaiah	Alair	INC (I)

SC Members of AP Assembly, 1983

S. No.	*Name*	*Constituency*	*Party Affiliation*
1	Syama Rao Gonipati	Palakonda	TDP
2	Kavali Prathibha Bharathi	Etcherla	TDP
3	Sumana Gantela	Payakaraopeta	TDP
4	Valtati Raja Sakkubai	Mummidivaram	TDP
5	JVB Maheswara Rao Aithabathula	Allavaram	TDP
6	Undru Krishna Rao	Nagaram	TDP
7.	Kota Bhaskara Rao	Achanta	TDP
8	Karupati Vivekananda	Gopalapuram	TDP
9	Purnanand Miriyala	Tiruvuru	TDP
10	Govada Mallikarjuna Rao	Nidumolu	TDP
11	J.R. Pushpa Raju	Tadikonda	TDP
12	Aareti Kotaiah	Santhanuthalapadu	TDP
13	Jogi Masthanaiah	Gudur	TDP
14	Satti Prakasham	Sulurpet	TDP
15	Manohar Talari	Satyavedu	TDP
16	Talari Rudraiah	Vepanjeri	TDP
17	Anjineyulu	Palmner	TDP
18	Settipalli Srinivasulu	Kodur	TDP
19	T.C. Mareppa	Kalyandurg	TDP
20	G. Guru Murthy	Singanamala	TDP
21	K. Basappa	Alur	TDP
22	Munuswamy	Kodumur	INC
23	Mahendranath Puttapaga	Achampet	TDP
24	Shankar Rao	Shadnagar	INC
25	K.R. Krishna Swamy	Vicarabad	INC
26	A.G. Krishna	Ibrahimpatnam	INC
27	N.A. Krishna	Secunderabad Cant.	TDP
28	Allam Sailu	Gajwel	TDP
29	Hadkar Laxmanjee	Andole	INC
30	Gangaram	Jukkal	INC
31	Gunda Mallesh	Asifabad	CPI
32	Sothuku Sanjeeva Rao	Chinnur	TDP
33	Mathangi Narsiah	Mydaram	TDP
34	Pati Rajam	Narella	INC
35	Goka Rama Swamy	Ghanpur	INC
36	Sammaiah Bochchu	Parakal	INC
37	Bheemapaka Bhupathi Rao	Palair	CPI
38	Eda Devaiah	Suryapet	TDP
39	Mothkupalli Narsimhulu	Alair	TDP

Note: The TDP candidates in Election Commission of India website were shown as independent candidates for technical reasons.

SC Members of AP Assembly, 1985

S. No.	*Name*	*Constituency*	*Party Affiliation*
1	Tale Bhadrayya	Palakonda	TDP
2	Kavali Prathibha Bharathi	Etcherla	TDP
3	Kakar Nooka Raju	Payakaraopeta	TDP
4	Pandu Krishna Murty	Mummidivaram	TDP
5	Gollapalli Surya Rao	Allavaram	TDP
6	Undru Krishna Rao	Nagaram	TDP
7.	Chittaranjan Alugu	Achanta	CPM
8	Karupati Vivekananda	Gopalapuram	TDP
9	Pitta Venkataratnam	Tiruvuru	TDP
10	Paturi Ramayya	Nidumolu	CPM
11	J.R. Pushpa Raju	Tadikonda	TDP
12	K. Addenna	Santhanuthalapadu	TDP
13	Balli Durga Prasada Rao	Gudur	TDP
14	Madanambeti Maneiah	Sulurpet	TDP
15	M. Suranjan	Satyavedu	TDP
16	Gummadi Kuthuhalamma	Vepanjeri	INC
17	Patnam Subbaiah	Palmner	TDP
18	Thumati Penchaliah	Kodur	TDP
19	Pakkerappa	Kalyandurg	CPI
20	K. Jayaram	Singanamala	TDP
21	Earanna	Alur	INC
22	M. Sikamani	Kodumur	TDP
23	Mahendranath Puttapaga	Achampet	TDP
24	M. Indira	Shadnagar	TDP
25	A. Chandrasekhar	Vicarabad	TDP
26	K. Satyanarayana	Ibrahimpatnam	TDP
27	S. Satyanarayana	Secunderabad Cant.	TDP
28	B. Sanjeeva Rao	Gajwel	TDP
29	Malyala Rajaiah	Andole	TDP
30	Begari Pandari	Jukkal	TDP
31	Gunda Mallesh	Asifabad	CPI
32	Bodha Janardhan	Chinnur	TDP
33	Mala Mallesh	Mydaram	TDP
34	Uppari Smbaiah	Narella	Janata Party
35	Bojapalli Rajaiah	Ghanpur	TDP
36	Jaipal V. Sammaiah Bochu	Parakal	BJP
37	Baji Hanumanthu	Palair	CPM
38	Daida Sundaraiah	Suryapet	TDP
39	Mothkupalli Narsimhulu	Alair	TDP

SC Members of AP Assembly, 1989

S. No.	*Name*	*Constituency*	*Party Affiliation*
1	Amrita Kumari P.J.	Palakonda	INC
2	Kavali Prathibha Bharathi	Etcherla	TDP
3	Kakar Nooka Raju	Payakaraopeta	TDP
4	Battina Subba Rao	Mummidivaram	INC
5	Veera Raghavulu Paramata	Allavaram	INC
6	Ganapathi Rao Neethipudi	Nagaram	INC
7.	Digupati Raja Gopal	Achanta	CPM
8	Karupati Vivekananda	Gopalapuram	TDP
9	Koneru Ranga Rao	Tiruvuru	INC
10	Paturi Ramayya	Nidumolu	CPM
11	Venkaiah Tiruvaipati	Tadikonda	INC
12	Venkata Seshu Gurrala	Santhanuthalapadu	INC
13	Patra Prakasa Rao	Gudur	INC
14	Pasala Penchaliah	Sulurpet	INC
15	C. Doss	Satyavedu	INC
16	Gummadi Kuthuhalamma	Vepanjeri	INC
17	Patnam Subbaiah	Palmner	TDP
18	Thumati Penchaliah	Kodur	TDP
19	Lakshmi Devi M.	Kalyandurg	INC
20	P. Samanthakamani	Singanamala	INC
21	Gudlannagari Loknath	Alur	INC
22	M. Madana Gopal	Kodumur	Independent
23	D.Kiran Kumar	Achampet	INC
24	Shankar Rao P.	Shadnagar	INC
25	A.Chandrasekhar	Vicarabad	TDP
26	Kondigari Ramulu	Ibrahimpatnam	CPM
27	D. Narasinga Rao	Secunderabad Cant.	INC
28	J. Geeta	Gajwel	INC
29	C.R. Damodar	Andole	INC
30	Gangaram	Jukkal	INC
31	Dasari Narsiah	Asifabad	INC
32	Bodha Janardhan	Chinnur	TDP
33	Matangi Narsiah	Mydaram	INC
34	Pati Rajam	Narella	INC
35	Arogyam Bhongiri	Ghanpur	INC
36	Jaipal V. Sammaiah Bochu	Parakal	BJP
37	Sambhani Chandrasekar	Palair	INC
38	A. Sudarsan	Suryapet	TDP
39	Mothkupalli Narsimhulu	Alair	Independent

SC Members of AP Assembly, 1994

S. No.	*Name*	*Constituency*	*Party Affiliation*
1	Tale Bhadrayya	Palakonda	TDP
2	Kavali Prathibha Bharathi	Etcherla	TDP
3	Kakar Nooka Raju	Payakaraopeta	TDP
4	Battina Subba Rao	Mummidivaram	INC
5	AJVB Maheswara Rao	Allavaram	TDP
6	Undru Krishna Rao	Nagaram	TDP
7.	Digupati Raja Gopal	Achanta	CPM
8	Babaji Rao Jonnakuti	Gopalapuram	TDP
9	Swamy Das Nallagatla	Tiruvuru	TDP
10	Paturi Ramayya	Nidumolu	CPM
11	GMNV Prasad	Tadikonda	CPI
12	Thavanam Chenchaiah	Santhanuthalapadu	CPM
13	Balli Durga Prasada Rao	Gudur	TDP
14	Parsa Venkata Ratnaiah	Sulurpet	TDP
15	M. Suranjan	Satyavedu	TDP
16	R. Gandhi	Vepanjeri	TDP
17	Patnam Subbaiah	Palmner	TDP
18	Vaddi Chennaiah	Kodur	TDP
19	B.C. Govindappa	Kalyandurg	TDP
20	K. Jayaram	Singanamala	TDP
21	Masala Eranna	Alur	TDP
22	M. Sikhamani	Kodumur	INC
23	P. Ramulu	Achampet	TDP
24	Bakkani Narsimhulu	Shadnagar	TDP
25	A. Chandrasekhar	Vicarabad	TDP
26	Kondigari Ramulu	Ibrahimpatnam	CPM
27	G. Sayanna	Secunderabad Cant.	TDP
28	G. Vijaya Rama Rao	Gajwel	TDP
29	Malyala Rajaiah	Andole	TDP
30	B. Pandari	Jukkal	TDP
31	Gunda Mallesh	Asifabad	CPI
32	Bodha Janardhan	Chinnur	TDP
33	Malem Mallesh	Mydaram	Independent
34	Suddala Devaiah	Narella	TDP
35	Kadiyam Srihari	Ghanpur	TDP
36	Sarahia Pothuraju	Parakal	CPI
37	Sandra Venkata Veeraiah	Palair	CPM
38	A. Sudarsan	Suryapet	TDP
39	Mothkupalli Narsimhulu	Alair	TDP

SC Members of AP Assembly, 1999

S. No.	*Name*	*Constituency*	*Party Affiliation*
1	Amrutha Kumari P.J.	Palakonda	Independent
2	Kavali Prathibha Bharathi	Etcherla	TDP
3	Chengala Venkata Rao	Payakaraopeta	TDP
4	Chelli Vivekananda	Mummidivaram	TDP
5	Chilla Jagadeeswari	Allavaram	TDP
6	Ayyaji Vema Manepalli	Nagaram	BJP
7.	Johar Mocharla	Achanta	TDP
8	Jonnakuti Babji Rao	Gopalapuram	TDP
9	Swamy Das Nallagatla	Tiruvuru	TDP
10	Govada Mariya Kumari	Nidumolu	TDP
11	J.R. Pushpa Raj	Tadikonda	TDP
12	David Raju Palaparti	Santhanuthalapadu	TDP
13	Balli Durga Prasada Rao	Gudur	TDP
14	Parsa Venkata Ratnaiah	Sulurpet	TDP
15	N.Siva Prasad	Satyavedu	TDP
16	Gummadi Kuthuhalamma	Vepanjeri	INC
17	M. Thippeswamy	Palmner	INC
18	Somineni Saraswati	Kodur	TDP
19	A. Saradamba	Kalyandurg	TDP
20	K. Jayaram	Singanamala	TDP
21	Moolinti Mareppa	Alur	INC
22	M. Sikhamani	Kodumur	INC
23	P. Ramulu	Achampet	TDP
24	P. Shankar Rao	Shadnagar	INC
25	A. Chandrasekhar	Vicarabad	TDP
26	Konduru Pushpaleela	Ibrahimpatnam	TDP
27	G. Sayanna	Secunderabad Cant.	TDP
28	B. Sanjeeva Rao	Gajwel	TDP
29	Palli Babu Mohan	Andole	TDP
30	Aruna Tara	Jukkal	TDP
31	Pati Subhadra	Asifabad	TDP
32	Bodha Janardhan	Chinnur	TDP
33	Mathangi Narasiah	Mydaram	TDP
34	Suddala Devaiah	Narella	TDP
35	Kadiyam Srihari	Ghanpur	TDP
36	Bojjapalli Rajaiah	Parakal	TDP
37	Sambhani Chandrasekhar	Palair	INC
38	Dosapati Gopal	Suryapet	INC
39	Mothkupalli Narsimhulu	Alair	TDP

SC Members of AP Assembly, 2004

S. No.	Name	Consituency	Party Affiliation
1	Kambala Jogulu	Palakonda	TDP
2	Kondru Murali Mohan	Etcherla	INC
3	Chengala Venkata Rao	Payakaraopeta	TDP
4	Viswarupu Pinipe	Mummidivaram	INC
5	Gollapallil Surya Rao	Allavaram	INC
6	Rajeswari Devi Pamula	Nagaram	INC
7.	Peethala Sujatha	Achanta	TDP
8	Maddala Suneeta	Gopalapuram	INC
9	Koneru Ranga Rao	Tiruvuru	INC
10	Paturu Ramaiah	Nidumolu	CPM
11	Dokka Manikya Vara Prasada Rao	Tadikonda	INC
12	Dara Sambaiah	Santhanuthalapadu	INC
13	Patra Prakasa Rao	Gudur	INC
14	Nelavala Subramanyam	Sulurpet	INC
15	K.Narayana Swamy	Satyavedu	INC
16	Gummadi Kuthuhalamma	Vepanjeri	INC
17	L. Lalitha Kumari	Palmner	TDP
18	Gunti Venkateswara Prasad	Kodur	INC
19	B.C. Govindappa	Kalyandurg	TDP
20	Sake Sailajanath	Singanamala	INC
21	Moolinti Mareppa	Alur	INC
22	M. Sikhamani	Kodumur	INC
23	Vamshi Krishna	Achampet	TDP
24	P. Shankar Rao	Shadnagar	INC
25	A. Chandrasekhar	Vicarabad	TRS
26	Masku Narasimha	Ibrahimpatnam	CPM
27	G. Sayanna	Secunderabad Cant.	TDP
28	Jetty Geetha	Gajwel	INC
29	C. Damodar Rajanarasimha	Andole	INC
30	Soudagar Gangaram	Jukkal	INC
31	A. Sridevi	Asifabad	TDP
32	G. Vinod	Chinnur	INC
33	Koppula Eashwar	Mydaram	TRS
34	Lingaiah Kashipet	Narella	TRS
35	G. Vijaya Rama Rao	Ghanpur	TRS
36	Bandari Sahara Rani	Parakal	TRS
37	Sambhani Chandrasekhar	Palair	INC
38	Vedas Venkaiah	Suryapet	INC
39	Kududula Nagesh	Alair	TRS

SC Members of AP Assembly, 2009

S. No.	*Name*	*Constituency*	*Party Affiliation*
1	Nalla Odelu	Chennur	TRS
2	Gunda Mallesh	Bellampally	CPI
3	Hanumanth Shinde	Jukkal	TDP
4	Koppula Eashwar	Dharmapuri	TRS
5	Suddala Devaiah	Choppadandi	TDP
6	Arepalli Mohan	Manakondur	INC
7.	C. Damodar Rajanarsimha	Andole	INC
8	J. Geeta	Zahirabad	INC
9	K.S. Ratnam	Chevella	TDP
10	G. Prasad Kumar	Vicarabad	INC
11	P. Shankar Rao	Secunderabad Cantt.	INC
12	Abraham V.M.	Alampur	INC
13	P. Ramulu	Achampet	TDP
14	Chirumarthy Lingaiah	Nakrekal	INC
15	Mothkupalli Narsimhulu	Thungathurthy	TDP
16	Thatikonda Rajaiah	Ghanpur (Station)	INC
17	Kondeti Sridhar	Wardhanapet	INC
18	Mallu Bhatti Vikramarka	Madhira	INC
19	Sandra Venkata Veeraiah	Sathupalli	TDP
20	Kondru Murali Mohan	Rajam	INC
21	Savarapu Jayamani	Parvathipuram	INC
22	Golla Babu Rao	Payakaraopeta	INC
23	Pinipe Viswarupu	Amalapuram	INC
24	Rapaka Vara Prasada Rao	Razole	INC
25	Pamul Rajeswari Devi	P.Gannavaram	INC
26	T.V. Rama Rao	Kovvur	TDP
27	Taneti Vanita	Gopalapuram	TDP
28	Maddala Rajesh Kumar	Chintalapudi	INC
29	Dirisam Padma Jyothi	Tiruvuru	INC
30	D.Y. Das	Pamarru	INC
31	Tangirala Prabhakara Rao	Nandigama	TDP
32	Dokka Manikya Vara Prasada Rao	Tadikonda	INC
33	Ananda Babu Nakka	Vemuru	TDP
34	Mekathota Sucharita	Prathipadu	INC
35	Audimulapu Suresh	Yerragondapalem	INC

Cont'd...

...Cont'd

36	B.N. Vijay Kumar	Santhanuthalapadu	INC
37	Gurrala Venkata Seshu	Kondapai	INC
38	Balli Durga Prasada Rao	Gudur	TDP
39	Parasa Venkata Ratnaiah	Sullurpeta	TDP
40	Kamalamma P.M.	Badvel	INC
41	Koramutla Srinivasulu	Kodur	INC
42	Labbi Venkataswamy	Nandikotkur	INC
43	Parigela Murali Krishna	Kodmur	INC
44	Sake Sailajanath	Singanamala	INC
45	K. Sudhakar	Madakasira	INC
46	H. Hemalatha	Satyavedu	TDP
47	Gummadi Kuthuhalamma	Gangadhara Nellore	INC
48	P. Ravi	Puthalapattu	INC

SC Members of Andhra and Telangana Regions in 1951 Lok Sabha Elections

S. No.	Name	Constituency	Party Affiliation
1.	Kaneti Mohana Rao	Rajahmundry (Madras-Andhra)	CPI
2.	B.S. Murthy	Eluru (Madras-Andhra)	KMPP
3.	Mangalagiri Nanadas	Ongole (Madras-Andhra)	Independent
4.	M.V. Gangadharasiva	Chittoor (Madras-Andhra)	INC
4.	P. Ramaswamy	Mahaboobnagar (Hyderabad)	INC
5.	M.R. Krishna	Karimnagar (Hyderabad)	SCF
6.	Sukam Atchalu	Nalgonda (Hyderabad)	PDF

SC Members of AP in 1957 Lok Sabha Elections

S. No.	Name	Constituency	Party Affiliation
1.	B. S. Murthy	Amalapuram	INC
2.	B. Anjanappa	Nellore	INC
3.	M.V. Gangadharasiva	Tirupathi	INC
4.	P. Ramaswamy	Mahaboobnagar	INC
5.	M.R. Krishna	Karimnagar	INC
6.	D. Rajaiah	Nalgonda	INC

SC Members of AP in 1962 Lok Sabha Elections

S. No.	Name	Constituency	Party Affiliation
1.	B.S. Murthy	Amalapuram	INC
2.	B. Anjanappa	Nellore	INC
3.	C. Dass	Tirupathi	INC
4.	J.B. Mutyala Rao	Mahaboobnagar	INC
5.	G. Venkataswamy	Siddipet	INC
6.	Laxmi Dass	Miryalaguda	CPI

SC Members of AP in 1967 Lok Sabha Eelections

S. No.	Name	Constituency	Party Affiliation
1.	B.S. Murthy	Amalapuram	INC
2.	B. Anjanappa	Nellore	INC
3.	C. Dass	Tirupathi	INC
4.	J.B. Mutyala Rao	Nagarkurnool	INC
5.	G. Venkataswamy	Siddipet	INC
6.	M.R. Krishna	Peddapalli	INC

SC Members of AP in 1971 Lok Sabha Elections

S. No	Name	Constituency	Party Affiliation
1.	B.S. Murthy	Amalapuram	INC
2.	D. Kamakshaiah	Nellore	INC
3.	T. Balakrishnaiah	Tirupathi	INC
4.	M. Bheeshma Dev	Nagarkurnool	TPS
5.	G. Venkataswamy	Siddipet	TPS
6.	V. Tulasiram	Peddapalli	INC

SC Members of AP in 1977 Lok Sabha Elections

S. No	Name	Constituency	Party Affiliation
1.	Kusuma Krishna Murthy	Amalapuram	INC
2.	D. Kamakshaiah	Nellore	INC
3.	T. Balakrishnaiah	Tirupathi	INC
4.	M. Bheeshma Dev	Nagarkurnool	INC
5.	G. Venkataswamy	Siddipet	INC
6.	V. Tulasiram	Peddapalli	INC

SC Members of AP in 1980 Lok Sabha Elections

S. No	Name	Constituency	Party Affiliation
1.	Kusuma Krishna Murthy	Amalapuram	INC(I)
2.	D. Kamakshaiah	Nellore	INC(I)
3.	Pasala Panchaliah	Tirupathi	INC(I)
4.	Mallu Anantha Ramulu	Nagarkurnool	INC(I)
5.	Nandi Yellaiah	Siddipet	INC(I)
6.	K. Rajamallu	Peddapalli	INC(I)

SC Members of AP in 1984 Lok Sabha Elections

S. No	Name	Constituency	Party Affiliation
1.	A.J.V.B. Maheswara Rao	Amalapuram	TDP
2.	P. Penchalaiah	Nellore	TDP
3.	Chinta Mohan	Tirupathi	TDP
4.	V. Tulasiram	Nagarkurnool	TDP
5.	G. Vijaya Rama Rao	Siddipet	TDP
6.	G. Bhoopathy	Peddapalli	TDP

SC Members of AP in 1989 Lok Sabha Elections

S. No	*Name*	*Constituency*	*Party Affiliation*
1.	Kusuma Krishna Murty	Amalapuram	INC
2.	Putchalapalli Penchalaiah	Nellore	INC
3.	Chinta Mohan	Tirupathi	INC
4.	Mallu Anantha Ramulu	Nagarkurnool	INC
5.	Nandi Yellaiah	Siddipet	INC
6.	G. Venkataswamy	Peddapalli	INC

SC Members of AP in 1991 Lok Sabha Elections

S. No	*Name*	*Constituency*	*Party Affiliation*
1.	G.M.C. Balayogi	Amalapuram	TDP
2.	K. Padmasree	Nellore	INC
3.	Chinta Mohan	Tirupathi	INC
4.	M. Ravi	Nagarkurnool	INC
5.	Nandi Yellaiah	Siddipet	INC
6.	G. Venkataswamy	Peddapalli	INC

SC Members of AP in 1996 Lok Sabha Elections

S. No	*Name*	*Constituency*	*Party Affiliation*
1.	K.S.R. Murthy	Amalapuram	INC
2.	Panabaka Lakshmi	Nellore	INC
3.	N. Subrahmanyam	Tirupathi	INC
4.	M. Jagannath	Nagarkurnool	TDP
5.	Nandi Yellaiah	Siddipet	INC
6.	G. Venkataswamy	Peddapalli	INC

SC Members of AP in 1998 Lok Sabha Elections

S. No	*Name*	*Constituency*	*Party Affiliation*
1.	G.M.C. Balayogi	Amalapuram	TDP
2.	Panabaka Lakshmi	Nellore	INC
3.	Chinta Mohan	Tirupathi	INC
4.	Mallu Ravi	Nagarkurnool	INC
5.	M. Rajaiah	Siddipet	TDP
6.	C. Suguna Kumari	Peddapalli	TDP

SC Members of AP in 1999 Lok Sabha Elections

S. No	*Name*	*Constituency*	*Party Affiliation*
1.	G.M.C. Balayogi	Amalapuram	TDP
2.	V. Rajeswaramma	Nellore	TDP
3.	N. Venkataswamy	Tirupathi	BJP
4.	Manda Jagannath	Nagarkurnool	TDP
5.	M. Rajaiah	Siddipet	TDP
6.	C. Suguna Kumari	Peddapalli	TDP

SC Members of AP in 2004 Lok Sabha Elections

S. No	*Name*	*Constituency*	*Party Affiliation*
1.	G.V. Harsha Kumar	Amalapuram	INC
2.	Panabaka Lakshmi	Nellore	INC
3.	Chinta Mohan	Tirupathi	INC
4.	Manda Jagannath	Nagarkurnool	TDP
5.	Sarve Satyanarayana	Siddipet	INC
6.	G. Venkataswamy	Peddapalli	INC

SC Members of AP in 2009 Lok Sabha Elections

S. No	*Name*	*Constituency*	*Party Affiliation*
1.	G. Vivekanand	Peddapalli	INC
2.	Panabaka Lakshmi	Nellore	INC
3.	Chinta Mohan	Tirupathi	INC
4.	Manda Jagannath	Nagarkurnool	TDP
5.	Sarve Satyanarayana	Siddipet	INC
6.	G. Venkataswamy	Peddapalli	INC

Bibliography

Books

Abbasayalu, Y.B., *Scheduled Caste Elite: A Study of Scheduled Caste Elite in Andhra Pradesh,* Osmania University, Hyderabad, 1978.

Ambedkar, B.R., *Annihilation of Caste,* Bheem Patrika Publications, Jalandhar, 1975.

——, *Buddha and the Future of His Religion,* Bheem Patrika Publications, Jalandhar, 1973.

——, *Caste in India, their Mechanism, Genesis and Development,* Bheem Patrika Publications, Jalandhar, 1973.

——, *The Untouchable,* National Herald Press, Lucknow, 1977

——, *Who Are Untouchables,* Bheem Patrika Publications, Jalandhar, 1948.

——, *States and Minorities: What are their Rights and How to Secure them in the Constitution of Free India,* Dr Ambedkar Memorial Society, Hyderabad, 1970.

Ambedkar, Mahesh, *The Architect of Modern India: Dr B.R. Ambedkar,* Dimond Pocket Books Pvt. Ltd. New Delhi, 2005.

Basham, Ardythe, *The Untouchable Soldiers,* Balaji Traders, Bangalore, 1980.

Basu, D.D., *Introduction to the Constitution of India,* Prentice-Hall of India Pvt. Ltd., New Delhi, 1980.

Bharati, Thummapudi, *A History of Telugu Dalit Literature,* Kalpaz Publications, Delhi, 2008.

Bose, Ajoy, *Behenji: A Political Biography of Mayawati,* Penguin Books, New Delhi, 2008.

Chandra, Mallapalli, *Christians and Public Life in Colonial South India: 1863–1937: Contending with Marginality,* Routledge Curzon, London, 2004.

Chandra, Ramesh, *Minority: Social and Political Conflict,* Isha Books, Delhi, 2004.

Das, Sisir Kumar, *History of Indian Literature 1911–1956: Struggle for Freedom, Triumph and Tragedy,* Sahitya Akademi, New Delhi, 1995.

Ghurye, G.S., *Caste and Race,* cited in Harold Issac's *India's ex-Untouchables,* Asia Publishing House, Bombay, 1965.

Guha, Ramachandra, *Makers of Modern India,* Penguin Books, New Delhi, 2012.

Hilgers, Tina, *Clientelism in Everyday Latin American Politics,* Palgrave Macmillan, New York, 2012.

Hande, H.V., *Ambedkar and the Making of the Indian Constitution,* Macmillan Publishers India Ltd., New Delhi, 2009.

Issac, H.R., *India's Ex-Untouchables,* Asia Publishing House, Bombay, 1965.

Jagjivan, Ram, *Caste Challenge in India,* Vision Books Pvt. Ltd., New Delhi, 1980.

Jeffrelot, Christophe, *Dr Ambedkar and Untouchability: Analysing and Fighting Caste,* C. Hurst and Co Ltd., London, 2005.

Karunyakara, Lella, *Modernisation of Buddhism: Contributions of Ambedkar and Dalai Lama XIV,* Gyan Publishing House, New Delhi, 2002.

Keer, Dhananjay, *Life and Mission of Dr Ambedkar,* Popular Prakasan, Bombay, 1962.

Kumar, Ashok Y., *Struggle for Economic Freedom and Social Justice of Scheduled Caste in South,* Kalpaz Publications, New Delhi, 2005.

Kumar, Vivek, 2006, *India's Roaring Revolution: Dalit Assertion and New Horizons,* Gagandeep Publications, Delhi.

Kshirsagar, R.K., *Dalit Movement in India and its Leaders,* MD Publications, New Delhi, 1994.

Kuppuswamy, B., *Social Change in India,* Vikas Publishing House, Ghaziabad, 1972.

Mathur, B.L., *Encyclopedia of Backward Castes: Commissions,* Vol. 2, Kalpaz Publications, Delhi, 2004.

Michael, S.M. (ed), *Dalits in Modern India: Vision and Values,* Sage Publications, New Delhi, 2007.

Mishra, N., *Socio-economic and Political Vision of Dr B.R. Ambedkar,* New Delhi, Concept Publishing Company pvt. Ltd., 2010.

Moffatt, Michal, *An Untouchable Community in South India,* Princeton University Press, New Jersey, UK, 1979.

Narayan, Badri, *Kanshi Ram: Leader of the Dalits,* Penguin Books, New Delhi, 2014.

Nim, Hotilal, *Thoughts on Dr Ambedkar,* Siddhartha Educational and Cultural Society, Agra, 1969.

Omvedt, Gail, 1994, *Dalits and the Democratic Revolution,* Sage, New Delhi.

Ouwerkerk, Lousie, *The Untouchable of India*, Oxford University Press, London, 1945.

Pai, Sudha, *Dalit Assertion and the Unfinished Democratic Revolution*, Sage Publications, New Delhi, 2002.

Pai, Sudha, *Dalit Assertion and the Unfinished Democratic Revolution: Cultural Subordination and the Dalit Challenge, Vol.3*, Sage Publications, New Delhi, 2002.

Paswan, Sanjay and Jaideva Paramanshi (eds), *Encyclopaedia of Dalits in India: Struggle for Self Liberation*, Volume 2, Kalpaz Publications, New Delhi, 2004.

Prasad, Chandra Bhan, *Dalit Diary: 1999-2003*, Navayana Publishing, Pondycherry, 2004.

Rajam, G. Venkat, *Damodaram Sanjivayya and His Times*, Hyderabad, Media House Publications, 2001.

Rajasvi, M.I., *Mayawati: Hope of Dalits and Faith of Bahujan Society*, Manoj Publications, Delhi, 2011.

Ram, Kanshi, *The Chamcha Age: An Era of the Stooges*, Kanshi Ram, New Delhi, 1982.

Ranga, N.G., *Harijana Nayakudu*, Guntur Kisan Publications, Guntur, 1987 (Reprint)

Rao, P.R., *History and Culture of Andhra Pradesh: From the Earliest Times to 1991*, New Delhi, Sterling Publishers, 1994.

Ratnam, P.V., *Socio-Political Philosophy of Dr B.R. Ambedkar*, Ambedkar-Lohia Socialist Centre, Hyderabad, 2005.

Reddy, L.V., *Education for Dalits*, Discovery Publishing House, New Delhi, 2004.

Sachchidananda, *Harijan Elite*, Thomson Press (India), Faridabad, 1977.

Sadangi, H.C., *Emancipation of Dalits and Freedom Struggle*, Isha Books, Delhi, 2008.

Satyanarayana, A., *Dalits and Upper Castes: Essays in Social History*, Kanishka Publishers, New Delhi, 2005.

Sen, S.N., *History of Modern India*, New Age International Publishers, New Delhi, 2006.

Singh, Balmiki Prasad, *The Indian National Congress and Cultural Renaissance*, Allied Publishers, New Delhi, 2007.

Shankar, Kalyani, *Pandora's Daughters*, Bloomsbury Publishing India Pvt. Ltd., New Delhi, 2013.

Srinivas, M.N., *Caste in Modern India and Other Essays*, Asia Publishing House, Bombay, 1977.

Xiang, Biao, *Global Body Shopping: An Indian Labour System in the Information Technology Industry*, Princeton University Press, New Jersey, 2007.

Zelliot, Eleanor, *From Untouchable to Dalit,* Manohar Publishers, New Delhi, 2001.

Articles-Journals/Working Papers/Chapters in Edited volumes

Charsley, Simon, 'Evaluating Dalit Leadership: P. Venkatswamy and the Hyderabad Example, in *Economic and Political Weekly,* Vol. 37, No. 52, Sameeksha Trust, Mumbai.

Hicken Allen, 'Clientelism' The *Annual Review of Political Science* accessed on 05.07.2013 www.polisci.annualreviews.org.

Hyderabad Political Economy Group, 'Laxmipet Dalit Killings', in *Economic and Political Weekly,* Vol. XLVII, No. 47 and 48, 1 December 2012, Sameeksha Trust, Mumbai.

Kumara, Swamy Nagam, 'Dalits' Autonomous Struggle for the Annihilation of Caste: An Appraisal of Experiments in Andhra Pradesh, *The International Journal of Social Science Research,* April 2013, Vol. 1, No. 4, pp. 35–55, www.ijssr.org/Aprilissue.html.

Land Reforms in Andhra Pradesh http://ebookily.net/pdf/andhra-pradesh-land-reforms-ceiling-on-agricultural-holdings-26549727.html.

Pathak, Bindeshwar, 'Relevance of Dr Ambedkar in Present Day Context' in S.N. Mishra (ed)*Socio-economic and Political Vision of Dr Ambedkar,* Concept Publishing House, New Delhi, 2010.

Ratnam, K.Y., *The Dalit Movement and Democratization of Andhra Pradesh,* East-West Centre, Washington, 2008.

Ross, Stanley, 'Hindu Customs and their Origins', cited in Kuber' s *Ambedkar: A critique,* PPH, New Delhi, 1977.

Satyanarayana, A., 'Dalit Protest Literature in Telugu: A Historical Perspective' in *Economic and Political Weekly,* Vol. XXX, No. 3, 21 January 1995, Sameeksha Trust, Mumbai.

Sivaji, Doneti, 'A Study of Adi-Andhra Reform Movement in Colonial Andhra: A Historical Perspective' in *Journal of Internatinal Academic Research for Multidisciplinary,* Vol. 1, Issue 5, June 2013, www.jiarm.com/Jun/paper3782.pdfý accessed on 14.11.2013.

Srinivasulu, K., *Caste, Class and Social Articulation in Andhra Pradesh: Mapping Differential Regional Trajectories,* Overseas Development Institute, London, 2002.

——, 'BSP and Caste Politics', in *Economic and Political Weekly,* 1 October 1994, Sameeksha Trust, Mumbai.

Tarakam, Bojja, 'Laxmipeta: Deadly Combination of Caste and Political Power', *Economic and Political Weekly,* Vol. XLVII, No. 28, 14 July 2012, Web Exclusive.

Zelliot, Eleanor, 'Congress and the Untouchables, 1917-1950 ' in Richard Sisson and Stanley Wolpert (eds) *Congress and Indian Nationalism: The Pre-Independence Era,* Berkeley, University of California Press, 1988.

——, 'Learning the Use of Political Means', in, *Caste in Indian Politics,* Rajani Kothari (ed), Orient Longman Ltd., Delhi, 1970.

Souvenir

Published by Sri Vemuri Ramjee Rao Memorial Educational Trust, Machilipatnam, 2000.

News Papers

The Hindu

The New Indian Express

The Times of India

Magazines

India Today

Web Sources

Anderson, Siwan et al., 'Clientelism in Indian Villages' Vancouver School of Economics./faculty.chicagobooth.edu/workshops/AppliedEcon/pdf /Francoisclientilism.pdf.

Hicken, Allen, 'Clientelism' The *Annual Review of Political Science,* www.polisci.annualreviews.org

Hopkin, Jonathan, 'Conceptualizing Political Clientelism: Political Exchange and Democratic Theory' Paper prepared at London School of Economics, London, 2006 http://www.academia.edu/2588134/ Conceptualizing_Political_Clientelism_Political_Exchange_ and_Democratic_Theory.

http://ebookily.net/pdf/andhra-pradesh-land-reforms-ceiling-on-agricultural-holdings-26549727.html.

http://indiankanoon.org.

http://www.britannica.com/EBchecked/topic/1916881/clientelism.

http://www.outlookindia.com/article/The-Grammar-Of-Anarchy/289235.

Padmarao, Katti., History of Karamchedu and What actually happened? http://roundtableindia.co.in.

Roniger, Luis, 'Political Clientelism, Democracy and Market Economy' in *Comparative Politics,* Vol. 36, No. 3, April 2004, published by New York University Press, pp.353–375 www. Jstor.org/stable/4150135.

www.eci.nic.in

www.epw.in

Index